Leading from Under the Sword of Damocles

Nabil Abu el Ata • Annie Drucbert

Leading from Under the Sword of Damocles

A Business Leader's Practical Guide to Using Predictive Emulation to Manage Risk and Maintain Profitability

Springer

Nabil Abu el Ata
URM Group
Omaha, Nebraska
USA

Annie Drucbert
URM Group, Europe
Cannes
France

ISBN 978-3-662-56299-4 ISBN 978-3-662-56300-7 (eBook)
https://doi.org/10.1007/978-3-662-56300-7

Library of Congress Control Number: 2017964489

Printed on acid-free paper

This Springer imprint is published by the registered company Springer-Verlag GmbH, DE part of Springer Nature.
The registered company address is: Heidelberger Platz 3, 14197 Berlin, Germany

To win without risk is to triumph without glory.
Pierre Corneille
One of three great seventeenth-century French dramatists

Foreword

Charlie Fote, CEO, Fotec Group, former CEO, First Data Corporation, board member of several companies during his career

Boards and C-level leaders are responsible for balancing risk and reward to achieve the highest returns for their shareholders. When risk is well managed, it creates opportunities for value creation and competitive advantage. But at any moment, unanticipated risks can disrupt even the best conceived plans. If strategic actions are not taken at the right time, the long-term stability and profitability of a company can be severely compromised.

It's both an exciting and frightening time to be the leader of a company. We live in a world of unprecedented change and rapidly evolving technology. The opportunities are endless, but we operate in increasingly complex environments. Cycles of volatility are accelerating, and new dynamics, caused by hyperconnectivity, amplify business risk. We are entering the age of hyper-risk, but risk management practices have not kept pace.

Regardless of technological acumen, years of experience, or academic achievements, no one can fully understand all the modern intricacies and dynamics of a global, multibillion-dollar business anymore. Instead, senior stakeholders are reliant on an army of subject matter experts, who may be the top in their field but possess just a portion of the necessary knowledge and foresight. Each domain assesses risk using their own methods and technologies.

Business strategies are built upon a conglomerate of constrained and often contradicting viewpoints limited by imagination and history. The biggest risks lay hidden in the blind spots. Surprises are inevitable because no one can comprehend how one small change can produce a ripple effect of unintended consequences. Within an operational environment comprising millions upon millions of dynamic interactions, direct and indirect influences produce unpredictable behaviors.

Vague predictions, disjointed or missing information, unknown timelines, and unquantifiable repercussions make it difficult for the C-suite to propose and defend any change that will cost the business money or alter the current status quo. Moreover, a focus on short-term goals, fostered by shareholder demands for returns, provides little incentive for management teams to solve long-term problems.

As a repercussion, the long-term outlook of many Fortune 1000 businesses is tenuous at best. Automation advances in the last 20 years have saved many businesses from failure but have created a Gordian knot. Layering of short-term fixes, without understanding the long-term risks, has created rigid organizations that are unable to respond to rapid change cycles driven by technological innovations and shifting market expectations.

New businesses will continue to displace market incumbents at an accelerating rate unless risk management practices evolve to deal with the modern realities of business dynamics. To create more resilient businesses and ultimately more value, it is necessary to build and maintain operational environments that deliver the best performance with the best economy but also allow the business to agilely adapt to constantly changing requirements.

New mathematical emulation techniques show great promise in revealing new sources of risk and guiding strategic decisions to ensure an optimal outcome that weighs both short- and long-term benefits. The question is, do senior stakeholders have the courage to abandon the mysticism of current risk management practices in favor of a more scientific approach that may reveal a sober reality filled with difficult choices?

I know from my own career, hope and optimism often outweigh reason. But change is inevitable. Companies that mature their risk management practices to preemptively understand and control dynamic complexity will prosper, while others will stagnate and struggle to continuously create value and competitive advantage. The era of hyperconnectivity, which creates hyper-risk, is upon us. We can resist the reality or embrace the opportunity.

For those that want to forge a clearer and more scientific path forward, *Leading from Under the Sword of Damocles* provides a practical guide that shows business leaders and risk management practitioners how mathematical emulation can be used to understand the impacts of hyperconnectivity and hyper-risk, as well as clearly identify when and which opportunistic actions should be taken to ensure the continuous efficiency and cost-effectiveness of business operations.

Fotec Group, Beverly Hills, CA, USA Charlie Fote

Preface

The famed *sword of Damocles* comes from the ancient moral parable popularized by the Roman philosopher Cicero in his 45 B.C. book *Tusculan Disputations*. The tale centers on Dionysius II, a tyrannical king who once ruled over the Sicilian city of Syracuse during the fourth and fifth centuries B.C. Though rich and powerful, Dionysius was supremely unhappy. His iron-fisted rule had made him many enemies, and he was tormented by fears of assassination.

The king's dissatisfaction came to a head one day after a court flatterer named Damocles showered him with compliments and remarked how blissful his life must be. "Since this life delights you," Dionysius replied, "do you wish to taste it yourself and make a trial of my good fortune?" When Damocles agreed, Dionysius seated him on a golden couch and ordered a host of servants wait on him. He was treated to succulent cuts of meat and lavished with scented perfumes and ointments.

Damocles couldn't believe his luck, but just as he was starting to enjoy the life of a king, he noticed that Dionysius had also hung a razor-sharp sword from the ceiling. It was positioned over Damocles' head, suspended only by a single strand of horsehair. From then on, the courtier's fear for his life made it impossible for him to savor the opulence of the feast or enjoy the servants. After casting several nervous glances at the blade dangling above him, he asked to be excused, saying he no longer wished to be so fortunate.

For Cicero, the tale of Dionysius and Damocles represents the idea that those in power always labor under the specter of anxiety and death and that "there can be no happiness for one who is under constant apprehensions." The parable later became a common motif in medieval literature, and the phrase *sword of Damocles* is commonly used to describe a looming danger.

Today every business executive leads from under a *sword of Damocles*, hanging by the thinnest of thread, capable of being cut at any moment by some unforeseen event or miscalculation. As our world becomes more global and digital, advancements accelerate the pace of change, and the thread between corporate growth and demise weakens. The next threat looms, but traditional risk management practices render business leaders helpless in predicting when and how the thread may be cut.

This book was written to show organizational leaders and risk management practitioners how to use our proposed methods of universal risk management and predictive emulation to more accurately understand risk and take strategic actions to improve business outcomes. The ways and means of achieving this goal are based upon our own real-life experiences, backed by scientific principles and the proven results we have achieved through consulting engagements with over 350 global organizations.

Omaha, Nebraska — Nabil Abu el Ata
Cannes, France — Annie Drucbert

Acknowledgment

This book, as was the case with our previous books, *Solving the Dynamic Complexity Dilemma* and *The Tyranny of Uncertainty*, would not exist without our perseverance—which led us to continuously question the status quo of risk as something many do not think about until it happens. We are grateful for our journey together as colleagues, coauthors, and friends. In writing a book, we assume a social and public responsibility that differs from delivering a scientific contribution or applying for a degree, which are individual acts. A book is an act of creation and a way to exchange—with lots of gestation and revelations but also at times risk adversity. In the end, we must succumb to the simple fact of life: nothing will be perfect or complete. There will always be some important task left undone or thought not yet communicated. But at a minimum we must start the journey. And it is our hope that this book sufficiently satisfies that goal.

Mathematicians are always looking for structures (even when none exist) and physicists are always looking for a phenomenon (even if they must wait a very long time for one to appear). But, today we must admit that there are still unexplained events that take us by surprise. And from this position, we must ask ourselves, *"Did we miss something? Or, were our predictions, right?"* The best results are always achieved when all efforts are directed at discovering, predicting, and acting based upon a solid scientific and rigorous engineering discipline.

Our Chairman, Charles T. Fote, is our greatest supporter and inspirer. His continuous encouragement helped us navigate the distance between concepts and practical application of our ideas. We are fortunate to have the collaboration of many great friends and colleagues—in particular we are grateful for our friend and co-thinker, Rudolf Schmandt—who possess the right level of expertise and experience to help us navigate the challenges of building a new management science designed to predict, master, and control risk. This book reflects the wisdom of these individuals. They helped us scope and define the new management science of risk and optimal business control (OBC) as well as the prescriptive management of risk—always challenging us to better meet the needs of businesses and faithfully pushing the boundaries of our thinking. Together we share a common objective to deliver a scientific platform that enables businesses to proactively solve dynamic complexity problems. We live in a time when these solutions are greatly needed—as the negative impacts of dynamic complexity-related risks grow and the opportunity to act shrinks.

A book that presents how businesses can practically manage the impacts of dynamic complexity-related risks through the application of advanced emulation technologies and modern risk management processes is admittedly overdue. For the last decade, we have seen the compounding effects of dynamic complexity on risk become an increasingly significant and counterproductive force within businesses. Yet, this book probably could not have been written earlier in our lives as practitioners, due to both the absence of the right solutions and an ill-framed general perception of risk.

To document and contribute meaningfully to the science of business management, one must have many opportunities to work on problems, which are endemic to business and work with a lot of people who are willing to share their experiences and the results of what they have could achieve using the proposed technologies and methodologies. Happily, the corporations we have worked with as well as our clients, partners, and joint collaborators have willingly supported our work and accompanied us in our achievements, which have brought us to this point.

Much of the work presented in this book was supported by real cases, which used the technology advances made possible by Annie Drucbert and Tomy Abu el Ata and their dedicated team at Accretive Technologies. We appreciate their commitment to our cause. We have made significant progress over the last decade—from being the first to identify the systemic risk posed by dynamic complexity to the present-day offering of commercial products and services that businesses use to diagnose and remediate dynamic complexity risks. We look forward to continuing our fight against dynamic complexity-provoked risk together.

Valerie Driessen kept us on track, imposed rigor and discipline of usefulness, and controlled the trajectory of the book until we landed smoothly. Her contribution was great in verifying and documenting sections of our book. Without Valerie's effort, this book would still be just a dream. To her we owe the deepest of gratitude.

Contents

About the Authors

Nabil Abu el Ata is the cofounder of URM Group and has invested over 20 years in maturing the science of risk management and the practical application of technologies to predictively expose and prescriptively treat operational risks caused by dynamic complexity. With over 15 patents and decades of experience providing consultative services to some of the world's largest and most complex organizations, he offers a breadth of analytical skills, risk management and business intelligence expertise, as well as IT and business process management knowledge. In the late 1970s, Dr. Abu el Ata's mathematical discoveries provided the predictive accuracy necessary to support innovative space exploration missions. By solving a dynamic complexity problem that was previously defined as unsolvable, Dr. Abu el Ata set the foundation for a new era of risk management, which today enables companies to more accurately predict future risk events and take strategic actions to improve business outcomes.

Dr. Abu el Ata's accomplishments include doctorate (Ph.D. and D.Sc. from Paris-Sorbonne) and bachelor's degrees in mathematics and a master's degree in physical sciences (Royal Observatory, Sussex-Cambridge Universities). He is a valued former doctorate fellow of the European Space Organization, former data processing director and advisor for the French Atomic Energy Authority, former CTO of First Data, and former CEO of Accretive Technologies. Dr. Abu el Ata is also an advisory board member of the European Strategic Program for Research in IT; a Steering Committee member for European programs: Pyramid, Europicon, and Itaqua; an advisory board member of French Employment Organization, French Ministry of Finance, French Postal Services, and one of France's largest banks and retail groups; an external professor for a number of universities in France, the UK, and the USA; and laureate of Computer World Honors 2008.

Annie Drucbert is a cofounder of URM Group and a recognized authority in the predictive and prescriptive analysis of economic, financial, and enterprise systems. Mrs. Drucbert's specialties include modeling, emulation, and performance management of complex database and corporate systems. Career highlights include the successful emulation of the 2007 financial meltdown and postcrisis analysis, which proved that the amplitude of the disaster could not be solely blamed on the subprime market collapse as popularly promoted and would not have had such a severe impact if the interdependencies of financial structures had not existed.

Mrs. Drucbert holds three US patents and has delivered strategic, tactical, and operational services using X-Act© OBC Platform for global clients including First Data, McDonald's, La Poste, Deutsche Bank, BNP, CLS, Reuters, Société Générale, Credit Suisse, GE Capital, and BT. Prior to cofounding URM Group and Accretive Technologies, Mrs. Drucbert was the automation division managing director of ATT/DATAID. During her tenure at ATT/DATAID, she managed the team that made the transformation of the French Social Security Platform possible with the creation of citizen health smart cards. She was also an active member of European Technology Initiatives ESPRIT and EUREKA programs. As a graduate of Paris-Sorbonne, Mrs. Drucbert holds a Ph.D. in chemistry as well as an MBA from Paris Dauphine.

Part I

Using Predictive Emulation to Expose and Control Risk

1 Introduction

> *To know that we know what we know, and to know that we do not know what we do not know, that is true knowledge.*
> —Nicolaus Copernicus, Renaissance mathematician and astronomer who formulated a model of the universe

We know that risk—especially operational risk—is commonly generated through excessive dynamic complexity, which ultimately threatens the sustainability of business models, profitability and competitiveness. Armed with this knowledge and scientifically proven methods of predictive emulation and analysis, we have helped hundreds of businesses expose the root causes of risk and identify the necessary actions to improve business outcomes. Ultimately, our goal is to help every organization improve their management practices by directly providing the tools and knowledge necessary for the self-discovery of risks caused by dynamic complexity paired with reliable methods to optimally control these risks.

Through our work presented in *Solving the Dynamic Complexity Dilemma*[1] and *The Tyranny of Uncertainty*,[2] we have shown that the hidden evolution of dynamic complexity in modern business systems leads to risks that cannot be anticipated using traditional methods of risk management. We know that dynamic complexity is produced in systems

[1] Abu el Ata, Nabil and Maurice Perks. *Solving the Dynamic Complexity Dilemma*. Springer Publishing. August 12, 2014. ISBN-10: 364254309X ISBN-13: 978-3642543098.

[2] Abu el Ata, Nabil and Rudolf Schmandt. *The Tyranny of Uncertainty: A New Framework to Predict, Remediate and Monitor Risk*. Springer Publishing. May 18, 2016. ISBN-10: 3662491036 ISBN-13: 978-3662491034.

N. Abu el Ata, A. Drucbert, *Leading from Under the Sword of Damocles*,
https://doi.org/10.1007/978-3-662-56300-7_1

through interdependencies among active components and risks can result from both external influences and/or a combination of internal factors and exchanges.

Due to a lack of sufficient methods to reveal the impacts of dynamic complexity, it is largely ignored in current management practices. When its effects suddenly appear as undesirable system behaviors, business leaders and/or system owners usually treat the symptoms without ever understanding the true cause of the risk. The reactive treatment of dynamic complexity symptoms leads to a growing number of negative impacts including cost inflation, quality degradation and/or a loss in capacity. This outcome can only be prevented if the role of dynamic complexity is well understood and the appropriate cure is proactively applied before problems appear.

Our methods link the cause to the effect. In most historical cases, when risk appears as a surprise or an unexplainable event, we have proven that dynamic complexity was the principle cause of risk. The real-life examples presented in *The Tyranny of Uncertainty* demonstrate how dynamic complexity can cause unexpected crises and disasters, like the 2007 financial crisis, which catch the business off-guard and threaten the long-term growth and profitability of the organization. But these threats can be largely avoided using scientifically proven methods. We can predict, diagnose and remediate the risks caused by dynamic complexity to optimally control service volume, quality and cost to support improved business outcomes.

Some well-regarded business management experts have suspected the presence of dynamic complexity without providing a thorough definition of what it is, how to measure it and predict its gradual appearance to ultimately control its evolution. We have transformed philosophy into science by outlining a process to address operational risk. We accomplish this by identifying negative trends as early as possible, and then predictively qualifying and quantifying the operational consequences. This allows organizations to anticipate and proactively apply the necessary remedial actions to treat dynamic complexity before any negative consequences appear.

The most dangerous risks in business today come from the *unknowns*, which cannot be predicted with historical reference models and often escape the imagination of risk committees. While some risk professionals would say, a precise answer is not necessary to support a business decision, we argue that we need to treat business decisions as a math problem with a specific answer. This allows us to quantify the risks and limit the severity of unanticipated surprises.

As always, our goal has been to define the metrics, processes and methods for evaluating dynamic complexity risk to prescriptively control business outcomes using advanced mathematics. To fill the gap between the limitations of traditional risk management practices and our vision of universal risk management, we have pioneered new technologies and methods of risk management that we believe contribute to the philosophical and scientific exploration of how to optimally manage the dynamically complex systems that support modern society.

Our scientific methods offer a mathematical solution to quantify dynamic complexity and reveal its impact on risk so that we can manage the outcome of business activities with more certainty. The positive reception of our ideas from executive leaders and within boardrooms worldwide point to the desperate need to solve the present-day risk management dilemma in which surprises and fear of the unknown often prevent organizations from meeting their stated objectives.

About This Book

In this book, we explain how our universal risk management concepts and methodology can be put into practice. Over the last 12 years, we have gained sufficient experience to prove the wide applicability of our methods. We have shown many businesses how to reduce uncertainty in their operations by predicting and managing dynamic complexity to prevent risk from hijacking the expected returns of various business activities. Herein, we provide a guide to enable the practical application of universal risk management so that business leaders can make risk-aware decisions and thereby strengthen the thread that precariously holds the *sword of Damocles*.

Icons Used in This Book

Throughout this book, we occasionally use special icons to call attention to important information. Here's what to expect:

	This icon points to the dangers of dynamic complexity as well as the short comings of current management practices that you will want to avoid if you wish to gain better control of risk.
	This icon points out information that is key to your understanding and practical application of the proposed universal risk management approach.

(continued)

	If you are a math wizard or science aficionado, this icon is for you. It provides the mathematical proofs and supporting evidence of the promoted scientific approach to risk management.
	When you are ready to put these methods of universal risk management into practice, this icon will help you locate the tips and information you need to practically apply the presented approach.

Beyond the Book

The impact of dynamic complexity as a predominant root cause of business risk is an expansively complex and ever evolving topic. There is only so much that we can cover in these pages, so if at the end of this book you find yourself wanting to learn more, just go to URMgrp.com.

2 The Looming Danger: *Mismanaging Risk*

Ignorance more frequently begets confidence than does knowledge: it is those who know little, and not those who know much, who so positively assert that this or that problem will never be solved by science.
—Charles Darwin, Naturalist and geologist, best known for his contributions to the science of evolution

In this chapter:

- Understanding the risk impacts of business modernization and digital technologies
- Examining the growing disconnect between the goals of risk management and capabilities of risk management practices
- Acknowledging that risk management failures can lead to business failures
- Outlining the requirements of a mature and future ready risk management practice

Endless amounts of time and resources are dedicated to the task of risk management, but every executive knows that the biggest threats to their business plans will be some new chain of events or unexpected surprises—none of which will be predicted using conventional wisdom or current risk management technologies.

It's the *unknown risks* that keep corporate executives awake at night—wondering how to prepare for and steer their companies clear from that which they cannot foresee. As our world becomes more dynamically complex through global operations and technological

N. Abu el Ata, A. Drucbert, *Leading from Under the Sword of Damocles*,
https://doi.org/10.1007/978-3-662-56300-7_2

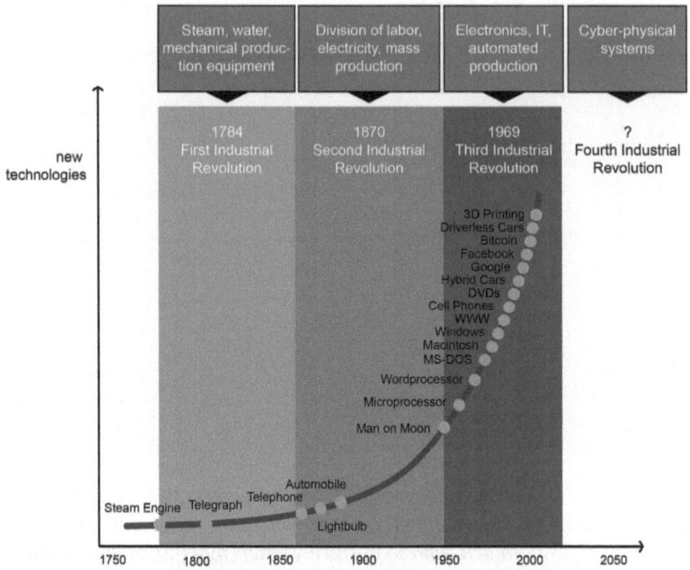

Fig. 2.1 Exponential technological breakthroughs will be the driving force behind the Fourth Industrial Revolution

advances that accelerate change, the window of opportunity to take corrective actions when problems arise is shrinking and risks are rising.

This problem will only get worse as the Fourth Industrial Revolution reaches its full force.[1] The speed of current breakthroughs has no historical precedent. When compared with previous industrial revolutions (see Fig. 2.1), the fourth is evolving at an exponential rather than a linear pace and it is disrupting industries worldwide. The breadth and depth of these changes are transforming entire systems of production, management and governance.

The possibilities of billions of people connected by mobile devices, with unprecedented processing power, storage capacity, and access to knowledge, are unlimited. The opportunities will be multiplied by technology breakthroughs in fields such as artificial intelligence, robotics, the Internet of Things, 3-D printing, autonomous vehicles, nanotechnology and quantum computing.

This acceleration of innovation and the velocity of disruption is difficult to comprehend or anticipate. The drivers of the Fourth Industrial Revolution will become a source of constant surprise, even for the best connected and informed businesses. The introduction of new technologies will create entirely new ways of serving existing needs and significantly disrupt existing industry value chains. While growing transparency, consumer engagement

[1]Schwab, Klaus *The Fourth Industrial Revolution: what it means, how to respond* weform.org Web. Accessed 12 Dec 2016.

and new patterns of consumer behavior will force companies to adapt how they design, market and deliver products and services.

The Goals Are Obvious, but the Means Are Lacking

Current risk management practices cannot arm leaders with the insights they need to navigate the uncharted territories and exponential change that is being driven by the Fourth Industrial Revolution. While the goals of risk management are clear, current probabilistic and experience based methods of risk management lack the means to reliably predict something that has not yet occurred.

☞ ***Risk management* can be defined as the identification, assessment, and prioritization of risks followed by coordinated and economical application of resources to minimize, monitor, and control the probability and/or impact of unfortunate events or to maximize the realization of opportunities. Risk management's objective is to assure uncertainty does not deflect the endeavor from the business goals.**

The growing deficiency of traditional risk management methods is clear based on the growing number and magnitude of recent disasters that have deflected businesses, economies and governments from their intended goals. Disasters are appearing more frequently as complete surprises and their impacts are becoming more significant.

Examples include:

- Major car recalls of Nissan, GM, Toyota, BMW, Ford and others.
- The Fukushima Daiichi nuclear disaster that melted down three out of six nuclear reactors through a series of malfunctioning components.
- The impact of regulatory directives, which unintentionally tightened the credit market following the financial crisis of 2007.

In retrospect, it becomes clear in these cases that the people in charge of managing risk were either unaware of the risk or did not correctly quantify it.

Today, as the repercussions of the Fourth Industrial Revolution begin to take hold, many corporations are fighting hidden risks that are engendered by the obsolescence of their cost structures, outdated business platform and practices, market evolution in reach and speed, client perception and pricing pressures that demand some form of action. But change is often a difficult choice as it implies a certain degree of unknown risk that cannot be revealed using statistical methods of prediction that are reliant on experience.

Under pressure, businesses often treat the symptoms rather than the risk potential, both quantitatively and qualitatively. This approach typically produces undesirable results that forms the impetus of the next crisis—launching an organization into a state of chronic crisis. Siloed sources of data, bad data, inaccurate predictions and over simplification compound the problems of risk management in the following ways:

1. ***Siloed Sources of Data***

   Today risk management is commonly divided by functions. However, managing risks within silos can lead to a host of problems including gaps in the analysis of risk, lack of a process to aggregate critical risks and difficulties in sharing risk information across the organization. When risk data comes from *siloed* sources of data it presents decision makers with a tunneled vision view of the risks. In this case, the aggregate effect of risk across domains is missing, so critical business decisions are made using incomplete data in combination with instincts. The results of these decisions typically unfold in a ripple effect of unintended consequences.
2. ***Bad Data Leads to Bad Decisions***

   It is easy to be misinformed by data. Air France's flight 447 crash provides a simple example of how bad data can lead to bad decision. Reports indicate that pilots pulled back in the middle of a stall because their sensor data incorrectly told them that they were going too fast.[2] This bad data may have caused them to make the situation worse. Just having a data gathering process in place does not guarantee accuracy. Many attempts to collect and interpret data not only miss key factors, but also lead to ill-advised actions with unforeseen consequences.
3. ***Limited Prediction Accuracy***

   Today most risk managers lack the foresight necessary to predict an unexpected disruption—or even understand the full impact of a crisis—until they have the benefit of experience and historical data to analyze. Often, we realize too late that the evidence of an impending crisis was always present, if only we had known where to look.

   The hype of *big data* promised to mitigate the risk of unknowns by correlating the experience and expertise derived from the known. But as hope gives way to reality, it is clear that decisions based on historical data will always be partial. It is the unknowns that will threaten resiliency when the next crisis hits, be it on a global scale, like the 2007 economic meltdown, or a micro-level, precipitated by an unexpected system failure

[2] Shaikh, Thair. *Air France crash pilots lost vital speed data, say investigators. CNN.* 29 July 2011. Web. 5 August 2015.

within a company. To ensure resiliency, leaders must be proactively prepared to take the right-time actions before a crisis unfolds.

4. ***Over Simplification***

   Many risk management practices deal only with ***total expected risk***, which is woefully inadequate. The very high risk of a banal impact is not identical to the minute risk of something devastating, but in a probabilistic model that is reliant on historical data, they are treated the same. Moreover, the probabilistic model cannot explain the circumstances under which a risk will manifest—meaning, *what will be the actual root cause of the risk?* Inter-domain dependencies can occur at any level as well as between levels of processes, implementations and resources-sharing. Through our work, we have proven that most business risk is due to these dependencies, which in turn produces dynamic complexity. But the impacts of dynamic complexity cannot be revealed using a probabilistic model.

We often look at risk as something we know but may be hidden in the historical records represented by *big data*. But recent, surprising risk manifestations have shown that past data is not always a predictor of future performance. The next crisis will come as a complete surprise—caused by a category of unknown risk if we lack a method to predict it.

Modern Businesses Require Modern Risk Management Practices

As adequately stated by Klaus Schwab, Founder and Executive Chairman, World Economic Forum, "We stand on the brink of a technological revolution that will fundamentally alter the way we live, work, and relate to one another. In its scale, scope, and complexity, the transformation will be unlike anything humankind has experienced before. We do not yet know just how it will unfold, but one thing is clear: the response to it must be integrated and comprehensive..."

Current risk management practices, which deal mostly with the risk of reoccurring historical events, cannot help business, government or economic leaders deal with the uncertainty and rate of change driven by the Fourth Industrial Revolution. As new innovations threaten to disrupt, our leaders lack the means to measure the risks and rewards associated with the adoption of new technologies and business models. Established companies are faltering as leaner and more agile start-ups bring to market the new products and services that customers of the on-demand or sharing economy desire—with better quality, faster speeds and/or lower costs than established companies can match.

As the systems that support business become more complex, more globally connected and more critical to sustainable business operations, a lack of agility can lead to the downfall of a business. Although, decision makers may want to proactively address risk and take advantage of new opportunities, they are given no means to prescriptively identify and validate the actions necessary for success.

In decades' past, the executive leadership of a company could understand all aspects of the business, but with the rate of change and rise of digital technologies, they are losing touch with how the goals of the business are implemented. Rapidly accelerating innovation cycles, growing maturity and shifting customer expectations are forcing a disconnect between the business and its implementation—ultimately producing crisis-prone business models.

Due to the continuous adaptations driven by the Third Industrial Revolution, most organizations are now burdened by inefficient and unpredictable systems. Even as the inherent risks of current systems are recognized, many businesses are unable to confidently identify a successful path forward.

In many cases the information gained through current risk management platforms is no better than astrology. Vague predictions, disjointed or missing information, unknown timelines and unquantifiable repercussions make it difficult to propose and defend any change that will cost the business money or alter the current status quo. Moreover, a focus on short-term goals, fostered by shareholder demands for returns, provides no incentive for management teams to solve long-term problems.

Fear and uncertainty foster stagnation. However, the problem is only growing in magnitude and businesses are becoming more exposed. Major corporations are failing at an increasing rate. Many of today's CEOs of global Fortune 1000 companies are like captains of sinking ships. As their crews focus on patching holes and bailing water, a tsunami is forming undetected off the port bow.

As frequent changes and reactive management practices accelerate risk and create unpredictable environments, no business will survive the coming storm unless risk management practices evolve to the point that they empower executives to confidently define and make the right disruptive moves at the right time to achieve better economy, control risk and support critical renewal.

To accomplish this goal, businesses must be able to pinpoint the nature and root cause of all potential problems before they occur—both those that have happened in the past as well as new, never experienced patterns of risk. And they must clearly understand which (and when) preventive and opportunistic actions should be taken to ensure the continuous efficiency and cost effectiveness of operations.

To respond to the rate of change engendered by the Fourth Industrial Revolution, the practice of risk management must mature and become a scientific discipline. Mathematical emulation supports this move by reliably predicting how changes will impact dynamic systems and prescriptively identifying which actions are necessary to continuously meet changing business objectives.

If you want your business to survive and prosper during the Fourth Industrial Revolution, your risk management practices must support the following four intersecting domains:

- Build a strategy and produce operational plans to discover, avoid and mitigate both known and unknown risks
- Predict the singularity (breaking point) of systems, as well as the distance to the singularity
- Understand the conditions or system behaviors that define the evolution of risk
- Put the system under surveillance, so that management may intervene at the right time to avoid a singularity.

This book is meant to show business leaders and risk practitioners how these four domains can be fulfilled using our proposed universal risk management approaches and predictive emulation technologies.

3 Dynamic Complexity: The Cancer of Business

We have also arranged things so that almost no one understands science and technology. This is a prescription for disaster. We might get away with it for a while, but sooner or later this combustible mixture of ignorance and power is going to blow up in our faces.
—Carl Sagan, one of the best brains of 20th century, astronomer, cosmologist and exceptional human

In this chapter:

- Understanding what dynamic complexity is
- Identifying how dynamic complexity creates business risk
- Learning why emulation is key to discovering the impact of dynamic complexity
- Reviewing an example of business risk caused by dynamic complexity

Defining Dynamic Complexity

We most commonly think of business systems as linear models with direct impacts, static references and 2-dimensional movements. But in fact, most modern business systems are exponential, non-linear, dynamic and multi-dimensional, and the behaviors of these systems are difficult to intuitively understand. Therefore, we are often tempted to cope with simple models rather than open systems and dynamic complexity. But simplifying a dynamic system into a closed loop model doesn't make our problems go away.

N. Abu el Ata, A. Drucbert, *Leading from Under the Sword of Damocles*,
https://doi.org/10.1007/978-3-662-56300-7_3

We often think of complexity as something that can be counted—a number of things, whether they be humans, machines, technologies, routes, processes or other moving parts and components of a system. However, *dynamic complexity* is something that is produced through component interactions, interdependencies, feedback, locks, conflicts, contentions, prioritizations or enforcements. Subsequently, dynamic complexity is revealed—often at a moment we do not expect—when a system begins to exhibit strange behaviors such as forming congestions, inflations, degradations, latencies or overhead.

Dynamic complexity always accelerates the appearance of risk in time and conditions versus what was expected or supposed to happen. Dynamic complexity is a characteristic of a dynamic system that is hidden until the structural interdependencies among components begin to play a counter-productive effect that may become predominant at a certain point in time and eventually be revealed as a surprise.

Dynamic complexity can best be defined as a detrimental property of any complex system in which the behaviorally determinant influences between its constituents change over time. The change can be due to internal events or external influences. When a set of constituents become stressed enough to exert an effect on a dependent constituent—such as a limit at some stage in a process—the diversion from the expected behavior is caused by dynamic complexity.

While dynamic complexity is created by design, its evolution is gradual. It starts as a small impact on the efficiency of a process and evolves to become the predominant negative contribution in a system's performance and behavior—causing over consumption of resources and lost opportunity. Dynamic complexity evolves over time when some conditions knock the interdependencies among system components, provoking the overutilization of intertwined structures rather than streamlining system performance, as was the original intention when the system was first conceived and constructed.

This process greatly resembles the Darwinian evolution model with the major difference being that the time between the cause and effect is much shorter in the case of dynamic complexity. Additionally, by using our methods of universal risk management, we can proactively intervene in the evolutionary cycle. By discovering the evolution of dynamic complexity, diagnosing the root causes and then prescriptively determining which actions will allow us to avoid a potential crisis, we can positively steer the course of evolution as needed to continuously meet stated business objectives.

Dynamic Complexity Creates Business Risk

A business can be primarily defined by its translation into systems—whether the system be an automotive production line, healthcare system, nuclear plant, financial system, or any other set of interacting or interdependent components forming an integrated whole that is created to achieve the objectives set forth by its stakeholders. In operations, dynamics generate risk that is produced due to external events as well as internal influencers generated through the way an organization or architecture is implemented.

When new systems are built or changes are made to existing systems, unintended consequences are a common result. In operations, surprises catch system owners off-guard because they did not understand the influences of dynamic complexity, and therefore could not fully understand the environment they were trying to manage or the hidden risks it contained.

Current risk management practices are challenged to discover these risks in time to remediate without negative business outcomes because business demands have expanded beyond the original intent of business systems. A gap is growing between the definition of the business and the defined behavior of the system that implements the business. The dynamic complexity that characterizes a business is growing at a much faster rate than can be managed using traditional practices.

As businesses change at an ever-increasing rate, so does the growth and severity of its dynamic complexity. Today the dynamic complexity that is generated due to business dynamics is reaching a much faster speed than the current business definition of stability can manage. Faster change in dynamics, and consequently faster growth in dynamic complexity, causes the eventual risk to come faster and therefore imposes a requirement on management to face the dilemma, anticipate the impact, and manage closely something that is hidden and can be suddenly revealed at any point in time.

Exposing Risks Caused by Dynamic Complexity

Dynamic complexity always produces a negative effect in the form of loss, time elongation or shortage—causing inefficiencies and side effects, which are similar to friction, collision or drag. Dynamic complexity cannot be observed directly, only its effects can be measured. Additionally, dynamic complexity is impossible to predict from historic data—no matter the amount—because the number of states tend to be too large for any given set of samples.

Therefore, trend analysis alone cannot sufficiently represent all possible and yet to be discovered system dynamics.

In the early stages, dynamic complexity is like a hidden cancer. Finding a single cancer cell in the human body is like looking for a specific grain of sand in a sandbox. And like cancer, often the disease will only be discovered once unexplained symptoms appear. To proactively treat dynamic complexity before it negatively impacts operations, we need diagnostics that can reliably reveal its future impact. System modeling and mathematical emulation allow us to provoke the existence of dynamic complexity through two hidden exerted system properties: the degree of interdependencies among system components and the multiple perturbations exerted by internal and external influences on both components and the edges connecting them directly or indirectly.

Successful risk determination and mitigation is dependent on how well we understand and account for dynamic complexity, its evolution, and the amount of time before the system will hit the singularity (singularities) through the intensification of stress on the dependencies and intertwined structures forming the system.

Knowing what conditions will cause singularities allows us to understand how the system can be stressed to the point at which it will no longer meet business objectives, and proactively put the risk management practices into place to avoid these unwanted situations.

☞ ***Perturbation:* A deviation of a system, moving object, or process from its regular or normal state of path, caused by an outside influence**

☞ ***Singularity:* A point at which a given mathematical object is not defined or not well-behaved, for example infinite or not differentiable**

How Dynamic Complexity Disrupts Business Operations

Below we provide an example of a client case where dynamic complexity played a key role in terms of resource consumption, time to deliver, and volume to deliver. Figure 3.1 represents a trading and settlement implementation used by a volume of business that continuously increases. The reaction of the system is shown by the curves.

In Fig. 3.1, the production efficiency increases until it hits a plateau after which the business is increasingly impacted by a slowdown in productivity and increase in costs. The amount of loss is proportional to the increase in dynamic complexity, which gradually absorbs the resources (i.e. the cost) to deliver little. The singularity occurs when the two curves (productivity/revenue and cost) join, which in turn translates into loss in margin, over costing and overall instability.

In client cases, such as the one presented in Fig. 3.1, we have successfully used predictive emulation to isolate the evolving impact of dynamic complexity and calculate risk as an impact on system performance, cost, scalability and dependability. This allows us

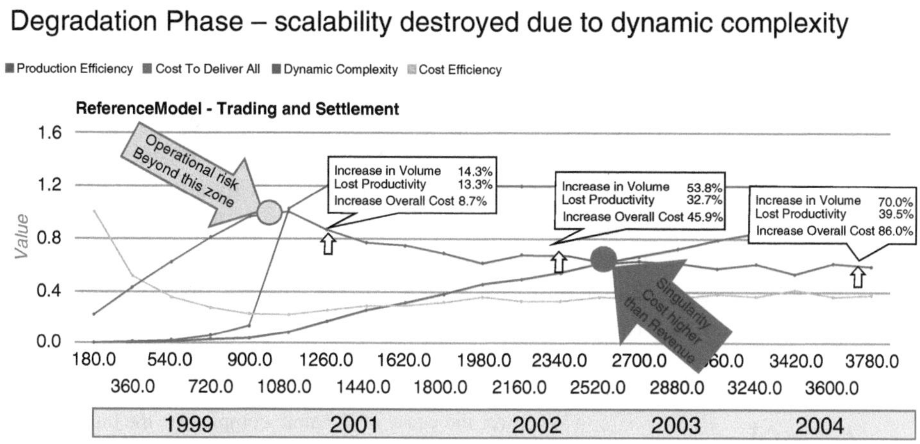

Fig. 3.1 Impact of dynamic complexity on productivity and service quality in a payment processing system

to measure changes in system health, when provoked by a change in dynamic complexity's behavior under different process operational dynamics and identify the component(s) that cause the problem.

But knowing the *how* and *what* isn't sufficient. We also need to know *when*, so we measure dynamic complexity itself, which then allows us to monitor its evolution and apply the right mitigation strategy at the right time.

Avoiding Dynamic Complexity as a Terminal Diagnosis

Any business implementation is precarious in nature, because businesses are dynamic and evolving over time, changing objectives will subsequently force multiple implementation changes. In some cases, dynamics can quickly lead to implementation obsolescence if the frequency and amplitude of changes are significant. For economic, political, industrial or management reasons, businesses often ignore the impact of changes on system health. Instead they stretch the implementation and hope it continues to meet business requirements. Sometimes the implementation continues to work for a while, but then the business is shocked when something abruptly stops working without warning or is severely handicapped due to some unknown cause. Often this point of discovery comes too late to execute a reasonable cure.

These events mainly occur when the tight coupling between business objectives and the corresponding implementation weaken. Over time the key importance of maintaining the relationship between business and the best-fit implementation becomes less clear to system stakeholders who rush to meet the changing demands of the business without fully considering the impact to system health. From experience gained over the last three decades, we have found that these surprises generally come when the business is strapped for time and does not possess sufficient means to face the challenge.

Once the dynamic nature of business begins to stretch an outdated implementation, it becomes the perfect breeding ground for dynamic complexity. Under these conditions, dynamic complexity can become a real threat to the sustainability of business operations and/or economics. The change in implementation that allowed dynamic complexity to thrive may have been foundational, but it also may have resulted from changes in perception (faster service, faster connectivity), or due to disruptive change in the functionality (sub-prime, algorithmic trading), or change in the process (hybrid mail, digital currency) or infrastructure (internet, nanotechnology).

Whatever the cause of dynamic complexity, the business can benefit by using a scientific approach to identify the right treatment plan to proactively slow down or eliminate the continuous growth in dynamic complexity. Armed with the right method, associated metrics and a process to discover the root causes of dynamic complexity, businesses can identify which level of their implementation needs to be optimized and cured. Our emulation technology delivers the prescriptive indicators that guide the necessary actions and predictively measures the expected gains

4 The Loose Cubic Dilemma

He, who every morning plans the transactions of the day, and follows that plan, carries a thread that will guide him through a labyrinth of the busiest life.
—Victor Hugo, French poet, novelist, and dramatist of the Romantic Movement

In this chapter:

- Understanding the impact of dynamic complexity through three-dimensional coordinates (volume, cost and quality)
- Why balancing business objectives versus architectural and infrastructure choices creates a dilemma
- How changing dynamics can force disruption as a business imperative

Delivering a topological representation of a business implementation, such as an industrial process, to conceptually understand the impacts of dynamic complexity is a challenge, however the industrial process can be depicted in the form of a cube as presented in Fig. 4.1. The edges of the cube represent the volume, cost and required quality of service. The cube itself represents the system content at a given moment—knowing that the content can sometimes change dramatically as business requirements change.

Now we can consider the industrial process represented as a function in time, where the exerted dynamics vary due to the three edges as well as the internal dynamic dependencies and a variety of the characteristics and behaviors of external influencers. Clearly, the business representation is dynamic, so it is wrong to assume, except over a short interval of time, that little or no changes will be required to support its automation and long-term survival.

N. Abu el Ata, A. Drucbert, *Leading from Under the Sword of Damocles*,
https://doi.org/10.1007/978-3-662-56300-7_4

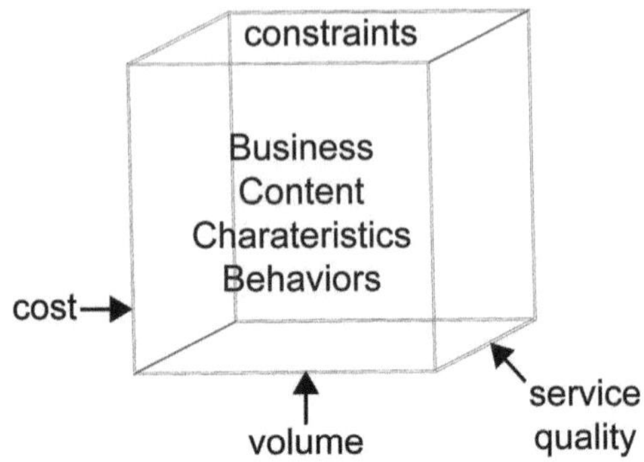

Fig. 4.1 Topological representation of an ideal business implementation

Therefore, the form of the cube is illusive. The physical cube deforms continuously during its lifetime due to its dynamic nature. The external perceptions of dynamics are dependent on the very position from which we look at a business implementation:

- **Users** want continuous service that is constant or improving in quality and offered at a competitive price.
- **Business management** wants a scalable implementation with a stable service condition that is adaptable to management objectives and supports cost of service/goods and time to market requirements.
- For **operational management**, the eyes are always on the operational risk, so they want to maintain an implementation with behavior that is easy to predict under different conditions, easy to fix if an odd behavior occurs and simple to project their return by maintaining the relationship between load and time to deliver.

The idea of the cube is a visual representation that embodies the definitions above and satisfies the different perceptions. However, one needs to accept the fact that such definitions are Newtonian in nature[1] and subject to continuous changes in inherent dynamics, which will deform continuously its topology.

In Fig. 4.2, the pink halo around the business implementation cube illustrates that various definitions will change as the dynamics change. The cubic form is only selected to provide a translation of business imperatives into three-dimensional space. Accordingly, the business implementation should also be considered as dynamic. Therefore, the cube is subject to optimization objectives, which are free of constraints imposed by the architecture or infrastructure of its implementation. In other words, if we can keep the objectives intact, we can select whatever architecture and infrastructure that fits the demands.

[1]Newton's third law: For every action, there is an equal and opposite reaction. The statement means that in every interaction, there is a pair of forces acting on the two interacting objects. The size of the forces on the first object equals the size of the force on the second object.

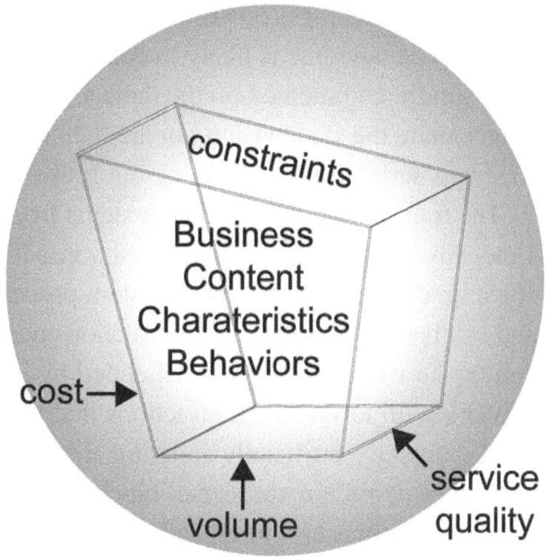

Fig. 4.2 Topological representation of a real business implementation

However, in most cases, the bridge is weak between the business imperative and the degree of freedom in choosing its implementation. From a pure process sequencing, information technology (IT) or factory design perspective, the goal of keeping the objectives intact is not realistic, as in many cases the choice of architecture and infrastructure is imposed depending on what knowledge is available at the outset. Additionally, trying to meet the objectives may generate excessive dynamic complexity due to successive infrastructure adaptations.

When we move to the business implementation, we face another dilemma in that the very definition of business is influenced by the implementation decisions and how the logical structure, the operational procedures and physical selections were defined. The following three examples further illustrate the loose cubic dilemma.

Bitcoin and Blockchain

Bitcoin and blockchain will likely be recognized as some of the most disruptive technologies of our time. However, many serious problems must still be addressed before full, unlimited adoption becomes possible. In February 2016, customer complaints of the most popular bitcoin wallet service hit a record high. How the creators of bitcoin chose to balance business objectives versus architectural and infrastructure choices was a significant factor. The constraints of the blockchain technology, which underpins the bitcoin, made it difficult for the network to handle the level of transactions, leading to higher fees and longer wait times. Basically, as network congestion occurred at high volumes, bitcoin users were paying more for less value.

Now a debate rages on how to resolve these problems through the future development of bitcoin. The outcome is likely to determine the fate of bitcoin. As Blockchain-info's CEO, Peter Smith, commented on the debate, "It became clear that large parts of the industry no longer share the same vision nor are they likely to pragmatically compromise to avert what I view as serious risk of running out rocket fuel before we get the ship to orbit.[2]"

The transaction delay problem stems from the fact that the blocks are limited in size to 1 megabyte, which means just seven transactions per second can be recorded. To put this in context, Visa says its payment system processes 2000 transactions per second on average and can handle up to 56,000 transactions per second if needed.[3] Additionally, some allege that the network is being overwhelmed by individuals that are purposefully spamming the network with low-value transactions that miners are unlikely to accept and verify on their blocks, thereby artificially inflating the list of unprocessed transactions. To support the objectives of bitcoin, the size of block must dramatically increase or changes must be made in how signatures are stored and spamming issues must be resolved so that the network can deliver a minimum of 1500–3000 transactions per second.

Whether the loose cubic dilemma is adequately solved to match architecture and infrastructure choices with business objectives under dynamic business conditions, will decide whether blockchain technology will be victorious in moving from hype to reality.

Relational Databases

A *relational database* is a database structured on the *relational* model—meaning that data is stored and presented in a tabular format, organized in rows and columns with one record per row. For the last 20 years, relational databases have been coveted by businesses as a sign of modern and mature data implementation. While we do not dispute the advantages of relational databases, there are conditions for success and as with all prescribed medicines, their use should come with some precautions.

Sometimes businesses change the architecture or infrastructure just to take advantage of the *technology de jour*. However, the loose cubic dilemma requires that the deploying organization consider how the move will impact business objectives. In multiple cases, we have seen the relational model handicap the deploying organization because it can add more restrictions than benefits. The required reorganization of data, cleansing and clustering activities can slow down access to data, increase the probability of proliferation of inefficient physical I/O's, and ultimately slow down transactions, while consequently increasing the cost and reducing the throughput to deliver.

Without strict observation of set theory and mathematical principles, the use of a relational model will follow the law of diminishing returns. In one case, we found that

[2]Gilbert, David. *Blockchain complaints have hit record levels.* Business Insider. Web. March 8, 2016.

[3]Visa Inc. at a Glance. visa.com Web. Accessed October 24, 2016.

moving a highly optimized file based data implementation to a relational model would increase the batch window from three hours to 32 days if implemented as a one-to-one conversion. Obviously, in this case the proposed infrastructure would not be able to meet the business objectives.

Overstretch Implementations

Many implementations that were constructed as part of the first wave of automation efforts were expected to last for the foreseeable future. This expectation has become a handicap to the deploying organizations. Now two competing strategies for implementing business dynamics have become a continuous challenge to maintain.

The first strategy that most businesses have chosen to pursue is to stretch whatever implementation is already in place to meet growing business demands. However, the system is inadequately prepared to do more, so this creates aging, inefficiencies and eventually obsolescence of systems.

The second strategy is to execute an infrastructure renewal project, when the first strategy fails. In many cases the renewal project yields temporary gains, but ultimately fails because the root cause of problems was not addressed. In many cases, the renewal project itself becomes obsolete before it can be implemented as the business keeps changing and the infrastructure never keeps pace. Additionally, the desired support of business objectives is often restricted by some decision to use the latest innovations such as publish/subscribe, distributed architectures, new protocols and/or smart search.

Disruption

Disruptive waves will always lead to major implementation renewals. In some cases, disruption may even challenge the accepted basics of industrial process implementation. Apple's iPod is an excellent example of how a company can drive innovation through a series of disruptive implementations that challenge the common wisdom of our time. Contrary to Apple's success story, Digital Equipment in late 1980s, Blackberry and GM in the early 2000s, as well as the great commercial success of IBM, are all cases where slow corporate strategy, and consequently the supporting industrial engineering and timely implementation handicapped the company from meeting its stated business objectives.

Such cases demonstrate that innovation is important only if the implementation and time to market are concurrently delivered at the right time. Moreover, any implementation that includes changes in business characteristics and dynamics should not cause frustration, cost escalation, unpredictability and manageability challenges.

Ultimately, business dynamics are difficult to encapsulate from the outset in a unique implementation. First, it is not clear if the business translation is exhaustive, as in most cases we are not able to imagine from the start all possible variations of dynamics and their origins. Our natural language is imprecise and can only express equivalences, therefore the transmission of business definitions is always imperfect. Finally, in most cases, the dialog between the business owner and implementation owner does not cover the definition of business. The business owner may consider some concepts obvious, while the implementation owner does not necessarily know what to ask or how to implement the definitions if told.

From this position, we can see that an implementation is immutable—as it represents an instantiation of understanding at a point in time, but in practice the understanding becomes changeable. As the implementation is stretched to represent a wider understanding, systemic changes will be required. This is one of the main origins of rapid implementation obsolescence that subsequently imposes implementation boundaries and uncertainties. Therefore, the flexibility of an implementation is important so that it can cover wider variations, but we should always be ready to profoundly question its survival in a world that changing faster than ever before.

No one can doubt that the characteristics of today's business environment differ greatly from those of a decade ago, which again differ greatly from those of the preceding century. Regardless of the populist speeches and conservative platforms that try to stop progress, the world is continuously moving to new horizons which operate at a faster pace with more dynamic complexity, permanent changes in dynamics and greater automation to do more for less and always questioning the role labor, value and cost play in the society.

Meeting Business Targets and Constraints 5

By three methods we may learn wisdom: First, by reflection, which is noblest; second, by imitation, which is easiest; and third by experience, which is the bitterest.
—Confucius, Chinese teacher, editor, politician, and philosopher

In this chapter:

- Challenges of delivering a business implementation according to plan
- How implementation choices and plan execution can negatively affect quality, cost and service capabilities of a proposed system
- Why time to market constraints and changing demands introduce unexpected risk

A business implementation is much wider than merely an automation process. Done properly, an implementation should translate strategic, tactical and operational objectives into processes, policies and constraints (see Fig. 5.1). However, most companies face significant challenges in obtaining such an ambitious goal.

While short-term objectives maybe easy to communicate between business and system stakeholders, longer-term objectives are generally more difficult to capture due to various human dynamics and our inability to predict the future. Most business requirements and constraints are communicated through natural language, and are not necessarily easily translated into systemic properties. In addition, the level of business or technology knowledge that various participants possess is not necessarily homogeneous. Due to hyper specialization and various centers of interest, the proposed implementation and its evolution is not thoroughly understood by all parties.

N. Abu el Ata, A. Drucbert, *Leading from Under the Sword of Damocles*,
https://doi.org/10.1007/978-3-662-56300-7_5

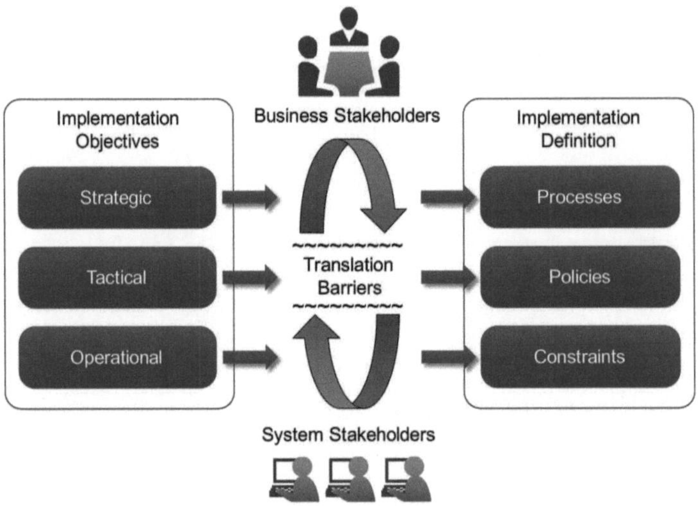

Fig. 5.1 Translation of business objectives into implementation

Additionally, it can be difficult to test assumptions, benchmark or prototype concepts prior to implementation. But, in most cases it is extremely difficult to roll-back, adapt or tailor an implementation in the final stages before delivery. Generally, the integration process is cumbersome and at this late stage of the development lifecycle, most parties become content on making it work, rather than postponing the deployment to optimize the implementation.

Deliver Per Plan

The timely delivery of a solution that satisfies business imperatives—such as competitive positioning, market and customer pressure, economic targets and process optimization—is the main goal of a business implementation. The pursuit of this goal may require changes to existing processes, management and monitoring, physical builds, or technology.

For example, a new blockchain implementation would be disruptive to how business is conventionally conducted—in that it is managed differently and its physical build and technology are different. To make the move to blockchain, the planned project must cover many dimensions and be flexible enough to solve any challenges that are identified along the way.

On the other hand, if we only need to propose a new interest rate to customers, the implementation plan could be accurately defined from the project outset. Still, caution should be taken to avoid aging the existing implementation, which can result when deviating from the original predictable architecture to a new one that may generate degradation.

Testing is another dimension that can significantly impact whether the implementation is delivered per plan. Prototyping, benchmarking and experimentation are not sufficient to fulfil the requirements of a rigorous testing plan—especially if the business faces security, safety and business continuity challenges. Due to economic and/or time to market pressures, many business applications are modestly tested before deploying into operations.

Partial testing often exposes operations to risk and jeopardizes the desired outcomes of projects. Additionally, a partially tested implementation accelerates aging because successive modifications become necessary to enhance system performance in production. Under pressure to keep the production system running smoothly, changes are made without questioning their impact on the original implementation principles. Thereby risk is increased without understanding the possible repercussions.

We need methods that allow project stakeholders to quickly and cost effectively test whether the implementation will be able to meet business expectations.

Meet Quality Requirements

In an isolated lab testing environment, it may be determined that it is possible to support the defined business objectives using the proposed implementation. However, the business may later find it difficult to fulfil the business objectives in a real deployment. This is a common occurrence because the proposed implementation often shares common infrastructure and resources, data updates and dependencies, or introduces technologies that were not sufficiently represented in the closed loop environment of the lab.

Implementations with shared resources are sensitive to both volumes and dynamic complexity at a point in time. In such circumstances, increasing volume will generally decrease the unit cost, but only up to a point at which additional volume will increase the unit cost or decrease the output—or in some cases do both. This is the effect of dynamic complexity, which ultimately leads to a degradation in service quality.

We know that the perception of quality can change over time and under different circumstances. A trade can be executed in microseconds or in few minutes depending on the pre-trade requirements, trade process and expectations. A postal service sorting machine can deliver 20 pieces of mail per second, but then it may take 8 hours to be transported to a regional hub, another few hours to be sorted for distribution and so on.

If we want to optimize the delivery time, it would seem clear that we should simply reduce the transport time. But if the sorting machine becomes unavailable, the mail won't be sorted until the next day. Therefore, right-time processing is the correct measure of efficiency and synchronization is critical for optimizing end-to-end services.

We need to be able to predictively test the dynamic impacts of production environments and prescriptively optimize the delivery to meet quality requirements.

Deliver at Lowest Cost

As more infrastructure and implementation scenarios have been made possible through innovation, the cost dimension of an implementation has become a primary concern. So much so that cost has become a major criteria of project acceptance. For this reason, many of the major activities that supported the success of an implementation project are sometimes reduced to a minimum if not entirely ignored.

Today testing, adaptability and maintainability are often sacrificed in favor of gaining competitive advantage by meeting time to market requirements. The cost dimension generally includes the project and operational cost. Curious enough, adaptation and optimization costs are considered part of management cost and not necessarily assigned to the corresponding implementation—even if some of the activities are dedicated to the rationalization, transformation and improvement of it. This position reduces any motivation to promote continuous improvement.

Costing analysis must cover a wider definition than just the cost of implementation and operations. The chronic cost associated with the loss of opportunity is a fundamental metric that may become a catalyst for disruptive moves. Fixed costs may lead to corporate re-engineering. The cost of dynamic complexity can become so intrusive that it prevents the implementation from delivering the required quantity with acceptable quality for the right cost.

Meet Time to Market Demands

Market requirements continuously evolve for a variety of reasons and with varying degrees of urgency in delivering the solution. Some joke that as soon as highways are built in United Kingdom, they will become saturated with traffic the very next day. In the case of transportation, obsolescence of infrastructure may happen over several years. In other cases, obsolescence may become a problem within months or even days of deployment.

Correctly timing the delivery of a market solution is a noble goal, but meeting timing constraints often causes system degradation. In which case, dynamic complexity may build in such a way that the original purpose and business goals of the project cannot be met.

Project stakeholders need reliable methods to confidently track projects to ensure the outcome will meet time to market requirements without sacrificing business goals.

Adapt Quickly

Often business goals and requirements change in the middle of a project. Sometimes, these changes would have had significant impacts on the choice of architecture, applications or supporting infrastructure if the requirements been known from the project outset. But in the rush to meet project timelines within budget, changes are quickly made and no one bothers to assess the overall implications to system performance or ability of the project to still meet all stated business objectives. In most cases, this rush to adapt eventually accelerates the aging of the system—ultimately leading to service degradation and cost escalation.

System stakeholders need to be able to quickly assess how proposed changes may impact risk in terms of service quality and cost as well as impact on volumes and consequently revenues.

Guarantee Uptime

> **warning**
>
> Establishing an operational goal of near 100% uptime/availability frequently translates into system constraints that are doomed to fail. When the complexity of structures and external influencers multiply, it leads to a degenerative availability risk. For instance, in a communication system, the error rate may prevent the system from meeting the availability objectives at the trader workstation.

System stakeholders need reliable methods to determine how any proposed changes will impact availability.

The Basics of Universal Risk Management 6

If you look up the synonyms for the word 'risk; you will likely receive results such as: danger, hazard, threat, peril, and gamble. So, why do people, companies, governments, and countries expose themselves to risk? The answer is simple: without risk there is no reward. Being that risk is an inevitable part of life, it is of great importance to mitigate the exposure.

Notice how I said mitigate versus eliminate. The reason behind this is that if we eliminate all risk, we essentially eliminate all return. Proper risk management ensures that financial institutions create a roadmap to achieve strategic goals. It allows companies to seize opportunities and to mitigate adversity.
—Kseniya (Kate) Strachnyi, Advisory consultant focused on risk management, governance, and regulatory response solutions for financial services institutions

In this chapter:

- Understanding how X-Act OBC Platform supports the goals of universal risk management
- Explaining the underlying methodologies that support universal risk management
- Reviewing key universal risk management concepts and definition of terms

Our proposed scientific method of universal risk management outlined in *The Tyranny of Uncertainty* is based on four pillars: causal deconstruction, perturbation theory, dynamic patterns and optimal business control (OBC). Further, methodologies such as *emulative*

N. Abu el Ata, A. Drucbert, *Leading from Under the Sword of Damocles*,
https://doi.org/10.1007/978-3-662-56300-7_6

Fig. 6.1 Step-wise approach to universal risk management

deconstruction theory and *model-based architecture* help us achieve the end goals of universal risk management. While the concepts and mathematics that support universal risk management are complex, the application of these methods are simple to implement through the use of our commercial universal risk management platform called, X-Act® Optimal Business Control (OBC) Platform.

Below we provide a basic overview of the technologies, methodologies and concepts that support a step-wise approach to universal risk management as presented in Fig. 6.1. For readers who wish to gain a deeper understanding beyond what is presented here, *The Tyranny of Uncertainty* provides further discussion and examples of these topics.

X-Act OBC Platform Overview

X-Act® OBC Platform was developed to provide users with access to the most advanced mathematical solutions for universal risk management without requiring that they be specialist in the art. X-Act® OBC Platform supports the goals of universal risk management by providing users with the capabilities needed to collect data, model systems, emulate the

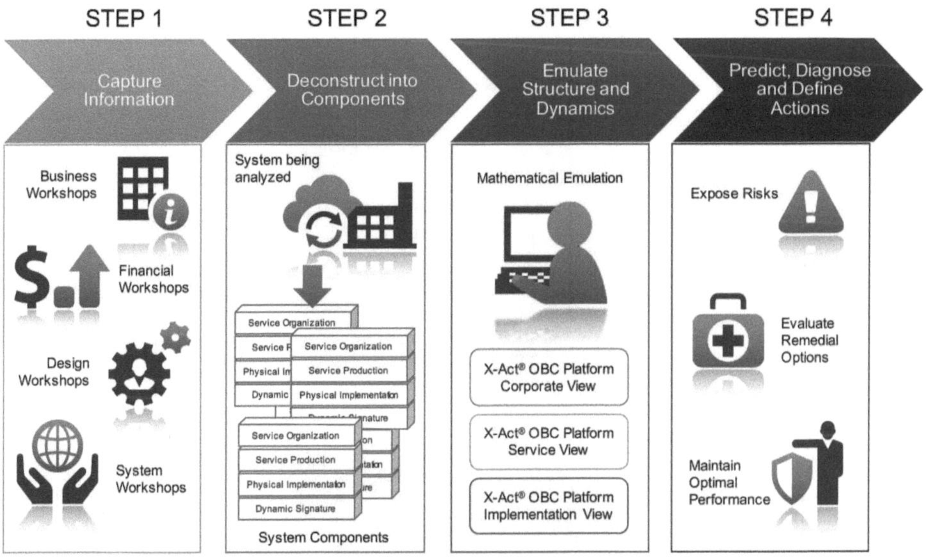

Fig. 6.2 Overview of X-Act® OBC Platform capabilities

implementation and perform stress testing to identify the impact of dynamic complexity on cost, quality and/or business (see Fig. 6.2). Additionally, X-Act® OBC Platform allows users to conduct sensitivity analysis to identify which actions are needed to remediate, improve or disrupt the business.

To analyze the impacts of dynamic complexity within open loops systems, X-Act® OBC Platform allows users to model the business process as wide as it spreads and deeply as is needed—including physical mapping all the way through to requests for resources (see Fig. 6.3).

X-Act® OBC Platform uses accurate, representative and reproducible mathematically converging algorithms to represent the dynamics of every object including processes, systems and physical objects in an operational structure.

Comprehensive, global as well as detailed metrics represent both quantitative and qualitative decision oriented support and interpretations. Such metrics represent both the dynamic complexity and the risk index as well as their lower level constituent metrics expressed in service quantity, quality and cost.

X-Act® OBC Platform computes the impact of dynamic complexity and the associated risk index that corresponds to situational evolution in volume, innovation or implementation changes. A lower level computation will provide the corresponding cost, service quality and productivity at different points in space time coordinates. Therefore, X-Act® OBC Platform provides two additional services: diagnosis to reveal the root cause of a risk at any level and the remediation options to fight a risk including using disruptive actions (see Fig. 6.4).

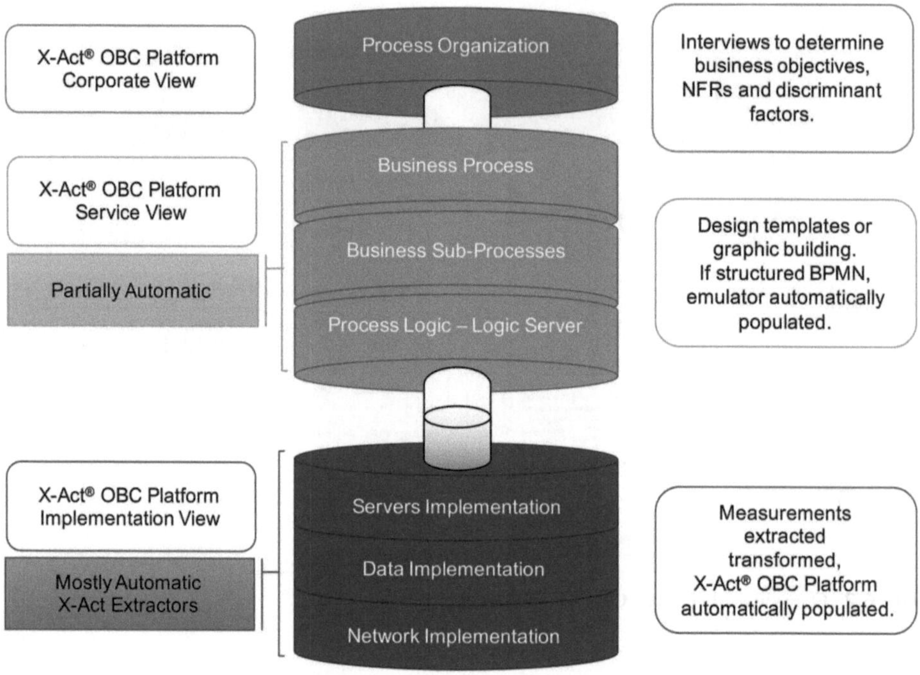

Fig. 6.3 Overview of X-Act® OBC Platform modeling capabilities

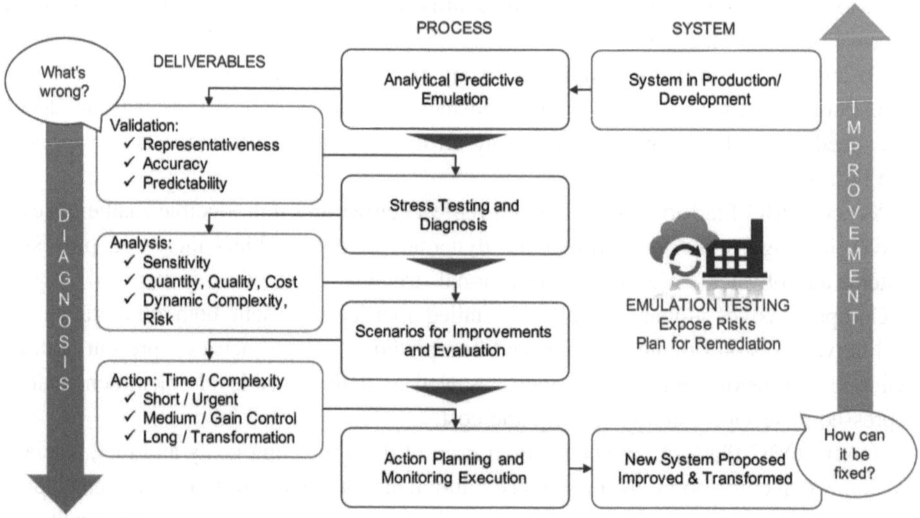

Fig. 6.4 X-Act® OBC Platform supports prescriptive analytics to diagnose problems and suggest improvements

Causal Deconstruction Method

Our causal deconstruction method is a seven-stage scientific methodology (Fig. 6.5) that is used to understand the constituent components of a system and any dependencies by establishing the base dynamics, deconstructing complexity, constructing an emulator, predicting singularities, comparing to the actual system, defining improvements and monitoring the execution.

Causal deconstruction allows us to uncover results that often defy the common wisdom that stops at the wrong level of analysis and usually produces a host of misleading conclusions. Using this method, we can promote the right approach of analysis and mathematics capable of solving the problem within an environment where dynamic complexity has become the major risk.

Emulative Deconstruction Theory

Emulative deconstruction theory is a set of methods, rules, and tooling that allows conceptual, virtual, and/or physical dismantling of structures into components, building blocks, interdependencies, interactions, and other dynamics to understand, predict, reconstruct, and operate improved, transformed or innovated structures.

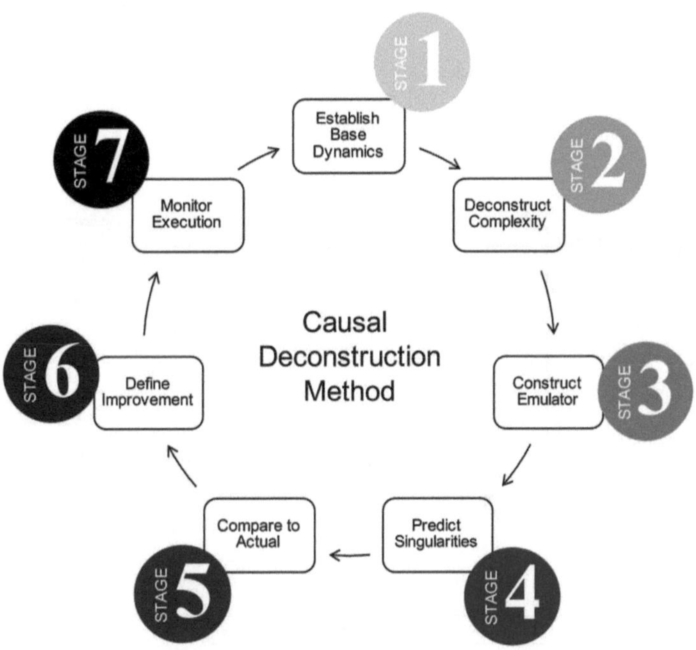

Fig. 6.5 Seven stage causal deconstruction method

Dynamic complexity is hidden in the complex web of processes, systems and physical objects that support modern day businesses that often operate 24/7 and are global in reach. To begin the dynamic complexity discovery process, we must deconstruct the system using *emulative deconstruction theory* to understand its constituent components and dependencies among them (see Fig. 6.6). Deconstruction is analogous to how a doctor, meteorologist, biologist, or engineer will diagnose an eventual problem. This step does not alter the system characteristics or behavior in any way other than is necessary to understand the interdependencies and dynamic properties that can impact each link and node.

To successfully achieve this goal, it is important to collect information and data that will allow us to map the interdependencies, topology of structures, justification of choices, operational constraints, modes of operations, and data available to discover the hidden structures that were formed over time.

We gather the information necessary for deconstruction (Table 6.1) using automated extractors, design templates, as well as graphical representations, such as Business Process Model and Notation (e.g. BPMN). Additionally, we conduct business, financial, design and system workshops to understand business objectives, non-function requirements (NFRs) and discriminate factors.

The goal of collecting this information is to model the system we wish to understand and build a representative mathematical emulation using X-Act® OBC Platform.

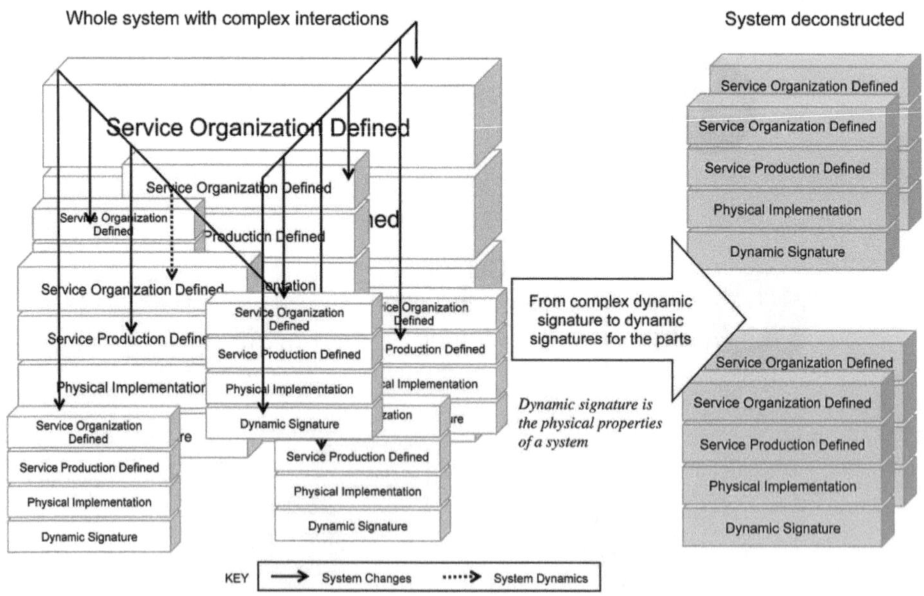

Fig. 6.6 System deconstruction

Table 6.1 Overview of information and data required for system deconstruction

Workshops (Characteristics and Constraints)	Technical analysis measurements	Patterns and peer evaluation	Fundamental analysis
• Corporate strategy • Business • Competition • Activity pricing • Operational implementation • Activity costing • Service management • Obligations • Resources and management • Business cycles • Resource utilization • Peaks/valleys	• Resources/events • Resources utilization • Outstanding issues	• Best in class • Implementation strategies • Specificities	• Impact of external events • Impact of internal services • Impact of external service • Impact of internal event

Mathematical Emulation

The mathematical emulation of a system encapsulates all characteristics, dynamic behaviors and dependencies among system components to reproduce the exact behavior and adhere to all the rules of thc system being emulated so that predictive analysis can be performed (see Fig. 6.7).

To emulate dynamic complexity using deconstruction theory, we need a hierarchical extraction of the dependencies. From this, we must identify the dynamic characteristics that define the behaviors of each participant in the structure (loads, constraints, speeds, and operational characteristics).

The structure starts at the organizational level, served through the generation of processes and sub-processes, implemented though a certain logic or layout (architecture, urbanism, or design), on a physical layer (factory, data center, sorting/transport configuration, or economic instrumentation) as depicted in Fig. 6.8.

As presented in Fig. 6.9, any layer may split into sub-layers to represent dependencies and combinatorial interactions that can appear or be produced vertically as well as horizontally. For instance, a business payment system might support several different business processes for various purposes.

At the physical level, the sharing pattern is predominant and it is crucial to understand the topology that allows the common service to be delivered as well as the behavior of the system at any moment of time, under different loads, and constraints.

Using the mathematical formulation and deconstructed characteristics, dependencies, and content behavior, X-Act® OBC Platform delivers a mathematical emulator that represents the system dynamics and dynamic complexity. Using this emulator, users can deploy the scenarios under different patterns of initial conditions and dynamic constraints to identify the risk and conditions under which the risk will occur, as well as the possible mitigation strategies.

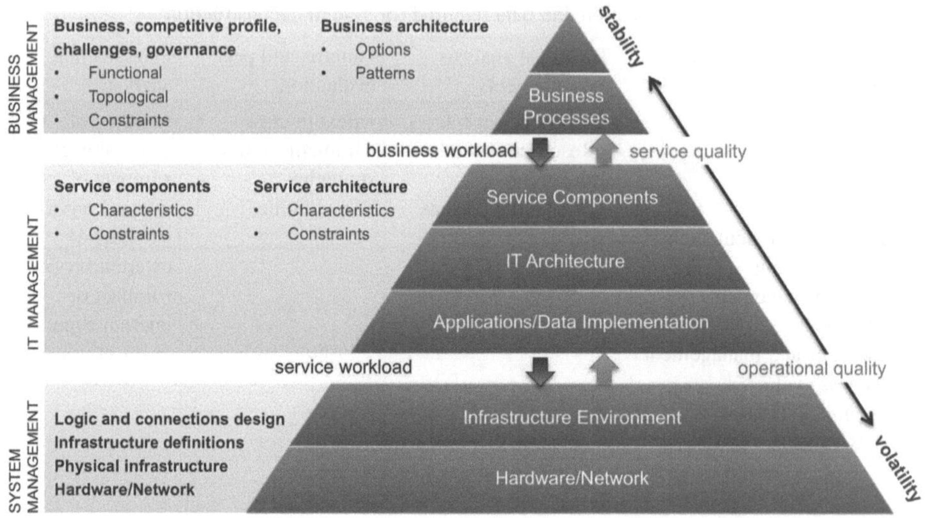

Fig. 6.7 Mathematical emulation covers all system characteristics, dynamic behaviors and dependencies

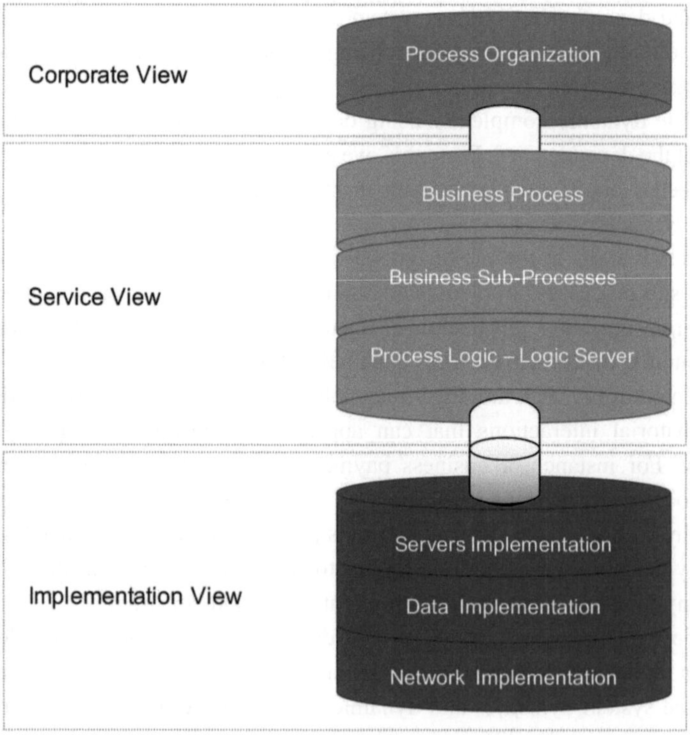

Fig. 6.8 Hierarchical view of a business system

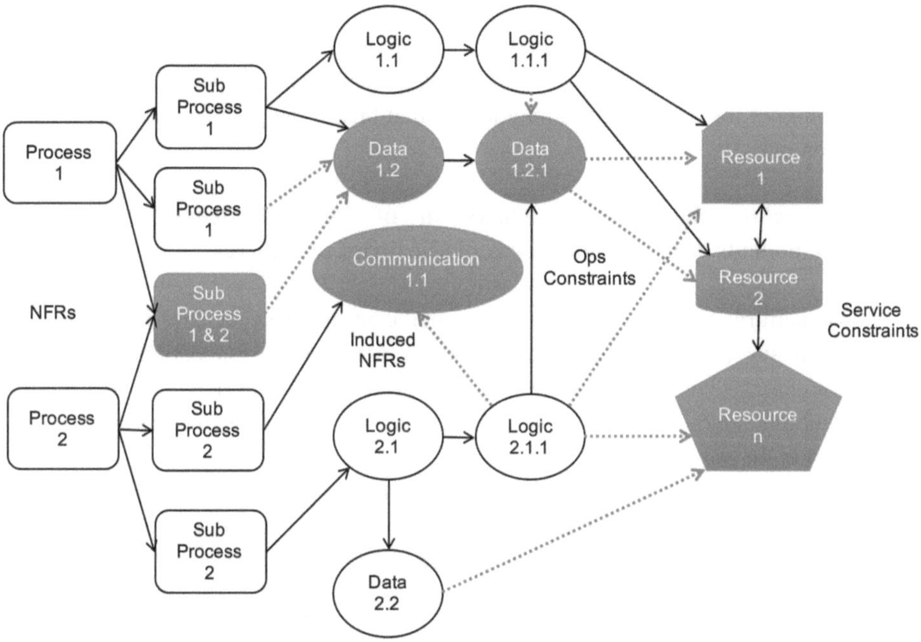

Fig. 6.9 Representation of dependencies and combinatorial interactions

Perturbation Theory

Many popular risk management methods rely upon approximations and assumptions that when applied to a dynamically complex system may result in deviations from real world observations and consequently diminish our ability to use these methods to predict with seriousness. The reasons for this deficiency include:

- Restriction on the size of the problem produces simplifications that may reduce considerably the whole purpose of formulation and consequently a real solution (e.g. as suggested by Issac Newton, we often reduce a 3-body problem to a 2-body +1 problem in modern space sciences).
- Restrictions in nature, kind, and type of disciplines covered by a specific theory may impact the representativeness or reproducibility of the solution (e.g. reliance on the fourth law of thermodynamics which assumes equilibrium and closed structure to compute the risk).
- Some methods may even generate errors with higher magnitude than some values of the parameters characterizing the problem (e.g. the use of curve fitting to derive a trend).
- For some methods, complexity can increase exponentially so that a decent mathematical average becomes problematic to obtain (or rationally be representative).

Perturbation theory uses mathematical methods to find an approximate (quasi-exact) solution to a problem, by starting from the exact solution of a related, simpler problem and continuously add more inequalities until the mathematical representation fits the real one. A critical feature of the technique is a middle step that breaks the problem into solvable and perturbation parts.

☞ ***Inequality*: the dynamic expression of interdependency between two components. Such dependency could be direct or indirect.**

We use perturbation theory to reveal the significant interdependencies in systems that produce dynamic complexity. Perturbation theory provides the foundational solution of dynamic complexity in systems that produces a large spectrum of dynamics and have an exact solution if and only if all or most individual and significant inequalities are explicitly represented in the solution.

Using this method, we can provide accurate formulation of dynamic complexity that is representative of the web of dependencies and inequalities as presented in Fig. 6.10. Additionally, perturbation theory allows for predictions that correspond to variations in initial conditions and influences of intensity patterns.

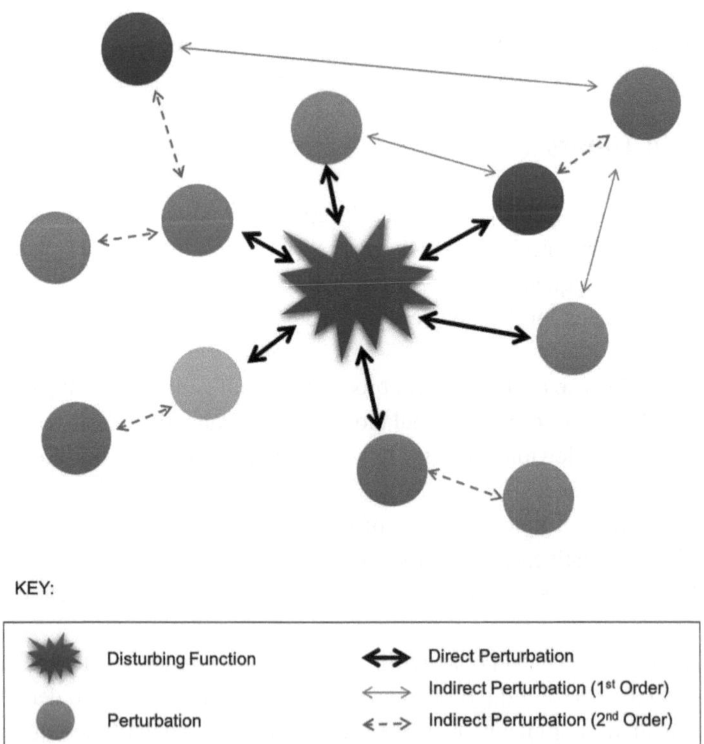

Fig. 6.10 Graphic justification of perturbation theory for critical systems

We have successfully applied perturbation theory in many case studies ranging from economic, healthcare and corporate management modeling to industry transformation and information technology optimization. In each case, we determined with sufficient accuracy the singularity point—beyond which dynamic complexity would become predominant and the predictability of the system would become chaotic.

Dynamic Patterns and Signatures

The use of experienced-based patterns can improve risk management practices if at any moment we can predict, identify and match observed behaviors against known patterns and react accordingly. However, the dynamic dimension of systems presents a challenge in the accurate identification and classification of patterns. To overcome this challenge, we use emulative deconstruction and perturbation theory to mathematically reproduce the dynamic behavior. Using these methods, we can identify whether we are observing a new pattern or a previously identified one.

We can then breakdown the environment or system into its constituents and create the dynamic signatures necessary to predictively emulate system behaviors under various conditions. We can then use emulation to discover system limits, identify chaotic boundaries, and proactively act to avoid an eventual crisis.

Dynamic Patterns

In most cases, patterns are attached to time and space dimensions—consider as examples different requests from a consumer using an ecommerce system or automatic teller machine (ATM). The requests can be regrouped in different patterns—each of which corresponds to a dialog script. A script will serve a purpose, for example, apply payment, obtain a statement, or transfer money for a claim. And each script is composed of multiple commands that replicate a specific dialog.

We define dynamic patterns through the identification of its constituents as illustrated in Fig. 6.11 and outlined below:

- A pattern has a functional purpose that may be a service, formula, process, etc.;
- A pattern has an implementation definition: a mode, kind, profile, structure, etc.;
- A pattern is implemented through a technology: type, constraints, use, evolution, etc.;
- A pattern has a dynamic signature: dependencies on others, performance, cost, service quality;
- A pattern has dynamic constraints: scalability, connectivity, limits, response, etc.;
- A pattern possesses a dependency matrix;
- And finally, a pattern has an aging index.

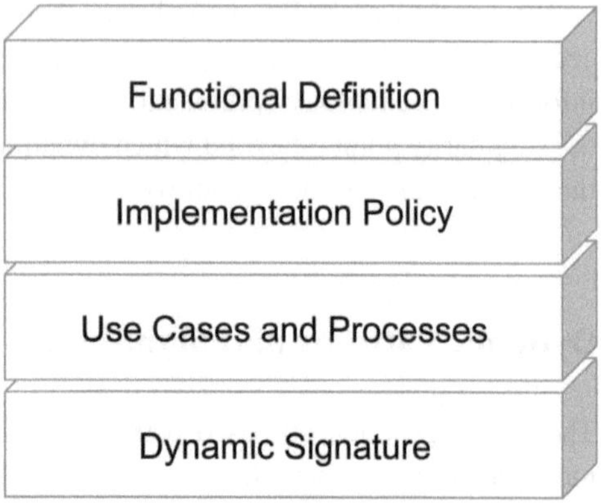

Fig. 6.11 Pattern breakdown (Abu el Ata, Nabil and Perks, Maurice J. *Solving the Dynamic Complexity Dilemma: Predictive and Prescriptive Business Management: Answering the Need for a New Paradigm.* Springer. 2014 edition. 12 August 2014. Print. ISBN-13: 978-3642543098 ISBN-10: 364254309X)

Simple dynamic patterns may form complex structures in which multiple layers of patterns are embedded to form a compound pattern (fractal). A fractal will have a structure definition, dynamic signature, and dynamic set of constraints determined by the way the structure, the dependencies, and how lower level dynamic constraints contribute to the ensemble.

Dynamic Signature

We use dynamic signatures to certify a dynamic pattern. From a system point of view, each pattern has a dynamic signature that requests resources, characterized by specific behaviors and business demands (e.g. authorization), and system infrastructure support (scheduling, recovery, and traceability).

The dynamic signature is determined by computing the amount of resources used to bind a compound pattern. For example, we may want to examine interconnected functional patterns that are each implemented to deliver part of the service. If we want to aggregate the patterns, we need connectors, interfaces, and management (implicitly or explicitly) to structure and bind the target structure. So, we may consider that each of the collaborating patterns will require a certain amount of resources to deliver its part of the service. From this we may establish the following:

T_{fast1} is the required time to deliver the rapid service for pattern 1;

T_{slow1} is the required time to deliver the slower service for pattern 1;

$T_{fast\ for\ slow}$ is the required time for the rapid server to deliver the slow service for pattern 1, if:

δ_{fast1} is the impact on the required time to deliver the processor service for pattern 1 due to other patterns;

δ_{slow1} is the impact on the required time to deliver the

(continued)

I/O service for pattern 1 due to other patterns

$\delta_{\text{fast for slow1}}$ is the impact on the required time from the rapid server to deliver the slow service for pattern 1 due to other patterns

From this we can mathematically express *Service Process A* as:

$$A = A_0 + \Sigma_i \left(\delta_{\text{fast (i)}} + \delta_{\text{slow (i)}} + \delta_{\text{fast for slow (i)}}\right) + \left(\delta^2_{\text{fast (i)}} + \delta 2_{\text{slow (i)}} + \delta 2_{\text{fast for slow (i)}}\right) + \text{Higher order perturbations}$$

$\mathbf{A_0}$ represents the service process dynamic signature attributes (that will be used to determine the signature: quality, quantity, and cost), free from any contention, management overhead or delays.

A is the perturbed service process.

$\boldsymbol{\delta}$ is the first order perturbation, $\boldsymbol{\delta^2}$ is the second order perturbation due to other impacts or the environment, and

$\boldsymbol{\delta^n}$ is the n order perturbation,

Or the binding energy E (resource used to aggregate, manage, and represent dependencies and complexity is:

$$E = A - A_0 = \Sigma_i \left(\delta_{\text{fast (i)}} + \delta_{\text{slow (i)}} + \delta_{\text{fast for slow (i)}}\right) + \left(\delta^2_{\text{fast (i)}} + \delta^2_{\text{slow (i)}} + \delta^2_{\text{fast for slow (i)}}\right) + \text{Higher order perturbations}$$

The optimization exercise targets minimizing the $\boldsymbol{\Sigma_i \left(\Sigma_n \delta_i^n\right)}$ and will be achieved by either modifying the architecture, implementation, or selecting the right technology.

The treatment of the above problem is easily generalizable to other services, missions, or enterprises where we use dynamic patterns to maximize predictability and minimize the management and context overhead (binding energy). In most industries, and in particular for financial and economic systems, such predictability is crucial.

Mathematically speaking, perturbation theory based solutions allow us to determine accurately the conditions that will make: $A \gg A_0$ or in mathematical terms, E tend to infinity i.e., starting to hit the chaotic boundaries.

Our approach determines the inflection point and through the associated discovery process, we are then able to identify the inequality or inequalities that caused the change. The chaotic situation may be caused by a tiny change in one of the parameters that impacts the initial conditions, an architectural or structural defect, or a change in the nature of dependencies among constituents.

The success of our approach is dependent on our ability to define the domain space and the initial conditions of its dynamics. While the identification of the right set of parameters influencing the dynamics is important from the outset, there is no need to statistically observe the system to derive robust conclusions as the ultimate phenomena will generally occur out of scope from any measurements.

Identifying System Limits and Chaotic Conditions

Finally, we propose the following formulation as the base for the dynamic patterns predictive computation that is used to determine both the system limits and inflection of chaotic conditions.

E (degradation due to perturbed impact) $= A - A_0 = \Sigma_i$ (first Order Perturbation) + Σ_j (n order Perturbations) + any other impact

Practical Use of Dynamic Patterns

Using the methods described above, we have mathematically modeled to predict and qualify over 10,000 dynamic patterns for a variety of industries, business processes, architectures, infrastructures, and platforms. These dynamic patterns, as represented in Fig. 6.12, are available to X-Act® OBC Platform users. The dynamic patterns are generated through confirmed, replicated and validated emulations that cover many business dimensions including characteristics and dynamic behavior of an industry, processes, infrastructure, physical resources and interdependencies.

X-Act® libraries cover a wide range of industries (postal services, supply chain, automotive, plane maintenance, traffic control and others), infrastructure (human services, robots, intelligent agents, sorting machines, schedulers styles, storage apps, queuing mechanisms and synchronization).

By making a library containing over 10,000 pre-built models and assets available to X-Act® OBC Platform users, even users with no previous modeling experience can easily use the libraries to build a representative model of all business and technology layers. When building a new emulation, users employ our libraries to speed up the emulation process and benchmark against best in class implementations.

The deployed process allows users to control and manage the targeted environment, predict the eventual crisis or singularity points, and augment X-Act® libraries with their own newly discovered patterns to gradually build and support more intelligent automation.

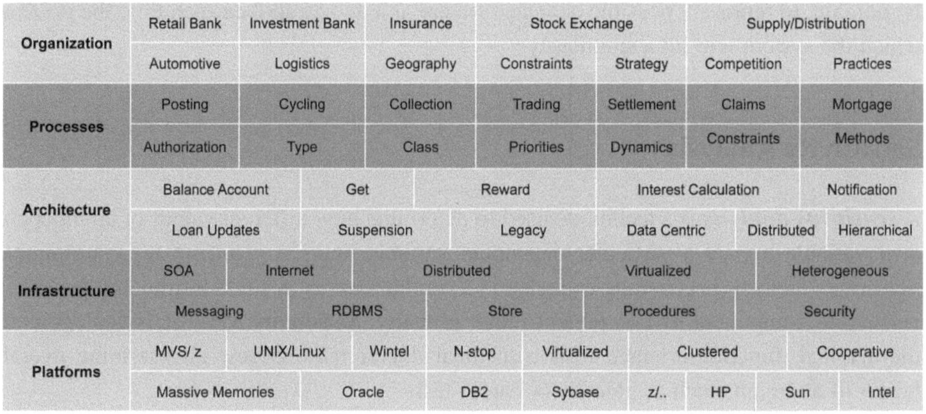

Fig. 6.12 X-Act® library of dynamic patterns

Causal Analysis

The basic principle of causal analysis is to find causes that you can treat rather than treating symptoms. A *root cause* is the basic reason why something happens and can be quite distant from the produced effect. We perform causal analysis through the emulation built using X-Act® OBC Platform. This allows us to represent not only the component's interdependencies discovered during the deconstruction, but also allows us to stress test scenarios for each component and connection to discover which ones provoke dynamic complexity. In this manner, we can discover the scenarios that may cause an eventual singularity, chaos, or rapid deterioration of system health. Consequently, this discovery allows for the timely mitigation of risk.

Stress Testing

Stress testing is a form of deliberately intense or thorough testing used to determine the stability of a given system. It is performed by applying predictive emulation scenarios that include extreme changes in volume and/or degradation of infrastructure or availability. To identify the risks or singularities that may be caused by dynamic complexity, we must test a system beyond normal operational capacity to find the breaking points and observe the results when various conditions change.

Using the emulator built in X-Act® OBC Platform, we deploy the scenarios under different patterns of initial conditions and dynamic constraints to identify the conditions under which risk will increase and use the corresponding information to diagnose the case. By modifying the parameters of each scenario within the emulator, one by one, by group, or by domain, to represent possible changes, we are able to extrapolate each time the point at which the system will hit a singularity.

Sensitivity Analysis

A ***sensitivity analysis*** is a technique used to determine how different values of an independent variable impact a particular dependent variable under a given set of assumptions. Sensitivity analysis is generally executed in a similar manner as stress testing, but the test is performed component by component rather globally. Sensitivity analysis is analogous to the detailed, function-oriented tests a medical doctor may request to determine overall health of an organ, such as glucose or cardio tests.

We use sensitivity analysis to identify which actions are needed to manage the risks posed by dynamic complexity. Using X-Act® OBC Platform, we can analyze the scenarios under different patterns of initial conditions and dynamic constraints to identify the conditions under which risk will decrease and explore viable and proactive remedial options that secure an acceptable risk mitigation strategy.

Optimal Business Control (OBC)

Optimal business control (OBC) provides right-time risk alerts and preemptive fixing of any identified problems by using quantitative and qualitative metrics to proactively discover risks that may cause situations of system deterioration. Using a knowledge library and machine-learning sciences, we can then define the optimal treatment of risk and use this knowledge to feed a decision engine that organically evolves to cover new and increasingly complex behavioral scenarios.

OBC uses situational data revealed by the predictive platform to provide surveillance of systems and identify cases of increasing risk. These cases are *unknowns* in big data analytical methods, which are limited to prediction based on data collected through experience. Within the OBC database, a diagnosis definition and remediation that cover both the experience based knowns and those that were previously unknown are stored together to allow for the rapid identification of a potential risk with immediate analysis of root causes and proposed remedial actions.

This approach to right-time risk surveillance, using a database populated by the mathematical predictive platform, represents a real breakthrough that alleviates many of the pains created by the traditional long cycle of risk management, which starts with problem-analysis-diagnosis and ends with eventual fixing well beyond the point of optimal action. OBC represents a clear advantage by shortening the time to discovery and time to fix risks.

As the database is continuously enriched by the dynamic characteristics that continuously evolve during a system's lifetime, the knowledge contained within the database becomes more advanced. OBC is also adaptive. By continuously recording within the OBC database foundational or circumstantial system changes, the predictive platform will identify any new risk, determine the diagnosis and define the remedial actions, and finally enhance the OBC database with this new knowledge.

Model-Based Architecture (MBA)

Through a goal oriented methodology that follows the principles of *computer-aided design* (CAD), referred to as Model-based Architecture (MBA), we help companies design future-proof architecture and validate that the proposed strategy will continuously meet business cost, scalability and performance requirements. This is achieved by continuously emulating the partial constructs of a system until it is fully defined. The method ensures that sufficient time and information is provided to system stakeholders so that any risks can be resolved before moving to the next step of system definition or implementation.

MBA is a patented methodology[1] that builds the conceptual context of remediation around the goal-oriented diagnosis of X-Act® OBC Platform. It contains three dimensions:

1. A generic architecture that separates the heavy-duty engines from the functional interfaces, the low maintenance from the fast upgrades, and the data on its own from its usage
2. An integrated emulation capability through X-Act® OBC Platform to validate the architecture (and its step-wise evolution) and monitor its implementation
3. A set of guidelines and principles that help manage the construction process and anticipate eventual problems through a large spectrum of best practices ready to be used in new implementation

Using MBA businesses can validate their risk management plans to determine the optimal path towards efficient, lean, and cost-effective implementation before significant resources are dedicated to any transformation project. MBA helps businesses reduce the impact of dynamic complexity by removing the interdependencies as far as possible, moving the interactions to the technology level, and selecting the right technology to satisfy the business requirements, which include non-functional and discriminant factors.

With the MBA approach, we have helped clients in many highly critical industries achieve 5–10 times the volume of traditional architecture for the same or less resources with a much higher quality of service. To maintain these advantages, architecture produced through mathematical emulation must be maintained using the same emulator. This allows users to keep the foundational principles intact and reduce/anticipate any possible aging due to adaptation, technology upgrade, or redundancies.

---

[1]2001 – US Patent 00703 1901 B2.

7 The Challenge: Escaping the Tunnel Vision, Identifying the Best Path and Evaluating the Reward

Ignorance bothers me less than the illusion of knowledge.
—Lawrence Krauss, 2015, Quantum physicist, cosmologist

In this chapter:

- How automation benefits create a tunnel vision that increases risk exposure
- Understanding why risk management must evolve to meet the requirements of the Fourth Industrial Revolution
- Why mathematical emulation is needed to identify the best path forward and evaluate the potential rewards of any proposed actions

Tunnel Vision Handicaps Business Leaders

The benefits gained over the last century through business automation were not questioned until the early 2000s. Mainly because no significant side effects or disorder could be observed as automation undeniably delivered economies of scale with better, more efficient delivery of products and services. For this reason, most management and system stakeholders focus solely on the benefits gained through automation and often disregard growing evidence of the harmful side effects. This entrenched perspective is supported by many unquestionable automation advantages that deliver business value, comforts and abundance including:

N. Abu el Ata, A. Drucbert, *Leading from Under the Sword of Damocles*,
https://doi.org/10.1007/978-3-662-56300-7_7

- Ability to popularize products and services that are supported by attractive cost versus price ratios
- Advancement of workforce skills as machines replaced humans for simpler, repeatable and sometimes dangerous activities
- Major reductions in the cost of raw materials and other industrial assets due to better mining, extraction and nuclear power
- Relative political stability, particularly for advanced and emerging economies, as political aggressions were refocused towards economic competitiveness and the achievement of targeted aspirations
- Creation of value through wider economic and financial performance supported by the gradual sophistication of a larger range of products and services

However, the past hundred years of coveted industrial evolution is starting to lose its momentum in terms of value and visibility. This decline has translated into successive recessions, economic crisis and massive unemployment for many reasons including:

- Globalization was certainly beneficial, but it also favored faster communication of crisis and instability from wider sources of risk.
- The advances in communication favored rapid changes and instability in process definitions. As such, many repeatable solutions were conceived to automate a process, but not necessarily adapted to handle a large amplitude of variations.
- The explosion of multi-media reduced the cost to enter new markets. Startups began to challenge traditional businesses by offering new tools, products and services that were better suited to meet market demands at a lower cost. Additionally, these companies operated leaner and were more suited to adapt to changing market conditions. Examples of new solutions that supported disruptions included money transfer, payment systems, componentization, miniaturization of processing power and integration, intelligent agents and internet.
- Changes in consumer perceptions and experience generated a wide range of new requirements that traditional systems were not able to fulfil without incurring a substantial deviation from the business' current economic equation.

Many Businesses Have Reached a Dead-end

Current business solutions and implementations are not compatible with today's business dynamics. There is a real disconnect between the business' requirements and the aging systems that were developed to meet those requirements. Many business leaders have anticipated that the benefits of automation would diminish over time, but now they face a practical dead-end. The cost of delivering goods and services through legacy business implementations is quickly spinning out of control while the implementations themselves are becoming increasingly difficult to adapt.

In our modern world, it is becoming clear that a business cannot continue to pay $40 to transfer $300. It is impractical to take five weeks to generate a picture ID or car title. Introducing a new banking service to clients in 9 months may no longer be fast enough to remain competitive. Taking 3 months to deliver a slightly customized car is longer than we can expect consumers to wait in our fast-paced world. And the required re-engineering effort necessary to meet these changing market dynamics can cost established global corporations tens of billions of dollars.

However, new innovations appear on the market every day that will be translated into opportunities for some businesses and the death knell of others. Retailers may become bankers, algorithmic trading may no longer be exclusive to traditional investment institutions, and driverless cars and alternative energy sources may cause the extinction of fossil-energy based conglomerates.

New business activities generate new implementations. Ecommerce surpassed $300 billion in 2015 with annual growth of 15%. Blockchain technologies will potentially save the banking industry billions of dollars while delivering better security. It will become much easier and much less expensive to provide healthcare through an individual health vault—and the same solution can be applied to the legal industry.

In the automation era, we built architecture and infrastructure solutions—hoping that they represented all possible patterns. But as dynamics shift due to changing requirements—whether they be business-driven or market-driven—established businesses are left treating new patterns as they appear with spaghetti structures that are nowhere near optimal and break the bridge between the business and its implementation.

Identifying the Path to Success

Once businesses acknowledge that the automation phase of the Third Industrial Revolution is quickly transitioning to the cyber-physical phase of the Fourth Industrial Revolution, they must redefine their forward path of progress. Through our work, it is becoming apparent that the next stage of modernization is dependent upon a business' ability to continuously and rapidly translate business dynamics into dynamic implementation. This objective will not be achieved by merely changing the infrastructure—as this approach has been increasing the risk exposure of businesses over the last 20 years.

Now, as dictated by Darwinian gradualism, a profound change is required to elevate the structure of a business to a level that corresponds to the current reality characterized by a continuous change in mixes, functionality, behavior, sophistication and complexity. This goal can no longer be served by the standard automation process that always leaves the implementation several steps behind the current direction of the business. Moreover, current methods that translate static business requirements into static implementations are now outdated.

The necessary business constraints of the future are applied in driverless technology through which all possible obstacles are predetermined implements at the command-center level. This necessitates that business implementations be built using variable geometry, variable-sweep wing or other adaptive control classes of technology. With more conservative classes of traditional business implementation, it will be important to collect as many business dynamic patterns as possible and use the most advanced emulative and predictive mechanisms to build the solution that best fits the dynamic instantiation.

The Importance of Emulation

Building the Right Implementation that Manages Risk for an Optimal Cost

Emulation comes from the Latin word *aemulat*, meaning "rivaled, equaled." The solution of the lunar 3-body problem is as an eloquent example of emulation—as the mathematical equation of any dynamics problem is an emulation.

Many industrial processes use emulation to speed time to production and avoid the costs associated with building prototypes. For example, new plane designs are most commonly conceived and tested through mathematical emulation. This type of emulation not only allows the designer to replicate the general characteristics of the system or object, but also makes it possible to accurately reproduce the dynamic behavior of the object and its behavior in connection to all other objects. Emulation is largely used in critical industries including space exploration, Dassault-Avionics, nuclear theoretical and experimental studies, and sensitive chemical projects and even in economic competition.

Some processes are unstable and sensitive to the environment, which leads to frequent changes in the initial conditions and therefore requires dynamic emulation through mathematical treatment involving multiple order of impacts. Most dynamic systems fall in such category.

X-Act® OBC Platform was conceived and built as an emulation technology to accurately represent the behavior of system dynamics. It replaces structures, characteristics and behaviors by perturbations exerted on dynamic equations through multiple order perturbations on dynamic coordinates such as volume, service quality and cost. The transformation of a system into emulation is foundational to our Model-based Architecture (MBA) methodology because once the emulation is successfully delivered it allows system stakeholders to quickly test and economically explore an unlimited number of change scenarios that would otherwise be complex, expensive or even impossible to test on a real system.

In comparison to other practices, such as simulation, emulation is clearly superior in its ability to accurately replicate a system, but its biggest advantage is that it allows for the discovery of previously unknown patterns, which cannot be determined using simulation.

Emulation Versus Simulation

A simulation is built from a fully understood process—in terms of operational characteristics—and will not necessarily cover a change in dynamics. While, emulation covers both the dynamic behavior—in time and space—and the comprehensive operational characteristics. Due to this fact, *we cannot simulate risk* because only the knowns are represented and so reproduced.

We can emulate risk because we can mathematically reproduce unknowns that may happen under certain conditions. This is possible using emulation because once we solve the dynamic equation and verify both its accuracy and reproducibility, we can change variables—such as volume, architecture, and infrastructure or perform sensitivity predictions on changing process dynamics—to observe the outcomes even if we have no historical record of these events happening.

To provide further clarification, the following examples highlight the differences between simulation versus emulation when applied to risk management scenarios:

- It is not possible to simulate an economic crisis if it has never happened before. But we can emulate the outcome of changing economic dynamics that impact the dependencies and explicitly represent internal and external influencers on economic systems.
- Using simulation for benchmarking is useless because the behavior of the system is not necessarily produced through well balanced and equally impacted behaviors of its constituents. Only emulation can predict the behavior of dynamic systems.
- Simulation can't replace prototyping because the simulated implementation may be difficult to build, so emulation becomes the only recourse.
- Predictive management of the supply chain is indispensable to avoid last minute modifications that may become difficult to implement as time runs critical and complexity of time-dependent tasks intensifies. Emulation can produce all possible scenarios that correspond to changes in operational and environmental parameters.

Over the last 15 years, we have worked on many cases where predictive emulation would have saved or did in fact save the business millions of dollars by identifying risks and the necessary corrective actions before investments and resources were committed. Sample cases include:

- In a newly delivered settlement and clearing system, we found that the system lacked any control over the number of cycles allowed before a match was made. Meaning that the outstanding number of cycles could become so large that the throughput of the system would severely suffer. Since the problem was found after the system was built, an additional effort of 16,000 man days was necessary to fix the problem. The proactive use of emulation testing could have prevented this problem.

- A wholesale business was exposed to an operational risk when they discovered it was not possible to verify the location of inventory through the point-of-sale (POS) terminals as planned. A new implementation had to be developed from scratch. Emulation testing would have allowed the business to verify that the proposed implementation would meet all business requirements from the outset.
- To improve operations, many businesses sought to expand and use a distributed processing environment. However, performance declined in most cases and an increase in dynamic complexity led to much more uncertainty on the outcome. Emulation could have revealed the impacts of dynamic complexity and the associated risks.
- A nation-wide social benefits implementation planned on using 13 datacenters with $2\times$ replication, but involved a risk of redundant fraud. Using emulation, we developed a plan that would use only two datacenters with a cross business continuity protocol that would minimize operational risk. The delivery of the solution was monitored and controlled using the same emulation to ensure the ongoing success of the project.
- A postal services implementation planned on using 75 sorting centers, but the emulation proved that 22 sorting centers would be sufficient and would not alter the service quality or volume capacity in any way.

8 Analytical Versus Numerical Solutions

If we knew exactly the laws of nature and the situation of the universe at the initial moment, we could predict exactly the situation of the same universe at a succeeding moment.
—Henri Poincare, French mathematician and father of the theory of chaos

In this chapter:

- Comparing the hype of big data analytics versus the reality
- Why the predictions of most analytics technologies are only valid for a short time
- Importance of taking an analytical approach to risk management

Many current popular analytic methods are in fact numeric—supported by big data hype, which promises users that the more *big data* they have, the better conclusions they will be able to ascertain. ***However, analytics can only deliver robust predictions and be data independent if the unknowns are discovered from the outset.***

N. Abu el Ata, A. Drucbert, *Leading from Under the Sword of Damocles*,
https://doi.org/10.1007/978-3-662-56300-7_8

Industry analysts continuously put forward their vision, estimation and predictions for the markets and technologies they cover. Some analysts' visions are aligned with evolution in Darwinian terms, but others' predictions lack seriousness and promote hype, as is the current case with big data analytics.

When considering the use of the term *analytics* in the last decade, it becomes clear that its popularization is mostly a marketing gimmick with little scientific support. Data exploitation and analysis is necessary to capture customer trends, market shifts and actual behavior or discover patterns in social media. However, the validity of analysis will always be highly dependent on the dynamics of the problem being analyzed.

If the dynamics of a system is continuously changing, the analysis will only be valid for the window of time during which the data was captured. Outside this window of time, an alignment with reality is unlikely, which is the case for most enterprise operational systems. In this case, it is necessary to use the type of mathematical analytics we promote to monitor, predict and support managing such systems because statistical methods are applicable only under two conditions:

1. The system is stable and the effects of dynamic complexity does not under any circumstance cause the system to deviate from its average behavior
2. The simulation is capable of accurately, representatively and predictably reproducing all system states—both known and unknown—under different initial conditions

In collaboration with our colleague Rudolf Schmandt (he comes from a theoretical mechanics background, as did I), we developed the following academic definition to explain the critical difference between an analytical and numerical solution:

> Suppose you have a mathematical model and you want to understand its behavior. That is, you want to find a solution to the set of equations. In this case, it is best to use calculus, trigonometry and other math techniques to write down the solution. Now you absolutely know how the model will behave under any circumstances. This is called an analytic solution, because you used analysis to figure it out. It is also referred to as a closed form solution.
>
> But this tends to work only for simple models. For more complex models, the math becomes much too complicated. So, you must turn to numerical methods of solving the equations, such as the Runge-Kutta or e method and Chebyshev's theorem. For a differential equation that describes behavior over time, the numerical method starts with the initial values of the variables, and then uses the equations to figure out the changes in these variables over a very brief time. It's only an approximation, but it can be a very good approximation under certain circumstances.[1]

[1]Abu el Ata, Nabil and Rudolf Schmandt. Email. 2017.

For numerical methods, a computer must be used to perform the thousands of repetitive calculations involved. The result is a long list of numbers, not an equation. This long list of numbers can be used to drive an animated simulation.

Numerical solution	Analytical solution
Produces a long list of numbers that can be used for simulation	Produces an equation that can be used for emulation
Approximate prediction of behavior	Precise prediction behavior
Valid under certain circumstances for short periods of time	Valid under any circumstances for long periods of time
Dependent on accuracy and volume of big data	Requires only a limited set of accurate data
Dynamic complexity cannot be accurately reproduced	Dynamic complexity can be accurately reproduced
Useful for closed loop systems operating in non-dynamic environments	Useful for open loop systems operating in dynamic environments

Using Technology to Achieve an Analytical Solution

X-Act® OBC Platform is an analytical representation that emulates system dynamics into mathematical expression—meaning a set of equations. This leads to the computation of an accurate solution that delivers the same values of metrics that would have resulted if we had taken real system measurements under the same set of initial conditions. Once validated, the system of equations can be reliably used for predictive diagnosis and prescriptive analysis.

There is also a middle ground between analytic and numerical methods—which is necessary because there are many important ***non-linear*** equations for which it is not possible to find an analytic solution. However, techniques such as the ***perturbation method***,[2] allow users to find approximate analytic solutions that are close to the true solution—at least within a certain range. The advantage of this method in comparison to a numerical solution is that you wind up with an equation (instead of just a long list of numbers) which allows you to gain additional insight. Others have added semi-analytic solutions to accelerate the delivery of the solution—even if is only valid for mid-terms. Such techniques are used to compute astronomical ephemeris and in quantum mechanics.

When marketers put together the two concepts of *big data* and *analytics*, they introduced—by impression, ignorance or hype—an incorrect coupling that delivers only partial results which are valid only within the initial conditions that seldom happen by accident. So, what analysts and vendors call analytics is in fact numeric. This inaccurate

[2]Laplace, Poincare, Abu El Ata, and Chapront.

use of terminology directly effects how analytics are perceived along with the projected value of the solution by blurring the input, the method and the output. The methods employed by X-Act® OBC Platform and our proposed method of universal risk management are truly analytic because they determine the solution to dynamic equations by applying perturbation theory.

Why an Analytical Approach Is Key to Risk Management

A high-level comparison between numerical and analytical approaches to risk discovery and mitigation is provided in Fig. 8.1.

When assessing risk, it is clear that some of the data we need will be available using historical information or *big data*. But some data will be missing because the event has not yet happened and can only be revealed under certain conditions. To expose the missing data, we must use emulation to reproduce the mechanics of various forward-looking scenarios and examine the potential outcomes.

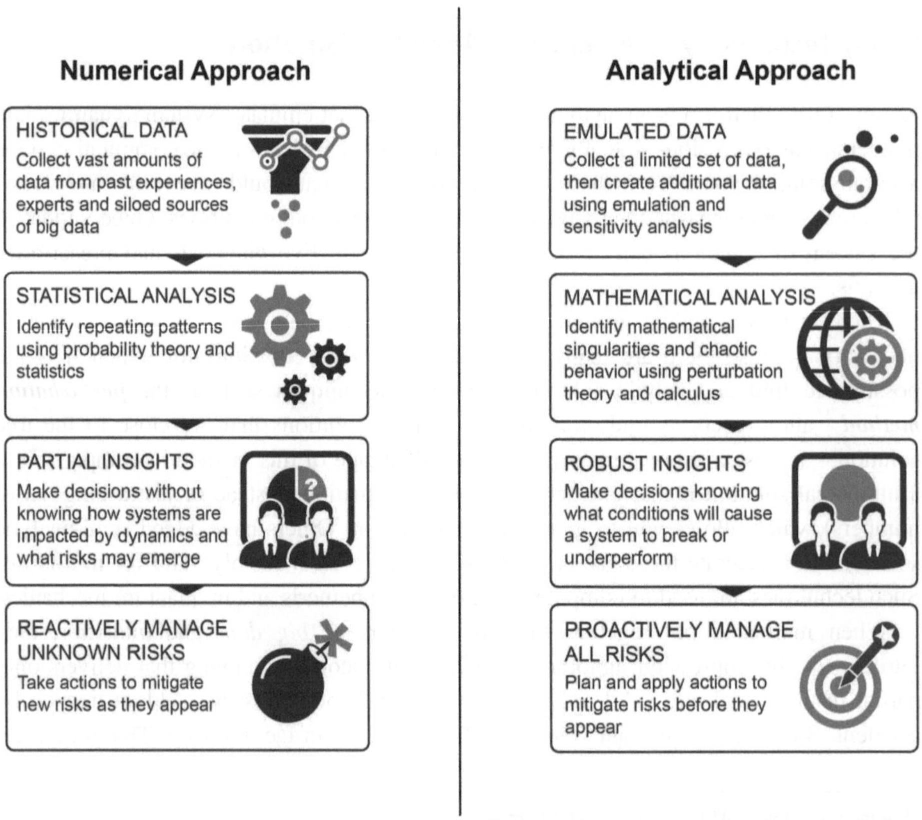

Fig. 8.1 Comparison of numerical versus analytical approach to risk discovery and mitigation

Emulation is used in many industries to reproduce the behavior of systems and explore unknowns. Take for instance space exploration. We cannot successfully construct and send satellites, space stations, or rovers into unexplored regions of space based merely on historical data. While the known data from past endeavors is certainly important, we must construct the data which is unknown by emulating the spacecraft and conducting sensitivity analysis. This allows us to predict the unpredicted and prepare for the unknown. While the unexpected may still happen, using emulation we will be better prepared to spot new patterns earlier and respond more appropriately to these new scenarios.

Once dynamic complexity is understood and its origins identified, management can move from reactive to a preventive stance. This will become the preferred way to manage risk—identify the dynamic complexity, evaluate the risk of degradation and singularities, measure the distance to the risk and take the right actions before negative business outcomes become unavoidable. The right predictive technologies will allow decision makers to evaluate proposed actions prior to implementation, determine the right path to optimization, transformation and/or innovation, and consequently reduce risk without inadvertently adding more dynamic complexity.

9 Using X-Act OBC Platform for Risk

Mathematicians carry the rigor of scientific reasoning into everyday life. Mathematical discovery is subversive, and is ever ready to break taboos, and depends very little on established authorities.

Many today tend to consider scientists, whether mathematicians or not, as people little concerned with moral standards, harmful, shut up within their ivory tower, and indifferent to the world outside. The Committee of Mathematicians is a brilliant illustration of the contrary.
—Laurent Schwarz, 1975, The French father of analysis

In this chapter:

- How X-Act® OBC Platform can be used to improve risk management maturity
- Discovering risk to diagnose potential problems and prescriptively identify solutions
- Why it is important to use technology to support a continuous chain of right-time decisions throughout the evolution of a business implementation

Under the pressure of time and circumstances, the identification of new risks and its necessary treatment are often ignored until a crisis hits. However, it is possible to proactively use emulation to build a risk signature of a situation, which includes the analysis of actions required for risk avoidance.

N. Abu el Ata, A. Drucbert, *Leading from Under the Sword of Damocles*,
https://doi.org/10.1007/978-3-662-56300-7_9

Through a wide range of built-in parameters that may change for a variety of reasons, the X-Act® OBC Platform emulator allows users to test options and build change scenarios, as well as perform sensitivity and stress analysis. Once an emulation is built and proven representative and accurate in comparison to a number of operational instantiations and demonstrates reproducibility, it will support decision activities and identify limits, degradation conditions and risk factors of business implementations to accomplish the following goals:

- Justify decisions
- Discover the origin of an eventual crisis
- Determine the distance until a potential disaster may occur
- Discover remediation actions, as well as prioritize and evaluate the actions in terms of complexity, the defined outcome and time to deliver
- Produce a blueprint for business implementations that correspond to business requirements and constraints
- Execute benchmarks and evaluate change options
- Test the implementation
- Alert system owners of any predicted degradation
- Predict the economic impact, opportunities and limits of changes that are proposed through change management programs

Using our methods, a higher level of business excellence can be achieved by continuously diagnosing and remediating risk at the right time rather than during the height of a crisis, when remedial options are greatly restricted by time and scope.

Five Ways to Use X-Act OBC Platform to Improve Risk Management Maturity

Using X-Act® OBC Platform emulation capabilities can help businesses establish risk management excellence in the following ways:

1. ***Project Command Center***

   Using emulation from the outset of a project definition allows system stakeholders to:
   - Verify that the business goals for the implementation will be met
   - Ensure the implementation will not lead to a high level of dynamic complexity
   - Test the dynamic options as scenarios in order to discover dynamic patterns
   - Keep volume, cost and quality constraints aligned

   Throughout the project lifecycle, the emulator can be used to discover possible operational risks and provide options for mitigation.

Risk can have positive impacts if it helps the enterprise maintain a competitive position, but out of control projects can quickly introduce negative outcomes. In both cases, the emulator will provide advance warning of evolving risks. Over the last 10 years, X-Act® OBC Platform has been used to help companies decide whether to maintain or cancel multi-year, multi-million dollar projects, as well as provide the oversight necessary to successfully manage projects to completion.

2. ***Monitor the Health of Implementations***

   Emulation represents an insurance mechanism to verify that the implementation will conform to the promise made to the business during the early stages of project definition. But even more importantly, emulation is critical over the lifetime of the implementation project because it provides a way to test different options, innovations or alternative scenarios and confidently determine if the scenario will provide measurable improvements—by accelerating implementation windows, reducing costs or increasing service quality and volumes. This allows system stakeholders to thoroughly test all options through the emulator to identify the opportunities for improvement and any associated risks before committing investments, time and resources to the change project.

3. ***Transform at the Right Time***

   Operating a profitable business and managing the transformation of a business implementation are complex endeavors. Once a transformation project moves from a conceptual to an active stage, many stakeholders, processes, practices, experience and skills become exposed to change. The scope of changes may vary in nature from superficial to profound, simple to complex, and precarious to durable. But only emulation can determine the right trajectory to success so that the journey is smooth, optimal and continuously justified at the right time with the right decision. In this way, emulation can become a great weapon that can be used to fight against the fear that often comes with any deviation from the status quo of current business operations.

4. ***Test Strategic and Tactical Moves***

   Executive management always faces an important dilemma as they consider whether to choose tactical excellence as a strategic objective or consider tactical issues as merely the tributary of strategies. The difference is foundational as strategies should allow for a stream of information that is necessary to support the adaptation of strategies to a dynamic environment, which is changing faster than ever. A strong, trustworthy predictive and prescriptive emulation can deliver the necessary optimal insights. Eventually this course of actions may well lead to disruption.

5. ***Monitor Risk in Real-time***

   The point above makes clear the need to test tactical moves to determine the correct strategies, but we should add that real-time operational information must be integrated to build a full picture and ensure that all efforts are focused on the right challenge. With

First Data in early 2000s, we were able to close the full cycle-operations to tactically feed the strategy. Running the cycle several times helped to form consensus as it was found that any major transformation would not be worthwhile since it was questionable whether the desired results could be achieved within the necessary window of time. This conclusion led stakeholders to instead consider optimization based on small predictable steps or a disruption as the only realistic scenarios. Over time it was proven that our emulation recommendations were correct and reconfirmed that emulation should always precede a strategic decision.

Discover Risk to Diagnose Problems and Prescribe Solutions

Emulation improves risk management excellence by ensuring that risk predictability leads to optimal prescriptibility so that decisions can easily be made in time to avoid negative business outcomes. Today crises appear more frequently than they did a decade ago. Currently in most of these cases, risk comes as a surprise and decision makers are forced to blindly react from unknown territory.

To clearly understand the situation and retain a proactive management stance, we need to determine the impacts of dynamic complexity on business implementations. This is a modern problem that needs a modern solution because dynamic complexity grows at a much faster pace today due to a wider impact of influences that have gained in speed and intensity. Further, we must accept that dynamic complexity evolves like a cancer within businesses. From this position, we know that the prescriptive treatment must be soundly based the correct root cause.

Emulation by its very definition recovers the origin of dynamic complexity. Emulation models are used to successfully determine the positions of stars at any point in time (past and future) and build astronomical ephemerides with sufficient accuracy of a few centimeters between two points on the moon. Space exploration would be too risky without such knowledge. In short, emulation allows us to discover the unknowns that are necessary to build accurate and impactful predictions which in turn aide in the prescription of timely business decisions.

What Information Do We Need for Prescription?

Before we can accurately prescribe a specific treatment of risk, we first need to discover all the causes of risk that may be manifested through the causes outlined in Table 9.1.

Table 9.1 Causes of business risk

Degradation	• Service quality • Cost escalation • Reduction of output • Predictability • Scalability • Latency • Resiliency
Aging	• Longer time to market • Cost inflation • Slow maintenance • Frequent failures • Slow delivery of service
Economic obsolescence	• Degradation in margin • Sensitivity to external influences and variations • Inflation in operations • Risk at the near horizon

What Universal Risk Management Delivers

As shown in Fig. 9.1, business implementations must evolve as business requirements evolve to avoid increasing risk. Figure 9.2 depicts how X-Act® OBC Platform provides the continuity necessary to support the evolution of business implementations through right-time decisions. X-Act® OBC Platform can be used to emulate the context of a business implementation and its dynamics at any moment in time to support a continuous chain of decisions such as:

- Improve the business performance through infrastructure optimization only if the project can be successfully managed and won't restrain the future direction of the business.
- Improve business implementation through architecture re-engineering. In cases when the implementation is over a few decades old, answer questions regarding the impact of continuing to use a system that is outdated, heavy and prone to problems.
- Improve business efficiency through business process definition, using emulation to explore the right questions, which includes not only the characteristics but also the variations in dynamics to form a common understanding.
- Transmute the business by redefining the business model, as may become necessary in case such as:
  - New business implementation rules: e.g. new regulation
  - New business foundations: e.g. blockchain

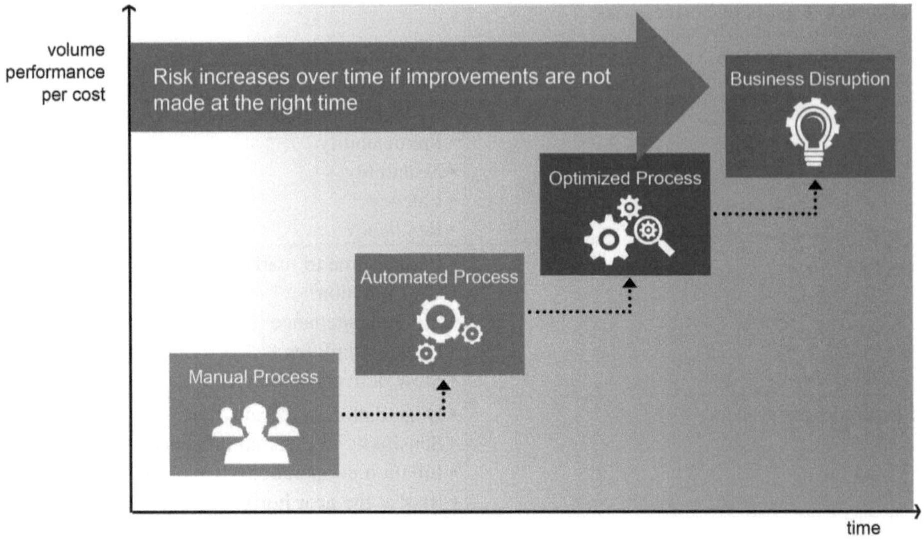

Fig. 9.1 To avoid increasing risk, business implementations must evolve as business requirements evolve

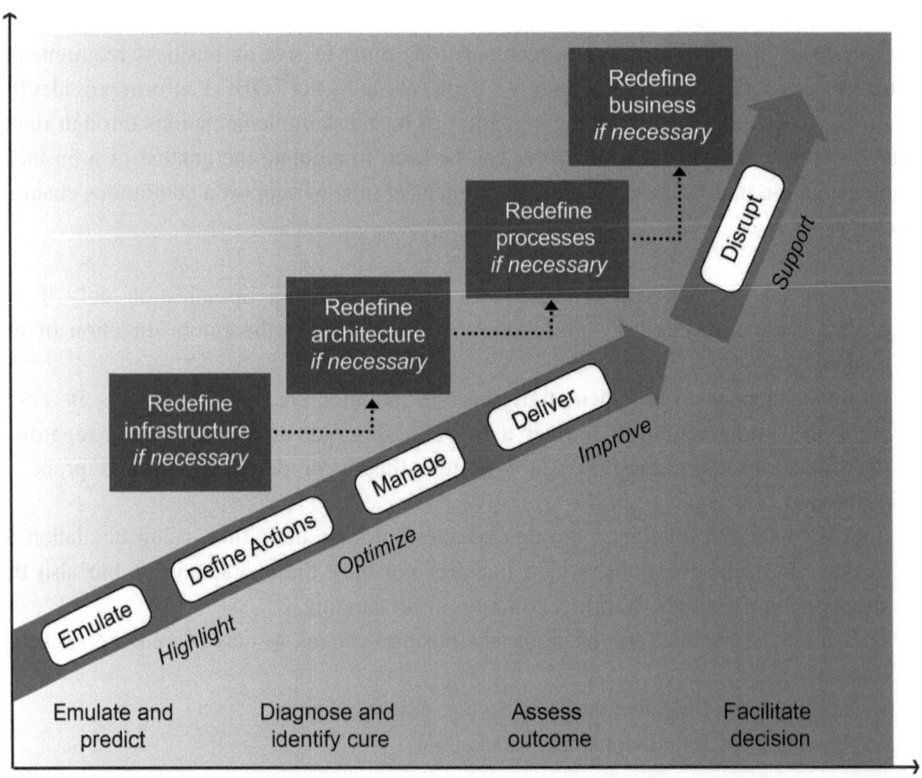

Fig. 9.2 X-Act® OBC Platform supports a continuous chain of right-time decisions

- New business context: e.g. cost, competition, time and space
- New market dynamics: e.g. ecommerce, IoT
- New environments: e.g. digital IoT

Predicting Outcomes, Limits and Conditions of Failure

X-Act® OBC Platform provides a mathematical replication of real world characteristics and dynamics. Once the emulator is built, the output will be a number of metrics that replicate the measurements of the actual environment. A predictive scenario can lead to multiple computations that correspond to multiple volumes as needed to discover the operational limit and consequently how far the system is from a potential risk.

Prescribing Actions, Execution and Monitoring

Once users of X-Act® OBC Platform emulate an implementation, they can use the emulation to explore various scenarios to find the actions that provide a potential improvement, remediation or transformation and disruption. The pre-modeled, sub-assembly components available through the emulation libraries help user quickly identify the best fit prescription for a potential problem. The emulation can also be used during project execution to solve any potential roadblocks and monitor the operation to mitigate any new risks as they develop.

Using Option Benchmarking for Management

X-Act® OBC Platform emulation is frequently used to compare a representative emulation to a best in class implementation. This comparison can take place at any level in the emulator's hierarchy from business process definition or implementation structure all the way down to infrastructure or supporting platforms. Using this comparison, the tool will measure any deviations between the current system and an ideal/optimized system—quantifying the differences and estimating the effort and cost to align the current system with the ideal system so that users can act on this intelligence.

X-Act® OBC Platform also computes decision level metrics such as:

- Loss of opportunity
- Cost escalation
- Quality of service degradation

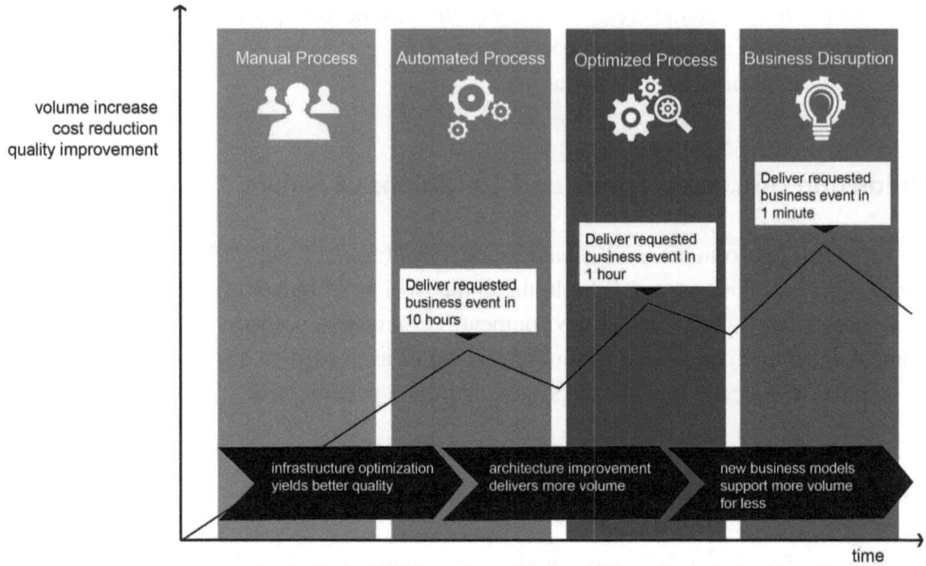

Fig. 9.3 Emulation can help businesses prepare for the transition between implementation phases

And decision supporting metrics such as:

- Dynamic return on investment (ROI)
- Aging ratio
- Complexity index and time to deliver

Figure 9.3 summarizes how X-Act® OBC Platform can be used to support the transition between implementation phases with the following benefits:

- When implementing a new business process, X-Act® OBC Platform delivers the blueprints for new architecture, justifies the selection of infrastructure and optimizes the performance
- To support the evolutionary requirements of the business, X-Act® OBC Platform delivers the right adaptation options, optimizes the service quality and ensures scalability with the objective to do more for less
- When disruption becomes necessary, X-Act® OBC Platform delivers the new blueprints to facilitate the use of the latest innovations so that the implementation is better able to support changing service quality and cost constraints while ensuring long term success.

Business Monitoring: Moving from Understanding to Implementation and Operations

10

Ignorance more frequently begets confidence than does knowledge: it is those who know little, and not those who know much, who so positively assert that this or that problem will never be solved by science.
—Charles Darwin, English naturalist, geologist and biologist, best known for his contributions to the science of evolution

In this chapter:

- Creating a dynamic signature through emulation enables predictive risk discovery and prescriptive treatment of risk
- The importance of taking a global and comprehensive approach to risk management
- How the foresights gained through X-Act® OBC Platform help businesses monitor and control risk

Predictive and Prescriptive Risk Management

	The use of emulation reveals knowns and unknowns to allow users to achieve both the predictive and prescriptive goals of universal risk management (see Fig. 10.1). By using advanced mathematics, X-Act® OBC Platform defines a dynamic signature, which reliably represents the dynamics of systems

(continued)

N. Abu el Ata, A. Drucbert, *Leading from Under the Sword of Damocles*,
https://doi.org/10.1007/978-3-662-56300-7_10

currently ignored by other false analytical methodologies. The dynamic signature is critical to predictive risk discovery and diagnosis, which ultimately leads the user to the best-fit prescription. In this way, emulation becomes the cornerstone of smart management. Using this approach decision making is continuously supported by a strong predictive capability that covers both the knowns and the unknowns to deliver robust prescriptive solutions to control risk and avoid undesirable business outcomes.

The Process

The universal risk management process supported by X-Act® OBC Platform is global, but represents each constituent at every level. Therefore, it imposes the following:

1. Fragmentation, dilution of responsibility, diffused accountability/ownership and obsolescence is counter-productive to the goals of universal risk management because risks hide in the gaps.

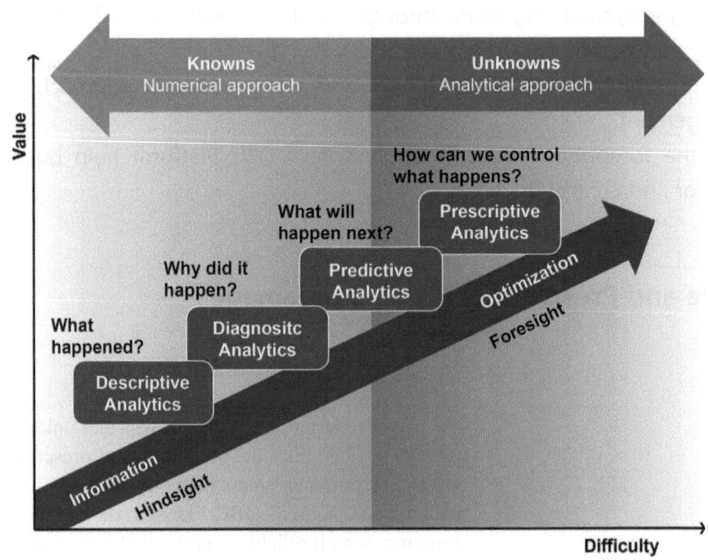

Fig. 10.1 Analytical approach supports the predictive and prescriptive requirements of universal risk management

2. The analytical solution must be globally controlled, explicitly and as far as possible by identifying all constituents and interdependencies that form the whole system so that it becomes possible to expose the negative effects of dynamic complexity.
3. It is necessary to monitor all levels of a business implementation and consolidate the information into a single model so that decision makers are armed with a clear and consolidated picture of the risks and rewards of any actions.
4. Simplification is necessary among stakeholders, between operational, tactical and strategic strata, as well as corporations and their suppliers.

The predictive treatment of risk is the only way management will be able to support the dynamics engendered by the Fourth Industrial Revolution. A short-term view of risk or only exploring known risks will not be sufficient to keep up with the accelerating pace of change. To help organizations thrive in the modern business era, business leaders must gain perspective of all possible sources of future risk and understand the economics of decisions as well as consider all possible scenarios based on the details of an environment and any discriminant factors.

Building the Necessary Foundation

X-Act® OBC Platform and our suggested universal risk management practices provide a solid foundation for the use of prescriptive and predictive risk management best practices. An emulation is built in X-Act® OBC Platform through the following steps:

- Construct the emulation of the operational point
- Validate that the construction accurately replicates the initial conditions and the baseline
- Test the representativeness
- Test the reproducibility

Placing Risk Under Control

Once the accurateness, representativeness and reproducibility of the emulation has been confirmed, it is ready for use and supports deeper analysis and the prescriptive treatment of risk through the following tasks:

- Construct as many emulators as necessary to explore any possible variations in initial conditions
- Replicate different volumes across each emulator
- Collect dynamic patterns that include characteristics, corresponding diagnosis and any prescriptive options
- Store the patterns to be used for real time monitoring of risk

Predictive Diagnosis

As shown in Fig. 10.2, the X-Act® OBC Platform interface shows which business processes are impacted by a dynamic complexity related risk through dashboard indicators and scoring metrics.

Prescriptive Remediation

Once a risk has been identified, users can drilldown to discover the cause of the risk as well as explore remedial options as shown in Fig. 10.3. X-Act® OBC Platform provides users with the information to understand the expected ROI, time to deliver and complexity of each remedial action.

Avoiding Evolving Risks

When it is discovered through operational system monitoring that one of the stored emulated risk patterns matches an observed pattern, the predetermined prescriptive actions can be applied without delaying for further analysis or diagnosis of the risk. In the case of

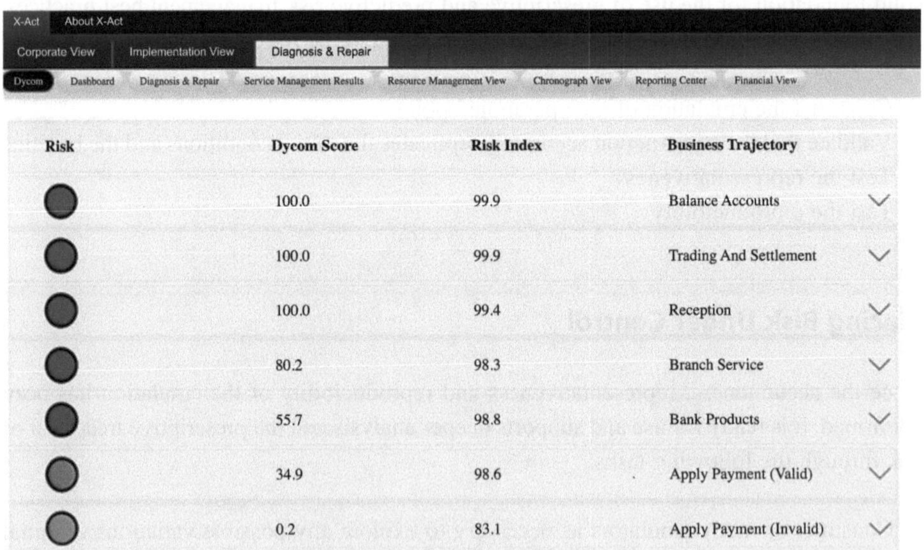

Fig. 10.2 X-Act® OBC Platform diagnosis and repair dashboard

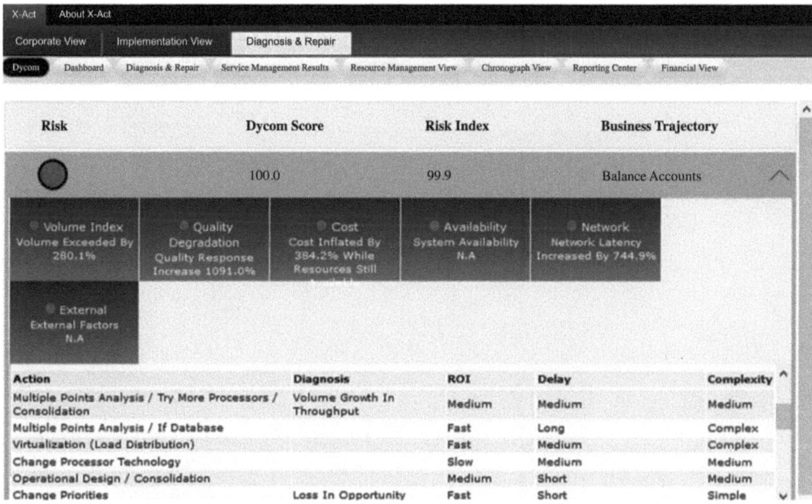

Fig. 10.3 X-Act® OBC Platform remediation dashboard

partially persisting patterns, the decision to act will be subject to business criticality. If no matches are found between the store patterns and the operational patterns, then all risks are under control and no remedial actions are required.

The Predictive Estimation of Dynamic Complexity

11

I have learned to use the word 'Impossible' with the greatest caution.
—Wernher von Braun, Aerospace engineer and space architect

In this chapter:

- Learning how metrics aide in the estimation and prediction of dynamic complexity
- Using X-Act® OBC Platform metrics to measure risk exposure
- Sample cases that show the practical use of X-Act® OBC Platform metrics

Discovering risk due to dynamic complexity is a foundational component of risk management. Towards this goal, we use the following three metrics for the estimation and prediction of dynamic complexity: (1) degree of complexity (dependencies), (2) complexity index (lost opportunity), and (3) complexity disruptors (vector of causes). These three metrics can be combined to provide one overall dynamic complexity indicator, which we call *Dycom*. These metrics are calculated by X-Act® OBC Platform to provide business leaders the insights they need to make risk-aware decisions.

N. Abu el Ata, A. Drucbert, *Leading from Under the Sword of Damocles*,
https://doi.org/10.1007/978-3-662-56300-7_11

Degree of Complexity (Dependencies)

At lower level analysis, degree of complexity (dependencies) is a qualitative and quantitative metric that varies from tight and strong coupling to loose and weak coupling. The quantitative part is more subjective and dependent on attitude and risk perception. Perturbation theory provides the metric as a number of orders involved or number of inequalities representing the direct and indirect perturbations in the solution. This metric is informative and can be used to discover the evolution of dynamic complexity and define the policy to reduce it or mitigate its inflation.

The example presented in Fig. 11.1 shows that the complexity gradient went up to 200, which means that the business has reduced access to resources and the scalability is substantially reduced for future business. In this case, the system did not hit the singularity point since the risk index is very small at 0.741.

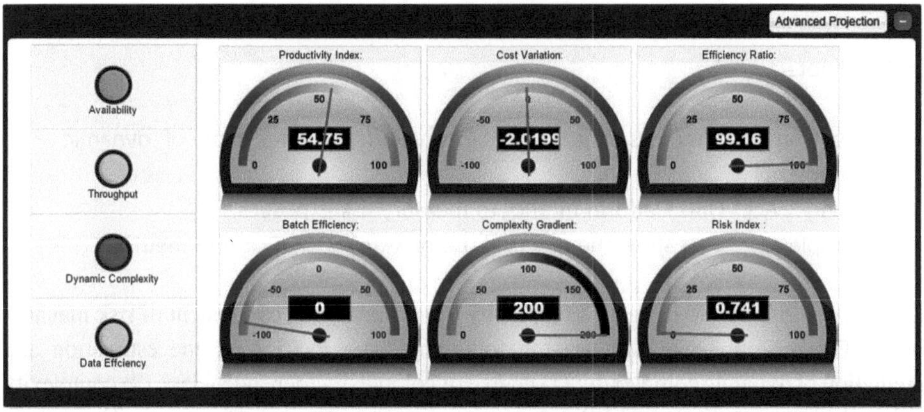

Fig. 11.1 X-Act® OBC Platform: dynamic complexity gradient and risk index dashboard

While the degree of complexity metric is essential for global control, discovery and management of risk, the next two metrics help identify the cause and possible mitigation options.

The X-Act® OBC Platform dashboard is color coded to indicate the degree of problems found.

- Green indicates that no problems have been found.
- Yellow should be considered as an alert that something may happen
- Red indicates a problem with an associated metric.

Complexity Index (Lost Opportunity)

Complexity index (lost opportunity) is computed by mathematical emulation. It represents the loss of opportunity due to contentions, conflicts, management overhead and combinatorial factors provoked by the presence of dynamic complexity. As an example, if the predicted value of the index is 20 it may mean that the company will produce 20% less cars than expected or the time to deliver will be extended by 20% or a degradation in cash flow or extended ROI by 20% more time. Obviously, 100% complexity index represents the ultimate risk, singularity, and chaos. This metric quantifies the risk and shows the cause and effect relationship.

Figure 11.2 shows a case where dynamic complexity was monopolizing resources that were supposed to produce more business, but instead resources were lost in conflicts due to dependencies and internal influences (database delays). *Column A1* shows conflicts due to dependencies and *Column A3* shows the external influencers, which represent the degree of interdependencies. Lost opportunities due to dynamic complexity are color coded in red.

Complexity Disruptors (Vector of Causes)

The complexity disruptors (vector of causes) metric represents causes that provoke the propagation of risk due to dynamic complexity. These causes may be direct or indirect, internal or external, dormant and appear under certain conditions or represent a design deficiency. Sciences such as biosciences, chemistry, system dynamics, nuclear physics, radiative transfer, optimal control and IT applications are full of disruptors that impact

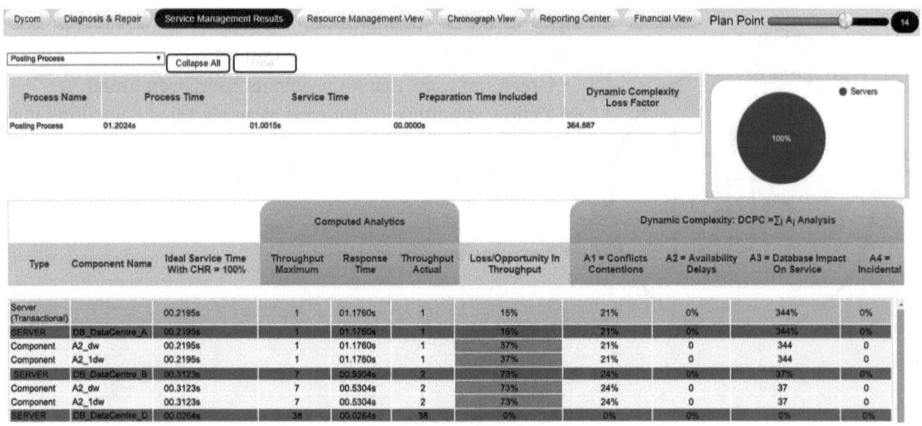

Fig. 11.2 X-Act® OBC Platform: service management results

dynamics. Knowing them is a guarantee of risk limitation; not knowing them can lead to incorrect diagnosis or reactive fixing of problems. Our intent is to provide management with the metrics necessary to control and monitor the focal points. The X-Act® OBC Platform screenshot in Fig. 11.3 shows the case of an IT business system in which the disruptors were the database design, memory size and SQL verbs.

In the X-Act® OBC Platform interface, a red circle in the status column indicates a critical status for the corresponding component.

Figure 11.3 shows a typical impact of computed dynamic complexity in which the delivery of business is reduced—in this case only 13.3 out of the 15.8 requested events per second are being served. The computation indicates that the database management system is not able to deliver in a timely manner the requested data and some of the data must be fetched at a much slower service (from the disk subsystem) with a much slower response time (RT) than if the request had been served directly from the memory (adding a few micro-seconds to the RT). The computed cache hit ratio (CHR) represents the amount of

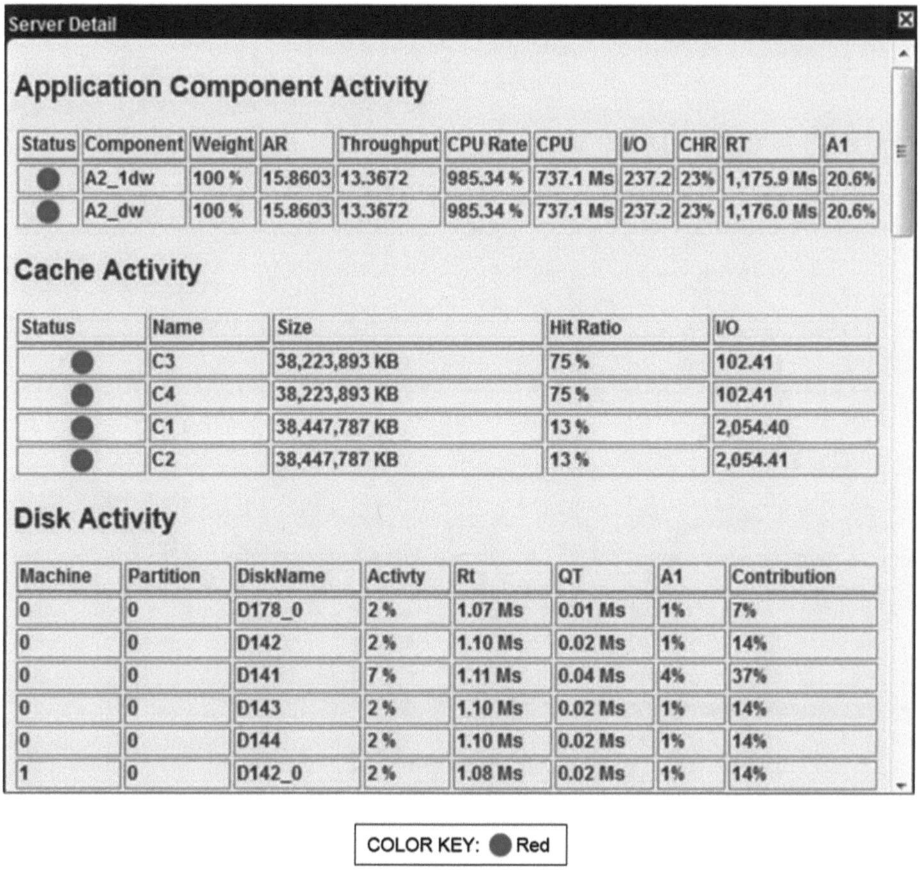

Server Detail

Application Component Activity

Status	Component	Weight	AR	Throughput	CPU Rate	CPU	I/O	CHR	RT	A1
●	A2_1dw	100 %	15.8603	13.3672	985.34 %	737.1 Ms	237.2	23%	1,175.9 Ms	20.6%
●	A2_dw	100 %	15.8603	13.3672	985.34 %	737.1 Ms	237.2	23%	1,176.0 Ms	20.6%

Cache Activity

Status	Name	Size	Hit Ratio	I/O
●	C3	38,223,893 KB	75 %	102.41
●	C4	38,223,893 KB	75 %	102.41
●	C1	38,447,787 KB	13 %	2,054.40
●	C2	38,447,787 KB	13 %	2,054.41

Disk Activity

Machine	Partition	DiskName	Activty	Rt	QT	A1	Contribution
0	0	D178_0	2 %	1.07 Ms	0.01 Ms	1%	7%
0	0	D142	2 %	1.10 Ms	0.02 Ms	1%	14%
0	0	D141	7 %	1.11 Ms	0.04 Ms	4%	37%
0	0	D143	2 %	1.10 Ms	0.02 Ms	1%	14%
0	0	D144	2 %	1.10 Ms	0.02 Ms	1%	14%
1	0	D142_0	2 %	1.08 Ms	0.02 Ms	1%	14%

COLOR KEY: ● Red

Fig. 11.3 X-Act® OBC Platform: dynamic complexity disruptors

data in memory that did not move to the disk subsystem in this case the CHR of 23% represented a risk to the business.

A CHR lower than 70% should be considered unacceptable for businesses that wish to maintain best practices in alignment with our optimal business control (OBC) methodology.

Identifying the Cure for Dynamic Complexity: Improve, Transform or Disrupt? 12

Many of life's failures are people who did not realize how close they were to success when they gave up.
— Thomas Edison, American inventor and businessman

In this chapter:

- Understanding how X-Act® OBC Platform supports a decision to cure the risk caused by dynamic complexity
- Explaining disruption as a viable path for the treatment of risk
- Reviewing areas of risks that may be best solved through disruption
- Why disruption is sometimes imposed by circumstances

Once we have identified the effects of dynamic complexity on a system and know the risks that come from maintaining the status quo, business leaders are faced with the decision of how to treat the risk. To face a potential risk, business leaders may need to improve, transform or disrupt their business and/or its supporting systems. X-Act® OBC Platform provides leaders with the information they need to know which path is required to cure or contain any identified risks and when these actions must be taken to avoid negative outcomes.

N. Abu el Ata, A. Drucbert, *Leading from Under the Sword of Damocles*,
https://doi.org/10.1007/978-3-662-56300-7_12

X-Act® OBC Platform helps support an optimal risk management decision by evaluating the sustainability of proposed remediation solutions as well as the optimal use of assets and how to limit any unnecessary exposure to risk. Additionally, economic, service quality and cost advantages of any proposed solution can be evaluated using X-Act® OBC Platform.

Knowing that the proposed improvements will lead to the desired results allows business leaders to make decision with confidence. Using emulation allows users to exhaustively explore all remedial solutions to find and justify the cost versus time to implement versus expected benefits of any required improvements or transformation projects. Even in the worst cases, when disruption may become the only option to cure the risk, X-Act® OBC Platform can justify the decision by showing the obsolescence—by predicting the loss of productivity, cost inflation or high degree of dynamic complexity, which may absorb most physical resources if no actions are taken—as well as the expected gains.

The Cure May Require Disruption

The term disruption generates considerable hype across many domains including philosophy, science, biology, cosmology and most recently governance. Much of this hype stems from fear and the perceived risks in taking a path of disruption—fear of the unknown, risks that come with changing established business processes or incorrectly managing the execution, and ultimately fears of losing economic or service quality competitiveness.

☞ ***Disrupt:* to cause something to be unable to continue in the normal way: to interrupt the normal progress or activity of something.**

Management's inability to predict the unknowns associated with disruption often leads to an overcautious and simplistic approach to risk. A partial analysis of risk leads to partial remediation, in which all plans to minimize, monitor, and control the probability and/or impact of unfortunate events will likely fail. When we treat only the symptoms of risk, new risks will always be exposed as a surprise and we will be forced to reactively manage the risk.

Disruption is a change that may come about slowly or quickly, be small or big, reasonable or radical, local or global. Additionally, disruption is usually accompanied by a changing trend that may be a hitting a singularity point or pointing to a new behavioral pattern.

The French word for disruption is *perturbation.* In English, the word *perturbation* points to a deviation of a system, moving object, or process from its regular or normal state of path, caused by an outside influence. So, if we can agree that *change* is synonymous to *disruption*, we can use perturbation theory to analyze, predict and manage a change with small or big influencers at any point in time and under a variety of conditions—knowing that the starting point and amplitude of change can be infinitesimally small or bigger than any known influence exercised at the regular or normal path.

Poincaré, Abu el Ata

We support the pioneering contribution of Harvard Business School professor and disruption guru Clayton Christensen[1] who was one of the first to point to disruption as a way to interpret the waves of innovation. We build upon his contributions by offering the mathematics necessary to emulate the inflection points that justify the disruption and prepare the organization to make a disruptive move. We help business leaders gain sufficient knowledge of the outcome in terms of complexity and time to deliver as well as ROI to confidently promote and execute a disruption as the best path for progress.

We offer a pragmatic approach to disruption by designing X-Act® OBC Platform to deliver robust prediction, aide in problem solving and guide necessary actions. Pragmatists contend that most philosophical topics—such as the nature of knowledge, language, concepts, meaning, belief, and science—are all best viewed in terms of their practical uses and successes. The philosophy of pragmatism "emphasizes the practical application of ideas by acting on them to actually test them in human experiences."[2] Pragmatism focuses on a "changing universe rather than an unchanging one as the Idealists, Realists and Thomists had claimed." To this end, we present cases to demonstrate areas where disruption produced value and allowed access to wider horizons.

[1]Christensen, Clayton. *Disruptive Innovation.* Claytonchristensen.com. Web. 5 August 2015.

[2]Gutek, Gerald (2014). Philosophical, Ideological, and Theoretical Perspectives on Education. New Jersey: Pearson. pp. 76,100. ISBN 978-0-13-285238-8.

Cases of Disruption

Based on our research and client cases, we have found that disruption can become a great opportunity to reduce a risk or ensure the survival of the business in the following categories:

Disruption Through Innovation

Sometimes disruption is forced by progress and innovation or as a byproduct of new concepts and industrial or business breakthrough. Many examples of disruptive innovation are included in Christensen's contributions, which have created some controversy. Christensen's initial research, which formed the kernel of the theory, was based mainly on the hard disk drive industry in the 1970s and 1980s.[3, 4]

Other scholars have published discussions of related case examples (notably about Polaroid Corp., Smith Corona, and the disk drive industry), but few quantitative tests have been performed. The ones that *have* been published fail to provide confirmatory evidence for the theory, suggesting instead that full-blown disruptions of the type that Christensen describes are rare and that most managers respond effectively to disruptive threats. In his defense, Christensen has said that the lack of numerical support is the result of the blunt measures used in statistical analysis.[5, 6] More nuanced case analysis, he argues, shows that the theory of disruptive innovation explains the failure of leading businesses, time after time and industry after industry.

Using X-Act® OBC Platform, we provide the dimension of numerical support that Christensen's theories necessitate. By providing mathematical proof, we can achieve wider validity than is possible through any form of statistical analysis. In some cases, it will become clear that disruption is the obligation of management if innovation is the only way to avoid the risk of obsolescence. By emulating the renewal of business models or business implementations, we can numerically prove if significant business and economic advantages can be achieved through innovation. Amazon, smartphones, blockchain,

[3]C.M. Christensen and J.L. Bower, "Customer Power, Strategic Investment, and the Failure of Leading Firms," Strategic Management Journal 17, no. 3 (March 1996): 197–218.

[4]C.M. Christensen, "The Rigid Disk-Drive Industry: A History of Commercial and Technological Turbulence," Business History Review 67, no. 4 (winter 1993): 531–588; Christensen and Bower, "Customer Power"; and C.M. Christensen, F.F. Suarez, and J.M. Utterback, "Strategies for Survival in Fast-Changing Industries," Management Science 44, no. 12, part 2 (December 1998): S207–S220.

[5]C.M. Christensen, "The Ongoing Process of Building a Theory of Disruption," Journal of Product Innovation Management 23, no. 1 (January 2006): 39–55.

[6]Christensen, "Innovator's Dilemma"; and C.M. Christensen and M.E. Raynor, "The Innovator's Solution: Creating and Sustaining Successful Growth" (Boston: Harvard Business School Press, 2003).

smart contracts and hybrid mail distribution are just a few examples of innovations that have forced disruption within industries. And in all cases, the path forward can be better defined using emulation to quantify the impacts of innovation and plan for the necessary disruption.

Business Disruption

According to Christensen, a disruption displaces an existing market, industry, or technology and produces something new, more efficient and worthwhile. In this sense, innovation is at once destructive and creative. In many cases, disruption continuously impacts the same industries over and over again, forcing extinction for companies that are unable to keep pace with changing market dynamics. Out of 200 major corporations that existed in the beginning of the twentieth century, only two have survived.[7] As we transition into the Fourth Industrial Revolution, the threat of business disruption will grow even more extreme. Only companies that are prepared to face the continuously accelerating rate of disruption will survive in the twenty-first century and beyond.

There are benefits to be gained by industries and corporations that accept disruption as a form of continuous renewal. Value chains, customer relationships, economic models and market positioning have repeatedly been disrupted in industries such as nuclear energy, credit cards, algorithmic trading, postal services and transportation. Corporations like GE, Alstom, Bombardier, Airbus and IBM have executed multiple disruptions to preserve their competitive advantage and/or renew their economic success.

Many of these disrupted industries and corporations will continue to face disruption. Nuclear energy must compete against green initiatives. Credit card companies must position themselves to support new ecommerce models. Information technology giants, such as IBM, must find ways to compete against smaller, more agile companies that may offer more attractive solutions at a lower cost. Postal service must deal with a decline in mail volumes and the explosion of hybrid mail. And undoubtedly, new disruptive forces will emerge in areas such as telemedicine, nano-technologies, genetic repair, self-reconfiguration and predictive-based-prescription. As the number and scope of disruptions grow, companies will increasingly need ways to analyze the risk of disruption and execute a successful strategy.

[7]Schrage, Michael. *Serious Play: How the World's Best Companies Simulate to Innovate.* Harvard Business Review Press. Print 1999. ISBN-10: 0875848141. ISBN-13: 978-0875848143.

Infrastructure Disruption

Over the last 50 years, infrastructure innovations have helped businesses face pressures to do more with less, deliver better quality, become more agile and retain more clients. Infrastructure disruptions can include gradual changes, such as retiring mainframe technology in favor of distributed processing, as well as the replacement of humans with robotics or intelligent componentization in industrial production.

But sometimes innovations force progress that forever change the principles of the game. Computer-based-manufacturing, enabled by the implementation of intelligent code, revolutionized all industries that relied upon mechanical processes. Later the internet produced yet another wave of disruption that ultimately laid the foundation for our global economy. Global banking, efficient supply chain management, cloud computing, internet of things (IoT), hybrid mail, blockchain and ecommerce all became possible because the internet removed the barriers that made global communications slow, complex and onerous.

As technological advances continue at an accelerating pace, companies will need new ways to evaluate the usefulness of infrastructure innovations, evaluate the level of dynamic complexity risks engendered by such solutions and successfully manage transformation programs.

Process Disruption

Industries, corporations, governments and human activities rely upon many processes to deliver products and services, perform activities, facilitate communications and manage interactions. Evolution of processes—in terms of content, characteristics and dynamics—are dictated by internal structures that lead to changes or external influences that impose modifications. In general, processes share the lower representation of other processes either through connectivity or through calls to the same resources. Dynamic complexity will start to evolve as conflicts, contentions and interdependencies intensify. In many cases, the evolution of dynamic complexity will lead to a risk of crisis or even a disaster, as dynamic complexity becomes so predominant that the process' *raison d'être* becomes questionable.

In these cases, disruption can provide the necessary efficiency innovation, business renewal and survival strategy. Below are a few examples in which we successfully used predictive emulation to guarantee that the renewal project would deliver the desired benefits both quantitatively and qualitatively:

- Advances in modern supply chain management that allow for faster delivery times and increasing delivery volumes at reduced costs.
- Introduction of hybrid mail to compensate for the continuous declines in traditional, physical mail—leveraging existing postal services assets, such as reach and connectivity, to build competitive advantage with new modes of service.

- Adoption of blockchain that allows for renewal by reintroducing the ancient concept of a continuously evolving ledger, now augmented by strong encryption and powerful protocols to support the future speed, volume and cost requirements of financial transaction processing and smart contracts while minimizing the impact of dynamic complexity.

Industrial Disruption

In the widest sense, industrial disruption can be considered as a call for better opportunities—including better products and foundational processes, as well as the pursuit of wider economics, competitive advantage or changing market preferences. Obviously, this level of disruption may be triggered by innovation or may encourage innovation. Whatever the incentive or trigger may be, the disruptive change spreads over a window of time, dependent on the speed of adoption and the coexistence of old and new systems. In many instances, this last point is critical as the concomitant existence of systems may produce the transitional degradation of both systems before the disruption fully takes place.

Some well-known examples of industrial disruption in recent years include the market move to electric, self-driven cars, the transition from blackberry to smartphones, the widespread adoption of the internet, solar avionics and the use of blockchain in healthcare, government and supply chain.

Economic Disruption

Economic disruption is an unavoidable side effect of progress. Today entropic practices, including legal and regulatory mandates, can cause major economic disruptions and even global crises. In examining the financial crisis of 2008, we found that dynamic complexity, caused by financial and real estate interdependencies, revealed an economic risk that quickly became an incommensurable disaster.

Lawmakers reactively treated the symptoms of the 2007–2008 financial crisis with new rules and regulations that have now been implemented by financial institutions, but we have yet to address the root cause of the problem. Therefore, a new crisis is still possible and will be triggered, not necessarily by a subprime market meltdown but by another dynamic complexity induced pattern that remains hidden.

For this reason, we are convinced that a substantial disruption to the foundation of our economy is necessary. We have the tools to test and predict the optimal constituents that will deliver the most effective economic outlook. The same methods can be applied at the corporate, enterprise, project or product level to evaluate economic risks and remedial solutions. Disruption in many instances is not a luxury or eventuality, it is a condition of survival, renewal or repairing systems which are no longer productive or economically advantageous.

Socio-economic and Political Disruption

Until recently, political disruption was considered an unintended consequence that could not be sufficiently anticipated or managed. Following the events of October 1990, December 1991, September 11, Arab Spring and most recently the Brexit, the socio-cultural status quo has been impacted by a high wave disruption. The French President, Francois Mitterrand, refers to the outcome of these events as a "rapport de forces."[8] Conceptually, these political events are a manifestation of socio-cultural dynamic complexity. The French, American and October 1917 revolutions produced the same manifestations of dynamic complexity—representing the same evolution, interdependencies and dynamics as the root causes of disruption presented above. We refer to these outcomes as the "Darwinian paradigm," meaning that the expected evolution is interrupted by a radical change in course.

In many cases, political disruption has propelled the impacted countries into blood-loss and chaos. There is no doubt that mathematical predictive emulation can help us measure and respond to the risk of political disruption. By measuring the behavioral evolution of one social group with respect all others, we can determine how the socio-cultural evolution may provoke political instability and become the catalyst of disruption. Using scientific-based studies, we can safely pursue aspirations of achieving positive benefits through a radical move.

Genetic, Biological Disruption

The evolution model presented by Darwin represents one of the most significant scientific contributions of our time. Darwin's model gave birth to further developments and progress in genetics, biomedicine, and research that revealed the root causes of many illnesses and biology. Darwin's genius in fact represented a much larger philosophy that allowed many other fields—including cosmology, nuclear physics, seismology and weather sciences—to express the evolution of disruptive behaviors by comparing a starting phase to subsequent phases to better understand the evolutionary and disruptive cycles.

Our discovery of dynamic complexity is a great example of Darwinism. Dynamic complexity creates an evolutionary process followed by a voluntary or involuntary disruption that then starts another evolutionary cycle, which again will be disrupted and so on.

Our methods of managing dynamic complexity include the calculation of a risk metric that allows us to enforce the disruption before the crisis occurs. We call this *controlled disruption*. And it is obviously a preferable management position than *uncontrolled disruption*, which almost always leads to unexpected outcomes. The 2007–2008 financial meltdown which led to a global economic crisis, the black Tuesday or Chernobyl disaster

[8] Power relations, balance of power.

of 1986, the Three Mile Island accident of 1979, and major tectonic and weather catastrophes are just a few examples of uncontrolled disruptions.

Disruption Imposed by Circumstances

Disruption should be considered as a last course decision that is made necessary by a change in environment, better opportunity, excessive dynamic complexity or obsolescence of current models. Evolution is the keyword that justifies the disruption. A Darwinian view shows disruption as the path for survival. In some cases, disruption will be justified as a business decision but in other cases disruption will be imposed as the only path to avoid obsolescence.

We must remain aware that the new world is different as the following examples illustrate:

- In the 1990s, credit card processing was a lucrative business. But the profitability curve has plummeted from its highly incentivized upward trend to a death spiral because the supporting infrastructure is too slow, cumbersome and costly. In the coming years, plastic will certainly disappear and ecommerce will evolve using more efficient cardless payment models.
- With the rise of blockchain, the role of intermediaries is being questioned. Today, the delegation of all or part of the verification process to third-parties is in many cases perceived as useless, complex, risky and costly.
- The growing popularity of the Internet, social media and internet of things (IoT) is changing the role of consumers and will lead to endless innovation opportunities.
- The global village has increased the speed of communications and guaranteed the secure and traceable delivery of new products, projects and processes.
- Increasing instability will lead to continuous business-disrupting surprises unless predictability and situational assessments are regularly executed at the right level and at the right time.

Remaining oblivious to these facts will most certainly leads to "death by obsolescence" as many companies have or will witness in the following cases:

- The world of mainframes is gone. The complexity of moving from mainframe to more agile, flexible and cost-effective implementations certainly posed a difficult dilemma for many businesses. However, the mainframe became an evolutionary handicap for any organization resistant to change due to its expense and complexity and fostering of a stagnant culture.
- System-based transactional processing is replaced by business event processing.
- Automation is a matter of definition and will be replaced by intelligent agents that will continuously compute a graph of interdependencies and provide timely triage whenever possible and optimal.
- The static singularity can't work anymore. Projected risk based on historical big data will always provide a static view of a dynamic world that is much more nuanced and sensitive to internal structures and external influencers.
- Lot of words that represented technological *innovations* have or will disappear in the near future including enterprise architecture, data center automation, LANs, TSO, pulse or rotary dialing, steam vehicles, VHS, floppy disk, pagers and CDs.

X-Act OBC Platform Metrics Guide the Disruption Decision

13

The greater danger for most of us is not that our aim is too high and we miss it,
But that it is too low and we reach it.
—Michelangelo, Italian sculptor, painter, architect, and poet of the High Renaissance

In this chapter:

- Understanding how X-Act® OBC Platform metrics guide a disruption decision
- Learning which metrics and indicators are calculated by X-Act® OBC Platform
- Reviewing the mathematical solutions that expose the impact of dynamic complexity on a system
- Using advanced mathematics to discover and control risk

Discovering the cause and effects of dynamic complexity is foundational to our risk management approach. Since conventional methods ignore the unknowns, risk often appears to management as a surprise that may potentially lead to disaster. To predict risk and anticipate the appropriate course of treatment, we must discover these unknowns and determine their current and future influence on system behavior.

To innovatively approach universal risk management and support the eventual avoidance of risk, we continue to build upon the mathematical solution that we presented in

N. Abu el Ata, A. Drucbert, *Leading from Under the Sword of Damocles*,
https://doi.org/10.1007/978-3-662-56300-7_13

earlier books.[1, 2] Our ultimate goal is to better expose how dynamic complexity is caused by the direct and indirect perturbations and allow management to confidently take action based on this knowledge.

The mathematical solution is presented within this chapter for those that wish to nurture a deeper understanding of our approach. However, X-Act® OBC Platform calculates and visually displays all the necessary metrics to support our universal risk management approach, so that advanced mathematical competency is not a requirement of success.

Using Advanced Mathematics to Discover and Control Risk

Perturbations are caused by the generally unknown internal interdependencies in a structure as well as the external influencers that consequently generate pressure, increase costs and cause time elongation. In turn, these conditions strain resources in ways that were not intended when the system was originally conceived and built.

Serious risk diagnosis and discovery requires the ability to identify the risk signature of a system that covers both the known origins and the unknown root causes of risk.

To build a risk signature, we must compute the impact of dynamic complexity on any component—including in the calculation the direct influence of adjacent dependencies as well as the indirect influence due to perturbed characteristics and behaviors of all components of higher orders. Around unperturbed characteristics, we add the effect of direct perturbations and the indirect high order perturbations to obtain a solution close to an exact solution for a representation such as:

$$X = X_0 + \sum_M X_M^{(d)} + \sum_N X_N^{(i)}$$

Where:

- X_0 is the initial value of a metric (e.g., function or characteristic);
- $X_M^{(d)}$ is the calculated direct impact due to M causes; and
- $X_N^{(i)}$ is the calculated indirect impact due to N causes.

In more detail, consider the following vector: $\sigma = \sigma(k)$ where $k = 1 \ldots k$ and where σ_k is a function of time and represents the metrics that describe corporate, financial, business and technology engineering characteristics and behavior.

(continued)

[1]Abu el Ata, Nabil and Perks, Maurice J. *Solving the Dynamic Complexity Dilemma.* Springer Publishing. 2014 edition. 12 August 2014. Print. ISBN-13: 978-3642543098 ISBN-10: 364254309X.

[2]Abu el Ata, Nabil and Rudolf Schmandt. *The Tyranny of Uncertainty.* Springer Publishing. 2016 edition. 17 May 2016. Print. ISBN 978-3-662-49104-1.

	Further consider that: • $\sigma^{(c)}$ represents the unperturbed value of a metric, or its minimum admitted value for simplicity; • $\sigma^{(d)}$ represents a measure of a perturbed metric due to the direct impact applied on the perturbing function X^d; and • $\sigma^{(i)}$ represents the indirect perturbation due to the perturbed effect of metrics against each other or the perturbing function $X^{(i)}$ due to an external impact. In general, the system of equations that represent the variations can have the form: $\frac{d\sigma}{dt} = X^{(c)}\left(\sigma^{(c)}\right) + X^{(d)}\left(\sigma^{(d)}\right) + \left(X^{i}\left(\sigma^{(i)}\right)\right)$ Where $X^{(c)}$ represents a basic function Further, assume that: σ' and σ'' are vectors representing σ through different coordinates, and that $\sigma^{(0)}$, $\sigma'^{(0)}$, and $\sigma''^{(0)}$ represent the unperturbed values of a metric. Then, the first order direct perturbation is: $\frac{d\sigma}{dt} = \sum_{k=1}^{K}\left(\frac{dX^{(c)}}{d\sigma_k}\left(\sigma_k^{(c)}, \sigma_k'^{(0)}\right)\sigma_k^{(d)} + \frac{dX^{(d)}}{d\sigma_k}\left(\sigma_k^{(c)}, \sigma_k'^{(0)}, \sigma_k''^{(0)}\right)\right)$

Four Fundamental Parameters to Risk Exposure

The impact of dynamic complexity on business system dynamics is significant. Therefore, the analysis, perception, predictive modeling and mitigation of dynamic complexity must become an integral part of modern management. To this end, X-Act® OBC Platform provides users with the following fundamental parameters: (1) Dycom "*Dynamic Complexity*", (2) RI "*Risk Index*", (3) E^2 "*Engineering Efficiency*" and (4) A^2 "*Aging Acceleration*" to provide a consolidated, yet comprehensive, view of system health and risk with both quantitative as well as qualitative significance. These parameters are meant to be self-explanatory so that they can be easily communicated to a variety of business and technical stakeholders and intuitively understood. An overview of these parameters is provided below, but the proposed mathematical foundation is presented in *The Tyranny of Uncertainty*.

Dycom: The Dynamic Complexity Indicator

Dycom represents the impact of dynamic complexity on business system metrics. Dycom is a vector (that combines the three complexity metrics—Degree of Complexity, Complexity Index and Complexity Disruptors—outlined in Chap. 11) to express entirely the non-functional requirements that qualify and quantify the system dynamics. From this we can identify if the system is approaching an operational risk. All the constituent metrics are computed by our proposed mathematical foundation.

RI: The Risk Index Vector

The Risk Index (RI) vector is an indication of the exposure to risk. It is directly derived mathematically from Dycom and AI, the average availability of the system during an event. The orientation of the vector will provide a good indication of the nature of risk. The gradient of the vector will indicate if the risk is internal or external through the mathematical definition.

E^2: Engineering Efficiency

The Energy Efficiency (E^2) parameter gives an indication of the ability of a system (company, IT-landscape, etc.) to change to more effective processing. It is defined via a function over time and will therefore indicate the ability to change system dynamics over time.

A^2: Aging Acceleration

Aging Acceleration (A^2) indicates how fast a system deteriorates over time. As discussed previously, systems will get more and more complex if no preventive actions are taken. This may be caused by bad maintenance practices or additional functionality that has been implemented. Also, the development of new products (e.g. derivatives in a bank) may contribute to the deterioration of the system through additional complexity. A^2 is mathematically defined by a decay function.

Understanding the Origin of Dycom and Other Management Indicators

Dycom is a vector that represents the dynamic complexity metrics:

- Represents the degree of interdependencies;
- Degree of dependencies that produce multiple impacts or feedback, for example, a feedback could be equivalent to *n* dependencies;
- Degree of deepness (elements like priorities, locks, volumes, or discriminant factors, such as pay-in at the right moment, default payment, etc.).

All elements of the Dycom vector are computed by perturbation theory, so the indicator will be given in the form of Dycom = $(x_1, x_2, x_3 \ldots, x_n)$

From Dycom, we derive three more management indicators:

- **Complexity Index** (lost opportunity) is the loss due to the degree of dependencies. Computed by perturbation theory, it is a vector that shows the loss or gain in each business and system process.
- **Complexity Disruptors** (vector of causes) will be the causes that make dynamic complexity visible and eventually disruptive. It is shown as a vector (where the cause, impact, and qualification appear one by one).
- **Operational Risk Index** is derived directly from Dycom.

The metrics used to determine the indicators are expanded to a number of ratios/ percentages for each of the service dynamic complexity metrics x_n

- $\boldsymbol{x_1}$ **is Throughput Index (TI)** = Actual Throughput/Maximum Throughput
- $\boldsymbol{x_2}$ **is Cost Efficiency (CE)** = Cost of Optimal Service Path/Cost of Actual Service Path
- $\boldsymbol{x_3}$ **is Quality Index (QI)** = Expected Quality (as planned)/Perceived Quality (response delayed for whatever reason)
- $\boldsymbol{x_4}$ is Service Continuity (SC) equivalent to Availability and Recovery of Service = Operable Time/Required Operable Time
- $\boldsymbol{x_5}$ **is Systemic Response Time Index (RTI)** = Service Time (as planned)/Response Time (aggregation of service components)
- $\boldsymbol{x_6}$ **is Operational Efficiency (OE)** = (planned number of people/actual number of people) × Effectiveness of Tools (%) and Efficiency of Process (%)
- $\boldsymbol{x_7}$ **is Loss of Service Guarantee (SE):** Current Service Index/Required Service Index: Best = 1
- $\boldsymbol{x_8}$ **is Loss in Quality (LQ)**: Perceived Quality/Best Quality: Best = 1

All metrics discussed here are directly delivered by X-Act® OBC Platform in a form that is associated to the risk and can be directly exploited by the decision maker to guide timely remediation.

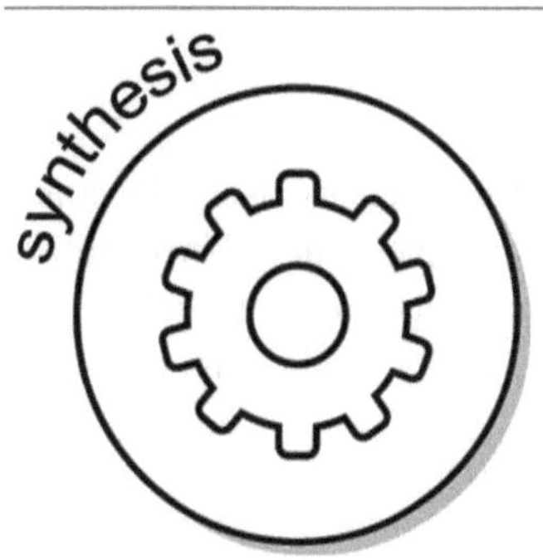

The Dynamic Complexity Efficiency Gradient (**Dycom**) of a service equals:

$$\nabla \boldsymbol{Dycom} = 1 - \left(\frac{1}{\boldsymbol{n} \sum_{n=1}^{n=m} \boldsymbol{c_n}} \sum_{n=1}^{n=m} \boldsymbol{c_n x_n} \right)$$

c_n Denote normalization coefficients and x_n is the dynamic complexity impact on a specific indicator

The Operational Risk Index Vector of a Service therefore equals

$$\overrightarrow{\mathbf{RI}} = \begin{pmatrix} \mathbf{Dycom} \\ \mathbf{AV - 1} \end{pmatrix}$$

(continued)

	Where AV is the normalized availability in a time window of the x_n The value $\lvert\overrightarrow{RI}\rvert$ yields from 0 to $\sqrt{2}$. The value will be a relative risk measure, values >1 will represent a maximum risk exposure. The angle will represent the source of risk, with $\Phi = 0°$ the risk is related to Dycom only, with $\Phi = -90°$ it is related to AV only. E^2 is represented as an exponential function. E^2 is the engineering efficiency metric: $\frac{d\vec{E}}{dt} = \overrightarrow{E_0}\ e^{\mu t}$ Where μ represents a cost function in time. **E^2 represents the ability of an organization to apply positive change to the system and put its complexity under control.** $\overrightarrow{A^2}$ The aging acceleration is represented by a decay function, such as: $\frac{d\vec{A}}{dt} = \overrightarrow{A_0}\ e^{-\omega t}$ Where $\vec{A}$ is the aging cost vector, **A^2 is a parameter representing the deterioration of a system over time.**
 	The X-Act® OBC Platform risk metrics are designed to address the following universal risk management objectives: • Discover and monitor the unknowns using **Dycom**; • Predict Dycom's impact on risk exposure with **RI**; • Determine **A^2** to understand how system aging will negatively impact the margin, income or quantities produced by the system; • Use **E^2** to measure whether a proposed engineering or transformation project will be able to decrease costs without negatively impacting the quality or quantity of units produced or full cost pricing.

All the vectors' elements are determined through perturbation theory using direct and indirect perturbations involving different elements of multiple orders (inequalities) impacted through internal interdependencies and external discriminant factors and integrates the disturbing function with the three variables: quantity, quality and cost.

$$\overrightarrow{Dycom}\ ,\ \overrightarrow{RI}\ ,\ \overrightarrow{E^2}$$

Dycom's Effect on Optimal Outcome and Evolutionary Risk

Through more than 350 cases, we have observed the impacts of dynamic complexity in a broad range of systems including corporations, factories, healthcare systems, postal services and information systems. Through our work, we have found that a degradation in productivity and cost inflation begins to appear after the point of maximum productivity and minimum costs has been reached.

Because we can determine in great details the effect of dynamic complexity on a system, our interpretation of these results is straightforward. After the maximum productivity and minimum cost point has been reached, the dynamic complexity starts to gradually absorb resources that were originally dedicated to a useful activity thereby reducing the system's ability to keep pace with evolving business demands. This explains the observed degradation, but also points to the most critical factor, which is the operational risk.

We can further examine this phenomenon as a simple equation:

Let us call the system productivity P if the maximum productivity is P_{max}

After we reach the maximum productivity and we try to do more, we obtain:

$$\mathbf{P = P_{max}(1 - Dycoml_n)}$$

Where Dycoml_n is the normalized dynamic complexity effect that translates the loss in productivity or the increase in cost of business. Its value is between 0 (best conditions) and 1 (worst conditions, which practically means productivity is nil).

If decision makers wish to proactively manage risk, they must be able to predictively examine the evolution of their business. If a persisting prediction confirms that the maximum productivity is about to be reached, the business should be prepared to either take immediate action before the degradation occurs or accept the limit and adjust business goals until re-engineering is possible to support improved capabilities. In all cases, X-Act® OBC Platform can help business leaders evaluate their remediation options and choose the optimal solution.

Obviously, the risk of hitting a point beyond which degradation becomes inevitable—*we call this reaching the ultimate health limit*—represents a challenge that deserves the attention of management. Philosophically, it is similar in part to the Darwinian evolutionary principle that ultimately produces the conditions for improvement or a clear disruption. As is the case in other areas that show complex dynamics, such as cosmology, nuclear physics, industrial experience and genetics, the determination of evolutionary risk at a point in time leads to the discovery of consequences, which then leads to the controlled or otherwise uncontrolled repercussions on the system. Conceptually, this is a very important property of a dynamic system.

After a gradual evolution towards an optimal behavior of maximum productivity and best cost advantage, the situation will degrade at a certain speed depending on the severity of dynamic complexity, which can be measured with Dycom and the consequential risk index (RI). These metrics then allow decision makers to handle the risk at the right speed.

Figure 13.1 shows in practice how the visual representation of mathematical computations available through X-Act® OBC Platform can be used to reveal the hidden, evolutionary effects of dynamic complexity and plan to take the necessary corrective actions. In this case, the computed predictive graph provided by X-Act® OBC Platform shows that the evolutionary risk will begin when the maximum productivity reaches approximately 980 business events processed per second.

From the graph, we see that as dynamic complexity increases sharply, it begins to absorb the resources that were originally available to support business goals and objectives. It can be clearly seen that as volume increases, the effects of dynamic complexity become more damaging by reducing the productivity and increasing the cost to deliver.

If this were a critical business system, these conditions may be severe enough to threaten the very existence of the business as productivity falls and costs rise. Armed with this

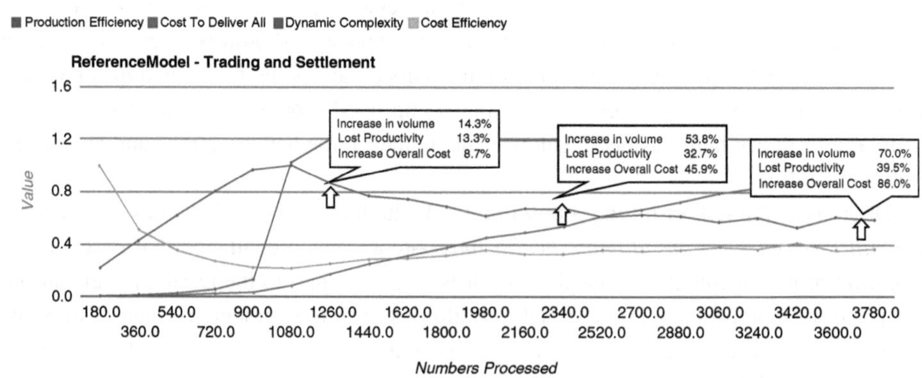

Fig. 13.1 X-Act® OBC Platform computed predictive graph reveals the impacts of dynamic complexity on productivity and cost to deliver

knowledge, users of X-Act® OBC Platform can monitor the evolution of dynamic complexity and execute a *controlled disruption* before this undesirable cycle occurs.

Risk Exposure Due to Discriminant Factors

The precarious definition of system stability is one of the major characteristic that determines the risk exposure of dynamic systems. This is mainly due to the interactions of internal system structure with *discriminant factors*. During the operational lifetime of a system, discriminant factors exert varying influences on the system due to changes in business requirements, the environment and workload.

☞ **Discriminant Factors** ***are the business factors that impact the performance, cost and service quality delivered by a system. They are generated by elements of the business architecture, business characteristics and dynamics behavior and methods of operations and create fluctuations in service behaviors and outcomes.***

Examples of discriminant factors include:

- In a settlement process, the pay-in condition and timing are primordial, so that if the pay-in arrives late, the settlement will be performed after a few empty cycles, causing the system to have a loss in productivity.
- In an automated teller machine (ATM) process, the mix of concurrent scripts vary from one moment to another. Certain mixes may potentially produce a system timeout and full failure.
- In postal services, the seasonality or mix of mail classes may produce desynchronized sequencing of services, thereby causing an accrual of unprocessed mail pieces and a considerable delay in delivery.
- In 2008, the subprime crisis caused the collapse of the financial system and a tightening of the money supply, which could not be predicted using traditional risk management practices.

While the involvement of discriminant factors in system risk is intimately related to the system operations, it is customarily agreed that most discriminant factors will be discovered or generated apart from the system definition—meaning their existence and consequences were unintended. Therefore, the potential outcome of discriminant factors is not usually accounted for when using traditional risk management practices. Only scenario-based predictive emulation allows for an exhaustive determination of their risk potential.

Risk Patterns and Risk Ephemerides

Systemic risk patterns can help us anticipate and control operational risks. A risk pattern is a dynamic representation of the internal, external and time-dependent parameters that instantiate and produce risk. A dynamic pattern is composed of the initial condition parameters presented to a system, the predicted evolution (if the mix of volumes are steady or reproducible) and the risk conditions. Any change in mix between groups results in new dynamic pattern with the proper corresponding evolution.

It is a goal of universal risk management to build dynamic pattern libraries which include all possible combinations, representing system dynamics at any point in time, under any initial conditions and the predicted evolution of risk for each. Additionally, each pattern stores the remedial options that will help management or system owners take the necessary preventive and prescriptive actions for timely risk avoidance. This same concept of pattern libraries, known as *ephemeris,* is broadly used in planetary studies, space exploration and many other industries. *Risk ephemeris* is a very interesting concept, as it allows for real-time risk discovery, analysis, and experience-based analytics, while it supports the research necessary to discover improved risk patterns that will yield tremendous business benefits and lead to the demystification of risk.

In our approach and following the construction of predictive emulation libraries using X-Act® OBC Platform, the ephemeris of patterns support optimal business control (OBC) best practices, which enables real-time surveillance and control of operational risks as outlined in Fig. 13.2.

The libraries become an indispensable knowledgebase that includes the characteristics and behaviors of system dynamics that then allows X-Act® OBC Platform users to quickly identify a system degradation and manage the continuous improvement process necessary to avoid negative business outcomes.

The number and sophistication of patterns will increase over time—allowing for more intelligence and a level of surveillance that surpasses what is achievable based on experience alone. OBC can be easily extended to provide multilevel alerts, reporting and a historical ledger.

Alerts are organized by function and follow management responsibility requirements in terms of risk and its persistence (see Fig. 13.3). At any point, a system may hit or approach a risk situation, but it is the predicted evolutionary speed and measurable impact of the situation that will trigger whether there is a need for action or not.

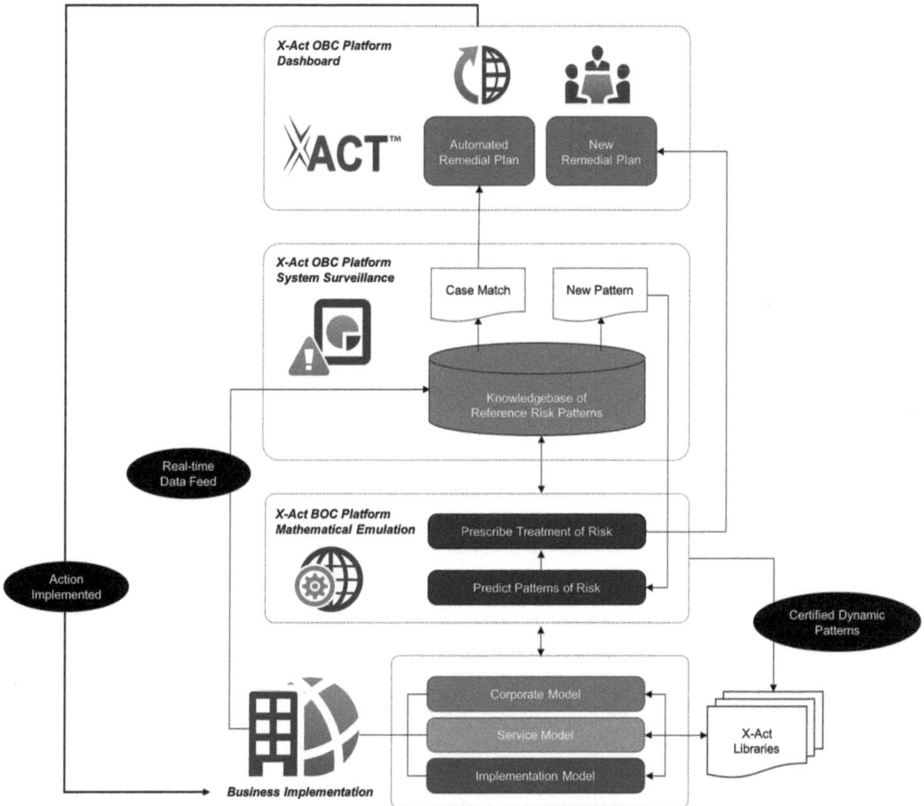

Fig. 13.2 Functional diagram of OBC real-time risk management using X-Act® OBC Platform

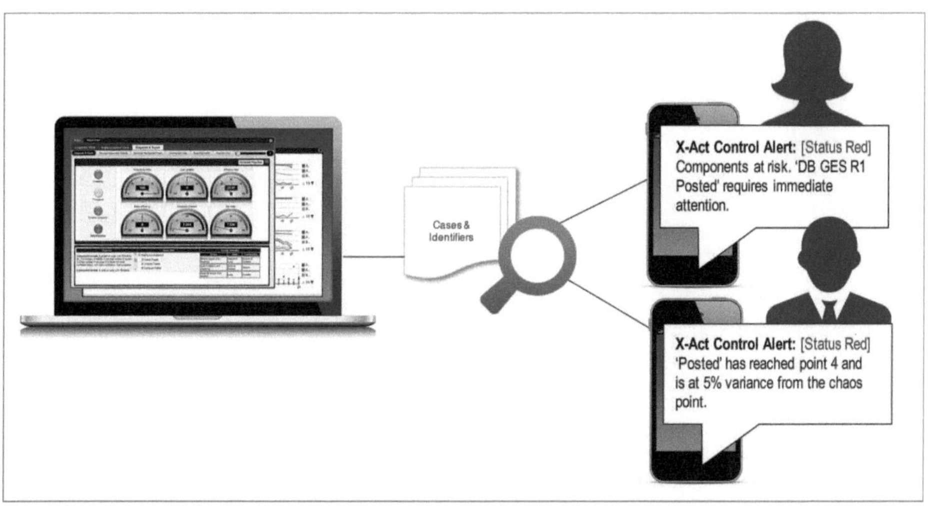

Fig. 13.3 X-Act® OBC Platform role-based action alerts

The Prescriptive Analysis: The Three + One Rule 14

What a scientist tries to do essentially is to select a certain domain, a certain aspect, or a certain detail, and see if that takes its appropriate place in a general scheme which has form and coherence; and, if not, to seek further information which would help him to do that.
—Subramanian Chandrashekhar, 1983 Physics Nobel Prize winner

In this chapter:

- Why a lack of communication and continuous change creates aging of automated systems and accelerates the appearance of risk
- How the Bridge Metric, a.k.a. *the Nabilian Vector,* is reliably used to measure and escape the risk posed by aging systems
- Timing a disruptive move to maintain continuity and better support evolving business requirements

The basic characteristics of automated systems popularized during the Third Industrial Revolution have endured to date, but they have not kept pace with the changes and evolution in business behaviors driven by the Fourth Industrial Revolution. Rapidly accelerating cycles of innovation, growing maturity and shifting customer expectations are creating a widening gap between the business and its implementation. The result is crisis-prone business models.

Continuously stretching system structures to fit an ever-changing world has accelerated system aging—both in terms efficiency and cost. Due to constant adaptation, most

N. Abu el Ata, A. Drucbert, *Leading from Under the Sword of Damocles*,
https://doi.org/10.1007/978-3-662-56300-7_14

organizations are now burdened by inefficient systems built on spaghetti structures and code. But, even as the limitations and inefficiencies of current systems are recognized, the enterprise continuously postpones addressing the problem based on a multitude of financial and short-sighted arguments. Many businesses are stuck in this current predicament—without the insights necessary to confidently define the forward path.

Aging systems add new sources of risks, which disrupt normal business cycles. Crisis prone systems are quickly becoming a handicap to the business they were designed to support. A lack of communication between business stakeholders and the people tasked with building the supporting implementation is a major contributing factor.

The bridge between the business and its supporting system is eroding, producing a perpetual gap between what the business wants to achieve and what the implementation can deliver. And this problem is not limited to traditional IT systems (i.e. financial systems), but includes all forms of business implementations such as supply chains, factories and healthcare systems.

The current one-way communication that comes from business leaders to system owners imposes a strict top-down hierarchy that impoverishes both the business and system implementation. The ability of system initiatives to contribute to or support the progress of business objectives at any point in time is severely limited by this widening gap.

In addition, most real-world implementations are exposed to hidden risks caused by the internal growth of dynamic complexity. Since most system owners currently have no means to accurately predict dynamic complexity risk, they cannot determine or communicate the severity of risk or when a crisis may occur. This forces the business to reactively manage the risk once it appears as a surprise.

It can no longer be denied that most business implementations operate in a state of declining health due mainly to the continuous growth in dynamic complexity. The longer the risk of dynamic complexity is ignored, the faster the implementation will age, ultimately making a cure even more difficult to achieve.

Performance Accretion and Bridge Metric

Today performance accretion is applied in many cases as a business survival tactic conceived by management to face a risk or to cure a circumstantial position. Examples of companies that have successfully executed a timely re-engineering of their business include Apple, Nokia and Samsung. Conversely, there have been other concepts and proposed paradigm shifts that have partially failed including SOA, AOL, Apple's Newton, Blackberry and Lotus Notes. While there are many examples of companies that were not able to make the right move at the right time including Digital Equipment Corp. and Braniff Airways along with 190 of the top 200 corporations of the twentieth century that no longer exist today.[1]

Why Corporations Fail

Corporations fail, but also states and projects fail for many reasons—mostly related to their inability to anticipate or predict a new risk in time to effectively cure the root causes. Some failures are a result of one or many of the following ten sins, but some environmental, competitive of structural dimensions may also lead to failures. Normally, the evolutionary process will lead in such cases to either untended consequences, obsolescence or uncontrollable growth in dynamic complexity.

The 10 Sins of Business Strategy and Execution:

1.	***Over and Under Syndrome***: Often due to business immaturity, the teams in charge of execution will overpromise and under deliver, leaving the business unprepared to face the resulting risk.
2.	***Ignorance is Bliss***: When organizations foster a culture of opaqueness and disorder by intentionally ignoring signs of risk.
3.	***Shortsightedness***: Rewarding selfishness supported by short-term gains and pleasing others over and above the virtue of righteousness.
4.	***Procrastination***: Always postponing preparedness by taking an unrealistic stance that problems will fix themselves.
5.	***Irresponsibility***: Disregarding the need for accountability and allowing people to commit to something without fully understanding the repercussions or how to control the outcomes.
6.	***Wait and See***: Reactively managing crisis that come as a surprise based on the belief that risk can't be preempted.
7.	***Tunnel Vision***: Letting partiality reign free, which promotes a tunnel vision view of risk and the required actions to preserve the goals of the business.
8.	***Micro Thinking***: Failing to see the big picture due to limitations in education of organizational leaders.
9.	***Greed***: Allowing personal greed to become the driving force behind the strategy and direction of the business.
10.	***Incompetence***: Letting incompetence and people who lack skills to become the majority within the workforce.

[1]• Schrage, Michael. *Serious Play: How the World's Best Companies Simulate to Innovate.* Harvard Business Review Press. Edition 1, December 10, 1999. ISBN-10: 0875848141 ISBN-13: 978-0875848143.

To prescriptively address the risk posed by dynamic complexity, we must ask if it is possible to predict a failure, disintegration or obsolescence with sufficient time to take the actions necessary to maintain a current position or further advance the position of a company. If we examine the following examples, we can see that major changes often trigger a major disruption or at least a fundamental change in corporate strategies:

- ***External factors for dynamic complexity growth***: Automation of trading processing had a positive effect in that it led to the acceleration of trading processes and reduction of trading latency. However, the outcome in terms of service quality and the concurrency of old and new is now less predictable.
- ***Following the hype or precipitations***: The adoption of unfit technologies produces negative consequences as they generate additional risk, delays and inexplicable cost burdens. This includes use of technologies that are not fully proven, only partially ready for generalized adoption, or not suitable for the chosen application—such as ADA language, un-modeled-relational data model, on-demand computing, self-healing, SOA, Next, and many other examples that now liter the technology cemetery.
- ***Early adoption of the still-to-be-proven innovations***: distributed object database, hybrid mail, self-driven vehicles, code-generators are few examples that show early adoption of technologies may lead to an uncertain outcome even if it provides a competitive advantage opportunity.
- ***Incompatible goals***: Sometimes the goals of the business are incompatible with the actual operating model. For instance, without changing the operational model of healthcare to embrace new ideas such as remote, tele-medicine and advance detection of diseases, the desire for improved wellness and economy is incongruent with today's dependence on manual processes and advanced specialization.
- ***Cost rationalization***: When cost escalation is driven by dynamic complexity and severe competition, a point will be reached when cost rationalization can no longer be achieved simply by applying directives.

The Magic Mover: The Nabilian Vector, Bridge Metric

To reinstate the two-way communication between the business and system owner's necessary to align implementations with the goals of the business, we need reliable methods to expose the severity of risk posed by dynamic complexity, predict when a crisis may occur and prescriptively detail the level of changes required to avoid the risk. We developed the *bridge metric* (Ŋ) to achieve this objective. It provides an indication of how urgent a change is, what level of change is required and when the change should be implemented.

The bridge metric helps decision makers decide if an optimization, transformation or disruption project is necessary to meet stated business objectives or imperatives. For instance, poor system performance could indicate that a change is necessary. In this case, it would be helpful to know if it is best to spearhead an optimization project, which could solve the problem by simply adding more resources or perhaps a re-organization of the production system, sun setting of old concepts and functions, or a limited re-engineering of some services.

If the predicted results of the optimization project show that it will be unable to deliver the desired long-term improvements, a transformation may be necessary to align revenue to mark-up cost, regenerate a value chain, do more for less, or initiate a fundamental change in processes, corporate structure or infrastructure. In this way, transformation may be fundamental to outperform the actual implementation through the key effort of reengineering.

Finally, if the predicted results of the transformation show the project will not be aligned with business strategies and the associated imperatives, it becomes clear that a business disruption is the only strategy capable of re-aligning the implementation with the business goals and objectives. For example, if the business goal is to increase the customer base by 10× within an environment with limited scalability, improve the ability to absorb an economic crisis (such as the 2007–2008 economic crisis) or use an innovation (such as blockchain), then disruption may be the only feasible course, but the bridge metric will help management validate whether the disruption is indeed the only option.

Therefore, the bridge metric can be used to confidently support business innovation by defining the necessary scope of a project, product, enterprise or sector-wide activity. It covers the following four possibilities:

1. **Maintain**: In this case, the bridge metric indicates that there is currently no need for a change. However, management should continue using predictive emulation to preemptively identify any risks that may prevent the implementation from meeting the stated objectives of the business. With a OBC monitoring process in place, issues can be proactively addressed before they negatively impact business outcomes.
2. **Optimize**: In this case, the bridge metric shows that an optimization is necessary and helps to identify how long the system can be maintained in its current state before a significant degradation becomes imminent. Optimization options can be explored to verify if the predicted improvements will meet business requirements. In general, businesses can expect that an optimization project will yield a 10–30% improvement in the performance of the implementation.
3. **Transform**: When the requirements of the business are beyond the scope of what can be achieved through optimization, the bridge metric will show that a more significant transformation is required to support the business plan or improve upon business imperatives. In this case, the business can typically expect that the transformation project will yield a one order of magnitude improvement.

4. **Disrupt**: Sometimes even a 10× change is still insufficient to meet the evolving requirements of the business. In this case, the bridge metric will show that a radical change through disruption is required. The predictive emulation will help determine at which level changes are required to meet a major change in business imperatives, such as innovations in ecommerce, disintegration of old business models, severe competition or pressures to re-invent the enterprise. A disruption project can typically deliver an improvement that is 10–100 order of magnitude better than the current implementation. For example, our work has shown that in certain cases, blockchain can deliver up to one billion transactions in 24 h in comparison to at least one order of magnitude less when using a traditional database model.

No business implementation can be built to last forever. At some point a disruption will become necessary. But at the same time, it can be fiscally irresponsible to make a major change when an optimization may be all that is required. As illustrated in Fig. 14.1, the bridge metric can be used to guide the necessary transitions between evolutionary phases of a business' implementation. When the business clearly understands the tradeoffs between the business' goals and an implementation's ability to support those goals, business leaders and system owners can confidently justify and prescriptively define the necessary transition between evolutionary phases.

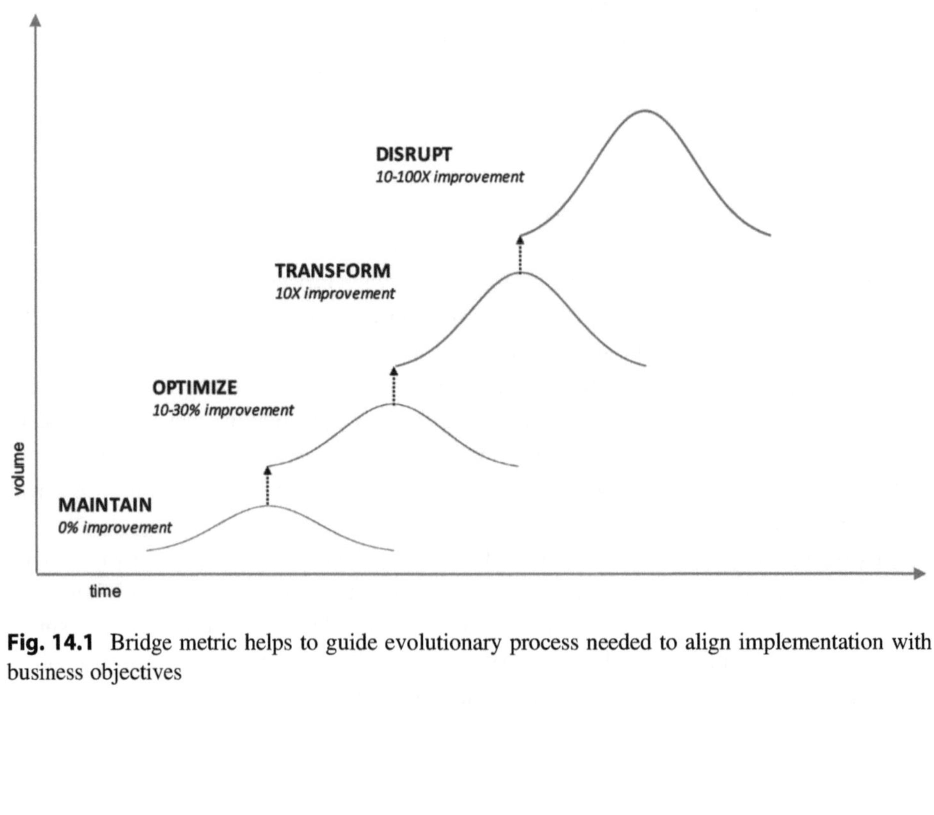

Fig. 14.1 Bridge metric helps to guide evolutionary process needed to align implementation with business objectives

The Nabilian Vector: Symbol Ŋ

Analytically, the bridge metric is derived from the Nabilian vector. It consists of three components that distinctively contribute to the overall performance of the business. The vector **Ŋ** = (**ɩ**, **ơ** and **ß**) represents the potential relative performance gained through a re-engineering effort for one of the components in comparison to the other two at a moment in time.

- The performance characteristics of the selected infrastructure is denoted by the symbol **ɩ**.
- The business and systemic business architecture performance requirements that justify an infrastructure selection is denoted by the symbol **ơ**.
- The performance (in business terms) of a deployment designed to meet specific business objectives is denoted by the symbol **ß**.

Using the Nabilian Vector to Define the Necessary Scope of Actions

The information provided by the Nabilian vector helps bridge the gap between the business and its implementation and supports bidirectional communications so that a decision to prescriptively address any identified issues can be made. Through the experience we have gained executing hundreds of projects, we have verified that the predictability offered by the bridge metric supports a business maturity model that prescribes the right dose of improvement versus effort versus outcome (see Table 14.1).

The Nabilian vector determines the degree of freedom available to preserve an acceptable condition using the current business implementation. This information can be used to guide an optimization, transformation or disruption decision based on the following criteria.

Table 14.1 Business model-based transformation

Phase	Improvement	Time	Outcome
Phase 1: Optimization	Optimize business system infrastructure	Short to medium term	Limitations will exist due to dynamic complexity. Can expect 10–30% improvement in the performance of the implementation
Phase 2: Transformation	Improve business architecture	Medium to long-term	Dynamic complexity addressed to deliver 10× improvement in performance
Phase 3: Disruption	Innovate business models	Long-term	New business is optimally engineered to deliver 10–100 order of magnitude better performance

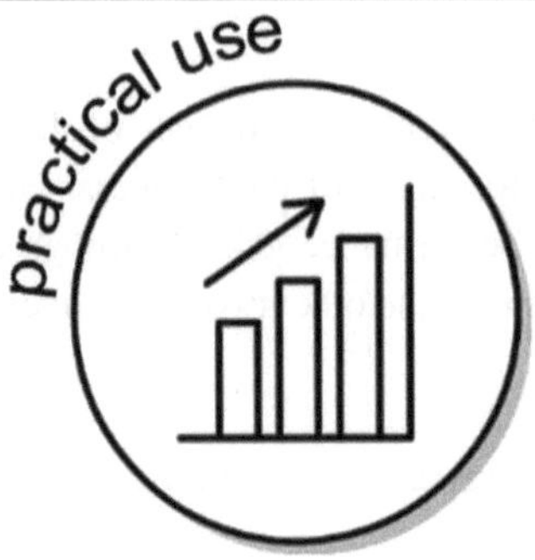

Optimization Decision: If left number (**ɩ**) of the Nabilian vector is the highest value, it presents the organization with the best opportunity to fix an imbalance in the bridge between the business imperatives and its implementation by making changes in the physical infrastructure (see Table 14.2).	**Ŋ** = **(10: 1: 1)**
Transformation Decision: If the middle number (**σ'**) of the Nabilian vector is the highest, it indicates that a re-engineering of the implementation is required to improve scalability, unit cost and/or performance (see Table 14.3).	**Ŋ** = **(1: 10: 1)**
Disruption Decision: If the right number (**ß**) of the Nabilian vector is the highest value, it indicates that the difficulty will best be overcome through a redeployment of the business model. This approach will require a strict top-down approach to identify an adequate architecture (**σ'**) and select the right infrastructure (**ɩ**) (see Table 14.4).	**Ŋ** = **(1: 1: 10)**

Using a Prescriptive Process to Time an Evolutionary Move

The following sections detail how the Nabilian vector can be used to manage the accretion evolution for dynamic systems as outlined in Fig. 14.2. By examining the requirements and benefits gained from each move, businesses can build a prescriptive process that will ultimately help to mitigate the risk of degradation or obsolescence. In addition, within the boundaries of each evolutionary phase, businesses can employ processes and advanced monitoring techniques to maintain an optimal outcome in terms of quality and costing, as well as avoid an acceleration in degradation and prepare for the next phase when the option becomes the optimal recourse.

Phase 1: Optimization of Business Infrastructure

The equation **Ŋ** = **(1:1:1) + 1** is representative of most systems that have evolved as a byproduct of the business automation phase of business. Moving from human intensive manual processes to automated services has allowed many businesses to do more for less. This has been the primary transformation objective over the last century and the efforts have delivered significant progress in how business activities are conducted. For this reason, no one anticipated any limits of the automation model. In fact, the automation

Table 14.2 Predictive optimization of existing business implementation

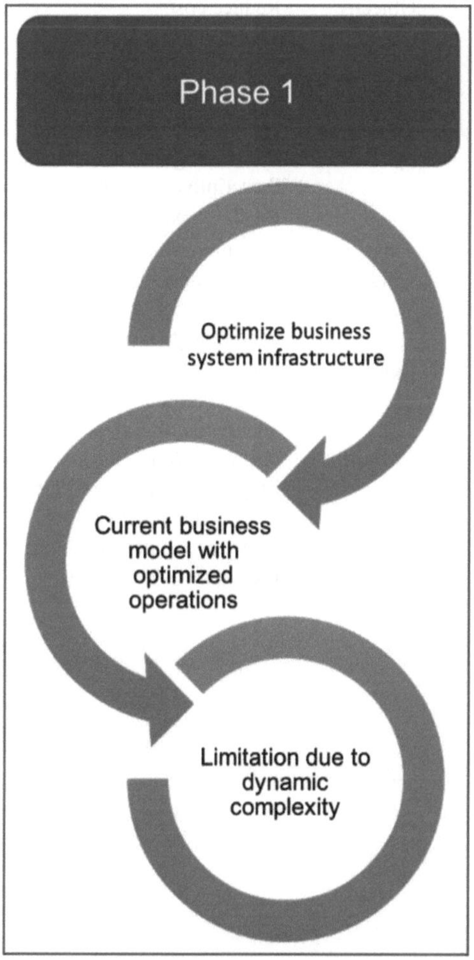

Objective	Identify the cause of cost increase Identify and optimize service quality Allow for more volume
Performed by	Production management, supported by: Predictive emulation Infrastructure suppliers Contributions from business and technical subject matter experts
Time window	Short to medium term Predicted level of gain Predicted limits and conditions that provoke crisis
Expected gain	Within 7% May deteriorate due to higher level dynamics (business and implementation obsolescence)

process has continued to evolve with new waves of adaptations every day as the results continuously confirm the original promise of wider, bigger and cheaper, while enhancing skills and improving the efficiency of management.

A scaler value of 1 added to the vector indicates that there is no change in the cost per transaction. A change in the cost per transaction can only happen in the following cases:

- **Case 1**: The implementation maintenance shows a degradation in the cost per transaction metric. This happens if resources become unavailable to maintain the service of volumes. In other words, the resources are used inefficiently due to formed hairballs or inextricable structures.

Table 14.3 Perspective implementation improvement of existing business

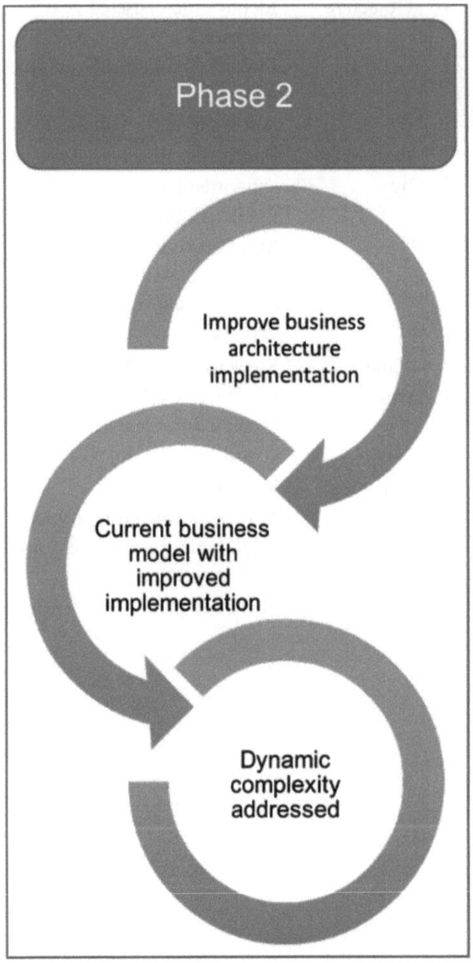

Objective	Reduce costs Improve and guarantee service quality Process higher volumes
Performed by	Architects and designers Prototyping and benchmarks Prescriptive emulation Business experts
Time window	Medium to long term Pre-certification of gains Predicted limits and conditions that provoke crisis
Expected gain	Within 25% of two times more volume for the same quality and 30% less cost per business event May deteriorate due to higher level dynamics (business strategy, competitive pressure)

- **Case 2**: Predictive projections come close to a zone in which dynamic complexity is so intense that part of the cost inflation is due to managing dependencies, conflicts and contentions that abstract the resource's abilities to deliver business.

In some environments, the two cases can happen simultaneously provoking an acceleration of risk. But for now, let us consider that only *Case 2* occurs and assume that the implementation stayed intact with no changes in the transaction characteristics. In this case, the business model stays dynamically stable and the definition of its related processes and presentation prove intact so that we are still using the same business model (e.g., a banking system that requires more bandwidth or opens branches in new geographic regions), the same architecture has been adapted to fit business requirements and new adaptive

Table 14.4 Prospective transformation of existing business

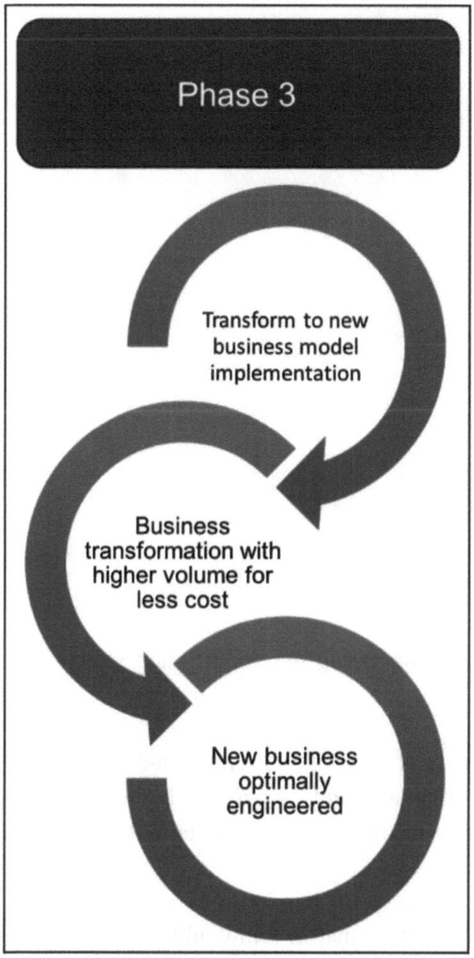

Objective	Reduce dramatically costs (competitive imperative) Rely on faster, wider and powerful advances Face the evolution in environment and the obsolescence of existing solution
Performed by	Business strategists Board rooms Business executives Business owners
Time window	Long term Timelines vs. transformation Predicted limits and conditions to provoke crisis
Expected gain	Typically, more than 70% or 10 times more volume, 20 times improvement in quality, and 50% less cost per business event Implementation flexible to fit changes in business re-engineering or adaptation

infrastructure helps serve any new constraints. The following two examples of *Case 2* have proved salutary for the impacted industries:

- **Banking**: Once automation was achieved in the banking industry, expansion became part of the strategy to merge, acquire and reach broader markets to do more with the same resources—leading to a race for more powerful, but less onerous infrastructure. Certainly, Moore's Law helped banks achieve this goal.
- **Automotive**: Who would question the improved performance of the automotive industry over the last century? Today, no one would want to buy a car that was manually produced even if cost was not a factor. Automation has resolved human errors and

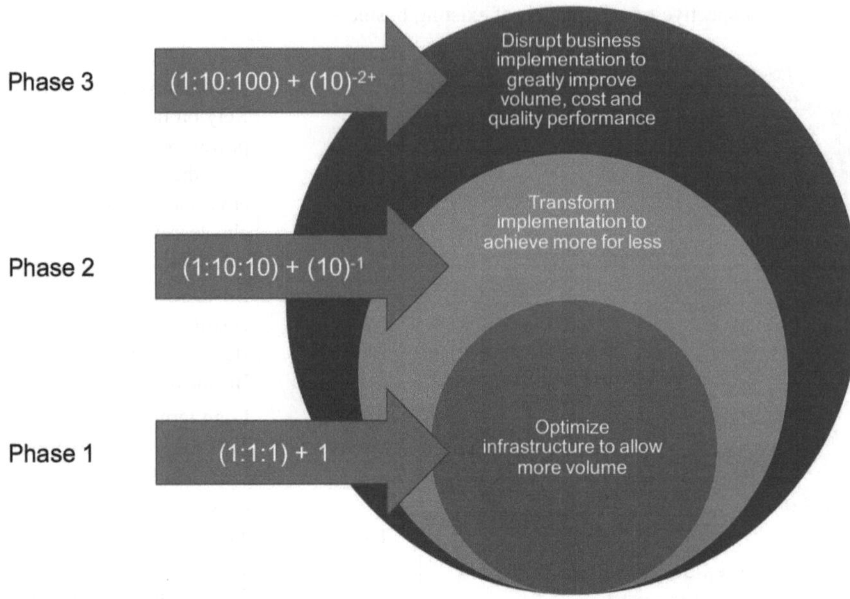

Fig. 14.2 Performance accretion

reduced time to deliver while significantly improving the security and safety of car manufacturing.

However, during the automation phase where $\mathfrak{N} = (1{:}1{:}1) + 1$ represented the expansion of businesses, we started to see deviations—at times largely aggravated by the inability of management to move at the right time or even recognize that a change in the vector was occurring.

The generation of excessive aging of business implementations came as a direct consequence of this problem—causing cost inflation that in turn could only be partially compensated for by a reduction in the cost of physical components. The real implications of aging were ignored—choosing instead to believe that IT could control problems through infrastructure upgrades, which then failed to deliver any benefits in the long term.

However, once the failure of infrastructure upgrades was recognized, IT executives and vendors would simply ask the business to support the decision to deal with the problems of business evolution from a high layer of the implementation through a re-architecture project. However, this isn't always the best course of action. Our predictions often show that a disruption may become necessary if a re-architecture is only able to provide modest headway until the next evolution phase.

As the degrees of freedom change, the corresponding benefits become orders of magnitude higher. During the 1980s and 1990s, the benefits of automation began to show limits and fatigue. However, advances in infrastructure and distributed platforms hid the need for re-architecture or disruptive business models altogether. Moore's Law supported the race for more physical integration and better miniaturization. The severe consequences resulted from the innovation opportunities of the past decades.

R&D and the resulting implementation solutions focused efforts on evolving physical objects—namely the hardware in cases of IT-based implementations—to further benefit IT vendor sales without disrupting their revenue models. Heavy investments in infrastructure including queueing mechanisms, relational models and transactional processing were necessary to support business automation and performance goals.

IT executives were sold solutions from IBM and other IT vendors that were trapped in dated models and did not move at the right time to support evolving business requirements—choosing instead to promote hype and false promises. The business decision makers that originally led automation initiatives ceased to be involved in IT purchases as they entrusted the adaptive evolution to IT executives. To leverage existing investments in infrastructure and save costs, IT continued to stretch and over-use the original paradigm to deliver successive evolutions. As the economy and cost equations blurred over time (with IT budgets representing up to 7% of annual budgets in a typical bank), IT costs increased as business implementations aged and the pursuit of new opportunities suddenly became cost prohibitive. In most cases, IT management became complicit in hiding known disasters in the making. The following two cases highlight this problem:

- A financial exchange settlement operator may be able process around two million events per day based upon a highly dependent sequence of steps. But will the system be able to process five times the volume for a certain period in the event of a crisis? The answer is no. It will not be possible even if the physical resources gain a good multiplier. The problem is the dependencies (internal and external) embedded in the implementation. New architecture is an option. Or a disruption can deliver 15 times the volume with higher quality and reduced costs.
- After enjoying a successful business model and high margins over a 30-year period, the largest credit card processor in the U.S. started seeing cost escalation because of aging assets, while revenues were declining due to pricing pressures. Optimization and performance improvements were continuously exercised but sufficient gains still could not be realized. Only a disruptive measure could guarantee corporate survival.

Obviously, there exist many other cases where infrastructure upgrades will be required and eventually sufficient to improve the outcome and present no need for transformation or disruption. Such cases gain improvement by using technological innovations and integration to face the requirements of performance and scalability and eventually economics, as is the current case with banking networks, production lines and reservation systems.

Phase 2: Transformation of Architecture

The equation $\text{Ɲ} = \boldsymbol{(1{:}10{:}10) + (10)^{-1}}$ represents the transformation phase of business, which is characterized by accelerated changes due to advances in communication, globalization and fierce competition. During this phase, the role of infrastructure shrinks and re-architecture becomes necessary. In this case, the business model remains intact but demand is growing or evolving in some way. New architecture becomes necessary to fit the new business functions, e.g. Internet adoption, online services, distributed and cooperative processing and data sharing, caching or implementation. A new adaptive infrastructure helps the business face new constraints.

From our experience, the transformation phase often becomes necessary and indispensable during periods of business expansion or when there is a need to reconfigure the cost equation or control the risks associated with an increase in dynamic complexity.

But some categories of business implementations have experienced major challenges due to their inadequate architectures. For instance, ATMs face challenges because the performance of the aggregate is not the aggregation of components' performance and CLS has found that a step-wise business flow does not necessarily lead to a step-wise deployment.

Phase 3: Disruption of Business Models

The equation $\text{Ɲ} = \mathbf{(1{:}10{:}100) + (10)^{-2+}}$ shows that new business strategies will drive better cost with higher volumes and less dynamic complexity. Examples could include removal of intermediaries through blockchain adoption, adaptive control, self-configured solutions, dependable systems and smart algorithmic implementation. In this phase, new architecture is built to fit new business requirements and new adaptive infrastructure allows the business to face the new constraints.

Over the last 40 years, businesses could trigger a disruption with little feedback from the systemic implementation. In most cases, the business dictated the move and the system owners reactively implemented the necessary changes. But this practice has resulted in aging implementations. The race to upgrade physical solutions to functional and logical requirements has ended by decaying the necessary bridge, leaving a one-way dialogue from business to system owners, which can no longer sustain the future needs of the business. Certainly, IT suppliers own the lion share of responsibility for this current predicament. They spearheaded large projects—mixing consulting services with product sales—while assuming barely any business accountability. Regardless of the fault, the next wave of disruptive evolution requires a new approach.

The use of the Nabilian vector can be foundational to planning when and how to make the move from one evolutionary phase of business to another. However, the following situations must be avoided:

- The buildup of excessive growth and frequent change pattern of dynamic complexity, which in turn forces the business to execute frequent and precarious actions to continually fix problems as they arise.
- A commitment to service constraints that are difficult to meet.
- A commitment to volume constraints that are difficult to meet without degradation in service quality.
- Loss of opportunity due to dated and inflexible implementation.
- Inability to respond to a disruptive event due to a lack of implementation adaptability.
- Inability to respond to business reinvention due to a lack of implementation maneuverability.
- Responding to problems too late and with too little effort, which in turn makes correcting the problem at a later date too difficult.
- Conservative, cautious behavior that imposes unrealistic time to deliver constraints.

In all these cases, predictive emulation capabilities can first be used to determine if these situations currently exist and guide the exercise to resolve any issues as needed to support the evolutionary advancement of the business.

Prescriptive Analysis of an Evolutionary Move Using X-Act OBC Platform

The Nabilian vector is calculated by X-Act® OBC Platform and visually represented in dashboards to help businesses make the move from one phase to another at the right time and under the right conditions. Below we present several cases to show how the dashboards can be used to compare current implementations versus optimized, transformed or disrupted implementation scenarios.

The case presented in Fig. 14.3 shows the trading and settlement activity for a global bank based on the current system as well as predicted results of the benefits that could be gained through proposed transformation and disruption projects. In this case, the ability of the system to absorb a volume increase at any moment in time without degrading service quality is a critical requirement. Therefore, a degradation in quality and increase in processing costs as seen in the "Reference Model" of the current system emulation in Fig. 14.3 would support a decision to optimize, transform or disrupt the system.

By emulating changes to infrastructure, architecture or business models through X-Act® OBC Platform, users can weigh the benefits, costs and constraints of each move to help system and business stakeholders agree upon the best-fit solution. Prescriptive emulative analysis of a system transformation followed by business disruption in Fig. 14.3 shows that

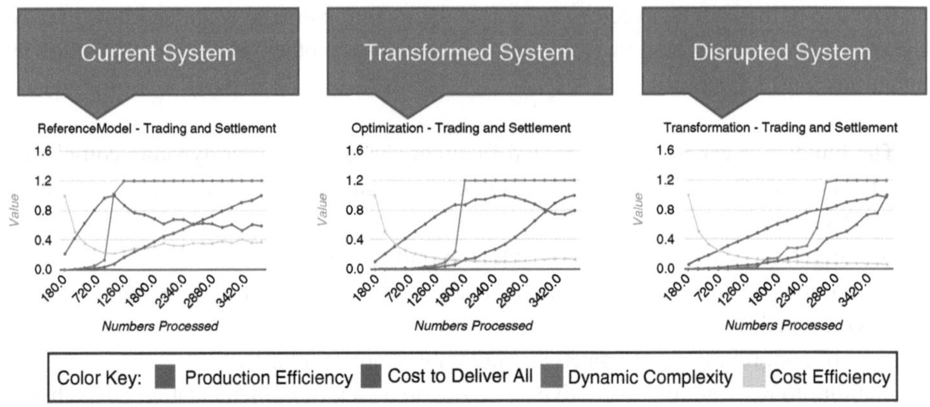

Fig. 14.3 X-Act® OBC Platform prescriptive analysis of trading and settlement activity for a global bank

changes to the architecture and business model would increase the system limit to allow the business handle increasing transaction volumes. Emulations show that the disrupted system could deliver at least 1.83 times the volumes of the transformed system. However, the transformed system would create unacceptable service quality conditions due to the decrease in production efficiency.

Armed with these insights, it becomes clear that the disruption is the only course of action that will meet business requirements, but the decision to make the move will be dictated by factors such as cost, time to implement and availability of resources, etc. The requirements of the move can be prescriptively determined using X-Act® OBC Platform to gain a full understanding of all the conditions of success. However, if the business decides not to make the move, the repercussions can be fully understood, thus reinstating a critical level of communication between system and business stakeholders.

Figure 14.4 shows a comparison between the transaction limits of the transformed and disrupted systems. The limit is found by identifying the point at which the *production efficiency* begins to decline. From this dashboard, it becomes clear that while the transformed system will process a maximum of 30,000 events per hour, the disrupted system will process 55,000 events per hour and at a better cost.

Figure 14.5 shows the Dycom and Risk Index (RI) comparisons for a settlement process within an optimized system that is scalable to a certain limit, but shows unacceptable Dycom and RI values. The Dycom is currently 100, but should be less than 30. The RI is 67.2, which is 7.2 points higher than the recommend score of 60 or below for optimized dynamic system limits. When emulating the same business model using blockchain protocols and the necessary supporting platform as a disruptive innovation, the results show a considerable gain in performance and metrics due to the elimination of intermediaries with a Dycom score of 0 and RI of 23.1.

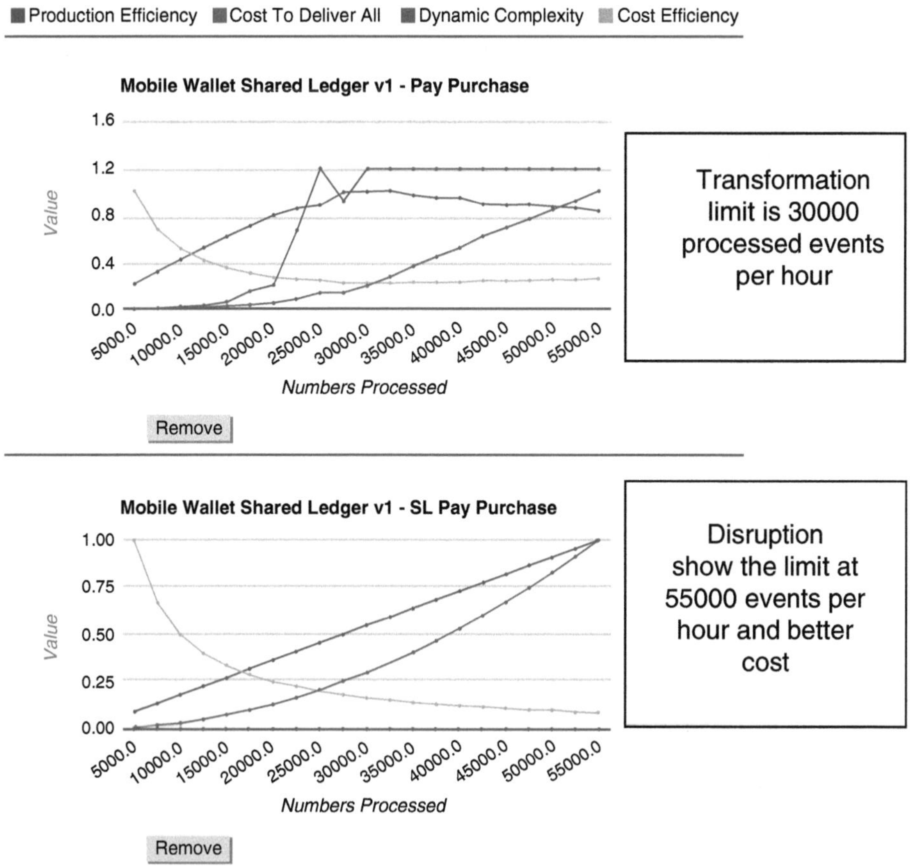

Fig. 14.4 X-Act® OBC Platform prescriptive analysis of system performance

Fig. 14.5 Dycom and Risk Index (RI) comparisons for a settlement process that is optimized through infrastructure changes or disrupted by adoption of blockchain technologies

Using such emulations, users can now definitively answer management's questions on whether a move to blockchain is the correct action to increase volumes and lower costs as necessary to maintain a competitive position or meet evolving market demands. In this case, the answer would be *yes*—if other conditions such as preparedness, organization, availability of convergence and risk rewards are defined, analyzed and adapted.

15 Getting Started with Universal Risk Management

Destiny is not a matter of chance, it is a matter of choice; it is not a thing to be waited for, it is a thing to be achieved.
—Winston Churchill, British statesman

In this chapter:

- Defining requirements of a step-wise approach to universal risk management
- Understanding the process and how technologies can be applied to discover the risk, construct the risk platform and monitor the risk
- Gaining a high-level overview of the universal risk management five stage process supported by X-Act® OBC Platform

Emulation-based universal risk management allows for the definition of a dynamic complexity signature, which represents the dynamics of a system ignored by other false analytic methodologies. The dynamic signature created by X-Act® OBC Platform becomes the critical foundation for risk discovery and diagnosis that leads to the appropriate prescription. In this way, emulation becomes the cornerstone of smart management. Using this approach, decision making is continuously supported by a strong predictive capability that covers both the knowns and unknowns to deliver reliable and robust prescription of any unwanted risks.

Our process is global, but represents the constituents at all levels. Therefore, it imposes the following points:

N. Abu el Ata, A. Drucbert, *Leading from Under the Sword of Damocles*,
https://doi.org/10.1007/978-3-662-56300-7_15

1. We must fight against fragmentation, dilution of responsibility, diffused accountability/ownership and obsolescence.
2. We must be able to globally control the analytical solution explicitly and as far as possible by identifying constituents and interdependencies that are necessary to form the whole system.
3. We must be able to monitor all levels and consolidate the information into a single model.
4. We must simplify the communication among stakeholders with numerical proofs and prescriptive propositions.

Additionally, we must apply a modern approach to management in which risk is predictively treated, not just in the short-term but exhaustively by understanding the economics as well as considering all options, details of the environment and every discriminant factor.

A good management practice requires a step-wise implementation that is regularly updated and revisited to allow the discovery of time dependent trends and an eventual change in the base-line. Our approach is dependent upon three functional domains: discover the risk, construct the risk platform and monitor the risk.

Discover the Risk

Businesses must first define the scope of risk evaluation by enumerating the types of risks and subsequently the areas of the business that may be impacted. Through this exercise, it is important to consider that all areas of the business may be impacted by various types of risk, and that many risks can co-exist. The goal of this exercise is to determine which dimensions of the business and the range of risks that should be evaluated, so that through X-Act® OBC Platform emulation, users can determine the effect of each conceivable risk on the entire system.

For example, we may discover that the subprime entropic behavior represents a risk on housing activities, but it is also possible that the resulting decline in the money supply can precipitate an economic crisis. Therefore, if the project is too narrowly defined, businesses may miss a major risk. Types of risks to consider during this stage include:

- *Service constraints* which should reveal a large spectrum of risks that may produce undesirable business outcomes such as a loss in productivity, efficiency, or availability. These in turn may threaten customer relationships, lead to contractual issues, impact project delivery or affect the return on investment (ROI).
- *Safety tolerance levels* that include all formal, stated procedural or undocumented positions that cover how the company works to avoid or minimize the possibilities of

danger, death or injury. This exercise should include project, product and workplace safety programs as well as any safety standards associated with system sub-processes such as transportation, mining, production-lines, and/or machinery.

- *Economic boundaries* represent a wide spectrum of risks that must be considered including risk on investments—even those that may result from a domino effect of hidden or unintended dependencies, market risks, risk of economic or financial products obsolescence or risks that result from money supply issues and unbalanced counterparties.
- *Competitive outlook* should consider the risks associated with a company's position within an industry. This analysis should include benchmarks between competitors within a market, conflicting investment opportunities within the same corporation, and corporations of different ages, sizes and risk perceptions, as well as readiness and sensitivity to risk tolerance.

Construct the Predictive Risk Platform

Risk appearance points to an evolutionary process. The conditions and impact of risk should be anticipated at the right time to provide sufficient opportunity for their mitigation through corrective actions. Which means that the predicted root causes of risk must cover both the known as well as unknown causes that may occur circumstantially due to the inherent dynamic complexity provoked by internal multi-order dependencies or due to external influencers.

By delivering predictive capabilities, X-Act® OBC Platform supports the goals of universal risk management in the following ways:

- Through the collection of pertinent information and data extraction, X-Act® OBC Platform compiles the information necessary to define the emulation, its objectives and the expected outcome as required to support a management decision.
- X-Act® OBC Platform comes with libraries of dynamic patterns to speed the emulation construction process by providing ready to use objects. Objects available for use and adaptation through X-Act® OBC Platform include a full industrial area (e.g., a retail bank, supply chain or postal service), business processes (e.g., payment system, telecommunication protocol, triage system or relational data model), or physical objects (e.g., a processor, truck, sorting machine, hubs or humans).
- Through a user-friendly interface that does not require any mathematical skills for use, X-Act® OBC Platform accurately emulates, computes and projects the necessary decision metrics under a variety of scenarios and dynamic, evolutionary options. The platform is the only commercial platform available today that ensures that all three of

the following key criteria are fulfilled and demonstrated by the mathematical computation:

- ***Representativeness*** requires that all processes, objects, sequencing, environmental and discriminant factors are explicitly represented;
- ***Accuracy*** requires that the computation results are highly accurate compared to the existing system;
- ***Reproducibility*** requires that all projections and predictive outcomes are aligned to the characteristics and behavior of the system at any point in time—indicating that the platform has successfully captured all *known* and *unknown* dynamics.

Risk metrics are expressed qualitatively and quantitatively through X-Act® OBC Platform to reveal the effect of dynamic complexity on the generation and acceleration of risk. To universally approach risk, we need to mathematically compute and capture all outstanding behaviors and characteristics that:

- Represent a safety threat, as early as possible for risk avoidance and treatment.
- Engender queuing, as explicit or virtual queuing are complex to fix and require either an upgrade in resources or reduction in system throughput. It is generally better to avoid or reduce queuing related problems through efficient distribution and better sharing mechanisms.
- Generate locks that may result in a timeout or inefficient utilization of resources.
- Increase the latency, which will impact the quality of service and reduce volumes to process and deliver.
- Consume the supply, as one of the major challenges decision makers face is the efficient use of assets and available supply. Inefficiencies will rarefy the resources because they are detoured to service dynamic complexity and auxiliary services without producing any real benefits.
- Cause excessive cost (business margin) that may ultimately make it difficult for the business to survive and/or threaten the continuity of the business, projects or services.
- Create instability that can prevent predictability and question the justification for action.
- Produce delays that makes a disruptive move or transformation difficult within an acceptable window of time.
- Prevent efficient surveillance and control management processes to be built.

Monitor the Evolution of Risk

The optimal business control (OBC) capability supported by X-Act® OBC Platform enables continuous risk surveillance. Based on predictive knowledge gathered during the emulation process and sensitivity and stress analysis, the pre-identified risks are stored in a knowledge base with an identifier, diagnosis and remediation actions. When a matching case is then identified in operations, the risk has already been evaluated and is ready to be immediately resolved. In this manner, OBC monitoring capabilities allow the organization to apply the proper action ahead of any negative business outcomes.

X-Act OBC Platform Five-Stage Process

X-Act® OBC Platform supports a five-stage process for universal risk management as represented in Fig. 15.1 to ensure:

- The constructed emulator will address the initially defined business challenge
- A structured collection of required inputs
- An easy construction of the target emulator
- The computed emulator will deliver the required outputs
- The emulator will support the predictive functions required for *what-if* scenarios

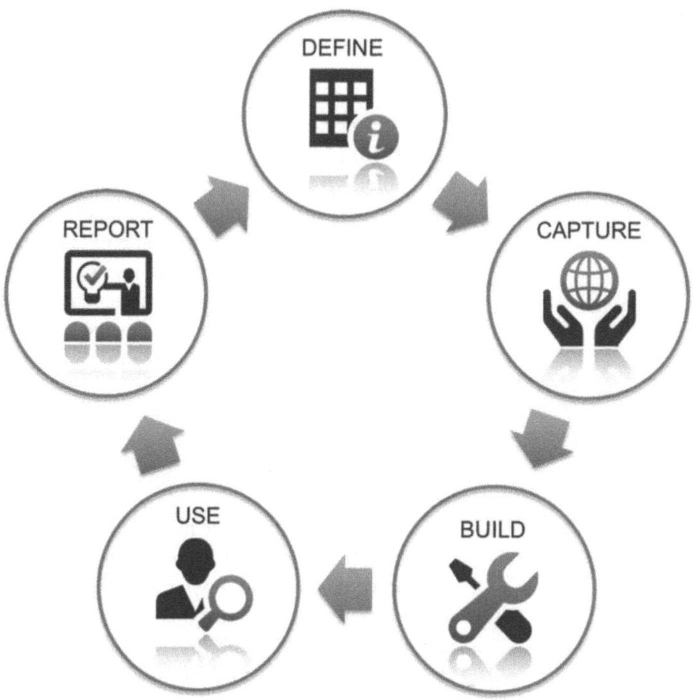

Fig. 15.1 X-Act® OBC Platform five-stage process

Step 1: Define
In this step, users should define the scope of the target emulator. This includes deciding which business function(s), service process(es), application(s), or other critical components to model. Clearly defining which business objectives and challenges the emulator is meant to address will help guide these decisions. This stage is key to the outcome and will define which actions must be taken to correctly build the emulator.

Step 2: Capture
In this step, users must capture the necessary business, service and infrastructure level information. While some information is captured through automated methods, much of the business and service level information comes from interviews and workshops. The quality of the future emulator will be highly dependent on the quality and completeness of the information captured, therefore access to the right business and IT leaders is critical to a successful outcome.

Step 3: Build
Using the X-Act® OBC Platform point and click interface, users are now ready to build the emulator. To accomplish this goal, users exploit the information provided in *Step 2: Capture* to construct the business, service and implementation views of the emulator. Once this is accomplished, they will calibrate the resulting model. At the end of this stage, the constructed emulator will be ready to compute and generate results.

Step 4: Use
Now users are ready to use the computed emulator to:
Predictively Diagnose Problems: Users can establish a precise and robust diagnosis of any identified issues through the analysis of results that are dynamically generated and visually represented through the X-Act® OBC Platform interface.
Prescriptively Identify Solutions: Users can use X-Act® OBC Platform prescriptive functions to find and evaluate the applicability of solutions using *what-if* scenarios.

(continued)

Step 5: Report

X-Act® OBC Platform helps users develop executive ready reports that detail the diagnosis of existing or potential problems along with any impacts and associated risks to the business. Additionally, X-Act® OBC Platform can be used to present remediation options and recommendations supported by value and benefit assessments. Often, *Step 5: Report* will expose new business challenges, leading users back to *Step 1: Define* to begin the process with new goals and insights—thereby delivering a continuous loop of predictive and prescriptive support for management decisions.

X-Act OBC Platform Walk Through 16

Many of life's failures are people who did not realize how close they were to success when they gave up.

—Thomas Edison, American inventor and businessman

In this chapter:

- Building an emulator and using predictive models through X-Act® OBC Platform
- Choosing between quick start and detailed emulation construction options
- Using emulation results to diagnose problems and evaluate prescriptive actions

This chapter provides an overview of the X-Act® OBC Platform interface and capabilities along with supporting methods that enable the construction of models, mathematical emulations, advanced analytical operations, and predictive and prescriptive results. This information is intended to provide readers with a robust understanding of how advanced predictive and prescriptive analytics technology can be used to support mature risk management practices and guide strategic business decisions.

Useful how to guides, best practices, case studies and additional training videos are available to X-Act® OBC Platform users to provide deeper understanding of how the technology can be applied to expose hidden risks and vet business decisions.

N. Abu el Ata, A. Drucbert, *Leading from Under the Sword of Damocles*,
https://doi.org/10.1007/978-3-662-56300-7_16

Model Construction Overview

An emulator is the representative mathematical system of an existing or future system and a model is the instantiation of an emulator under specific initial conditions. X-Act® OBC Platform emulations are computed based on models built to support the following three views:

1. **Corporate View** shows the top/down organization of the business. For example, this might be a division, sector or activity within any industry (insurance, retail banking, credit card, automotive, etc.) mapped to its business service trajectory—whether it be settlement, trading, payment, car production, mail processing, etc.
2. **Service View** includes the business service processes, the architecture logic and dynamic constraints. The view shows the service trajectory for whatever the service maybe (mail delivery, credit card settlement, etc.) and the hierarchy of service business processes (such as input, posting, cycling, etc.), business components (e.g., customer processing, payment processing, etc.), up to the lowest logical level (e.g., balance accounts, update information, etc.) and the logical server (be it human, truck, mainframe, database messaging, etc.)
3. **Implementation View** includes all lower level supporting components and is divided into two levels:
   a. **Local level**: the logical server is transformed into one or many physical servers—each with its own processing mode, physics, space and energy characteristics
   b. **Global view**: shows geographical distribution of components over a larger structure (e.g., the location of datacenters or distribution centers on Google maps)

X-Act OBC Platform Information and Data Collection

The quality of the emulation is dependent upon the quality of data captured, therefore it is important to keep in mind the following objectives when executing *Stage 2: Capture* of the X-Act® OBC Platform five stage process. To build an emulator which will correspond to the multiple models that are necessary to support predictive and prescriptive universal risk management, the user must collect the information covering the full stack shown in Fig. 16.1 and broken down by model view in the following sections.

Model Construction: Corporate View

The corporate view provides an organizational view of the business structure and business constraints. Figure 16.2 shows a corporate view of a bank within X-Act® OBC Platform as an example. The components of the interface are outlined in Table 16.1.

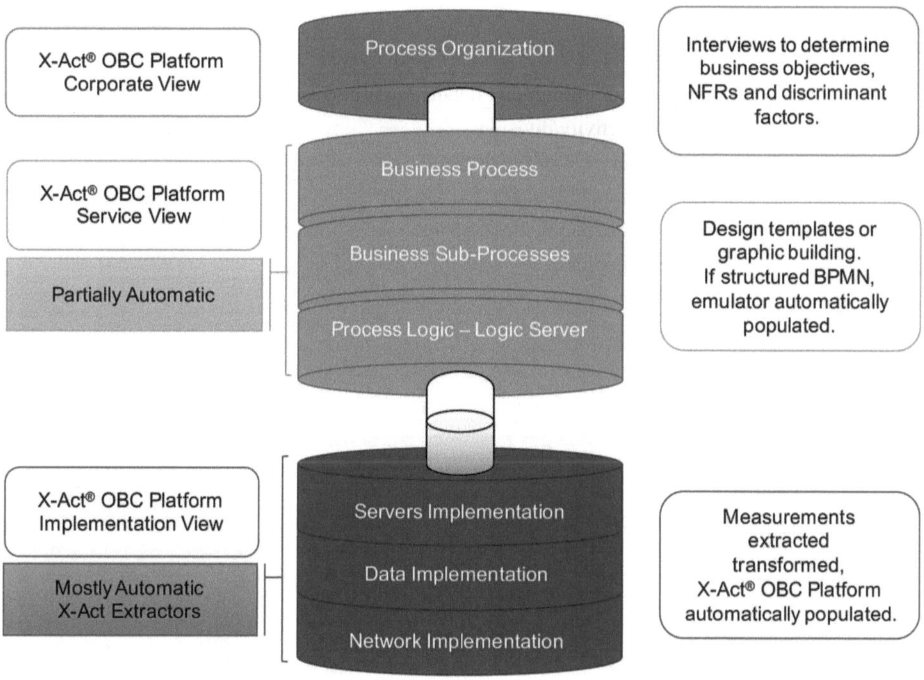

Fig. 16.1 Collection of data: scope and structure

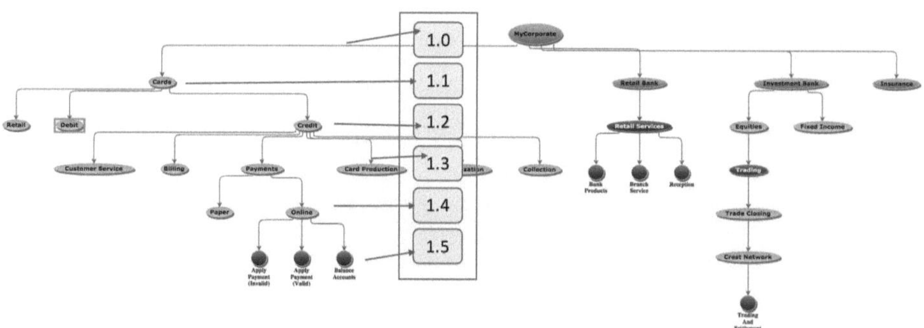

Fig. 16.2 X-Act® OBC Platform: corporate view

Table 16.1 Corporate view interface definitions

Label	Definition
1.0	Corporate definition that details the organizational link to different divisions
1.1	Business activity/division
1.2	Various services of the division
1.3	Business function of service activity
1.4	Dynamic characteristics of a service
1.5	Business process

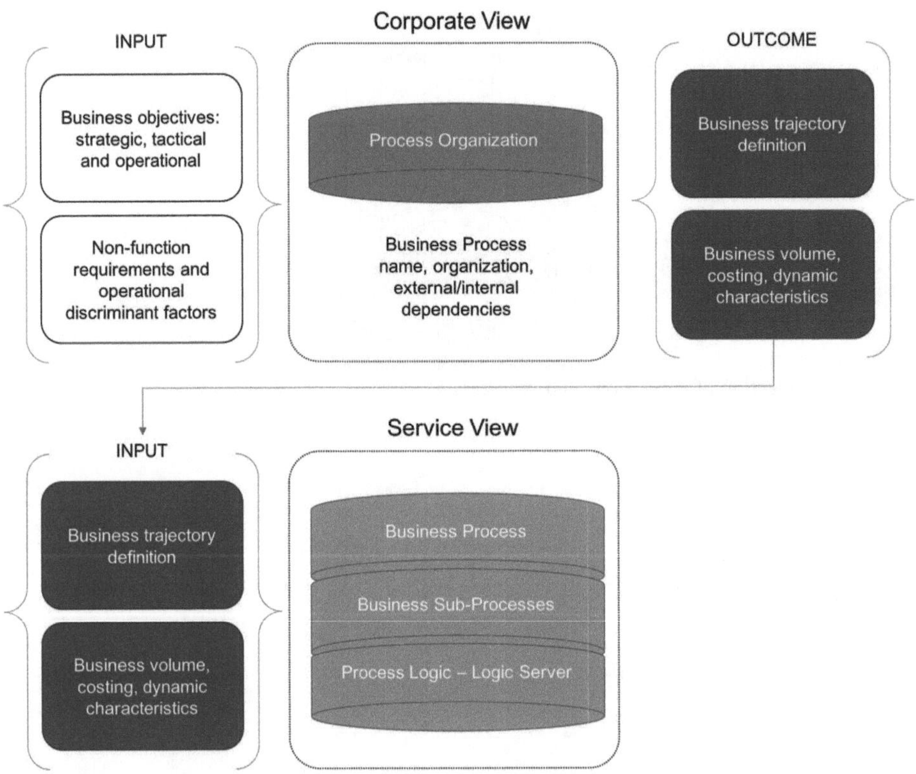

Fig. 16.3 Overview of corporate view model construction

Corporate View: Data Collection

As the corporate view shows a top-down view of a business division, sector or activity—such as insurance, retail banking or credit card—in relation to business service trajectory, whatever it may be, e.g. settlement, trading, payment, car production or mail processing, it is critical to collect the necessary information before building the model.

Figure 16.3 provides an overview of the inputs necessary to build the corporate view model and the outcomes which then become the inputs necessary for construction of the

Table 16.2 Corporate model details

Purpose:	Supports understanding and representation of the service structure, dependencies, sharing (data, resources, functionality, locations, arrival mechanisms, arrival distributions, service quality constraints, cost effectiveness constraints, seasonality)
Collection methods:	Interviews and collection of documentation including architecture diagrams, workflows, future cases of business services and service constraints
Data required:	• Business service workflows • Arrival (rate, mechanism, seasonality, sources, windows, priorities) • Asset sharing, dependencies, etc. • For each process or service branch: hierarchy, dependencies, feedback (if any), lock (if any), branching, parallelism, conditional branching, etc. • Performance constraints: service level agreements (SLAs), cost effectiveness, availability target, per window and per branch • Critical success factors • Priorities: high, medium and low • Business process continuity • Business changes, transformation and competition: triggers, functionality, arrival modes, access strategies, diversification, consolidation

service view. Table 16.2 provides a deeper overview of the purpose of the corporate view model, data collection methods and details of the information required to build the model.

Model Construction: Service View

The service view provides a hierarchical view of the service architecture. The number of the levels is based upon the goal-oriented deconstruction. Figures 16.4 and 16.5 show example service views of a trading system within X-Act® OBC Platform. The components of the interface are outlined in Table 16.3.

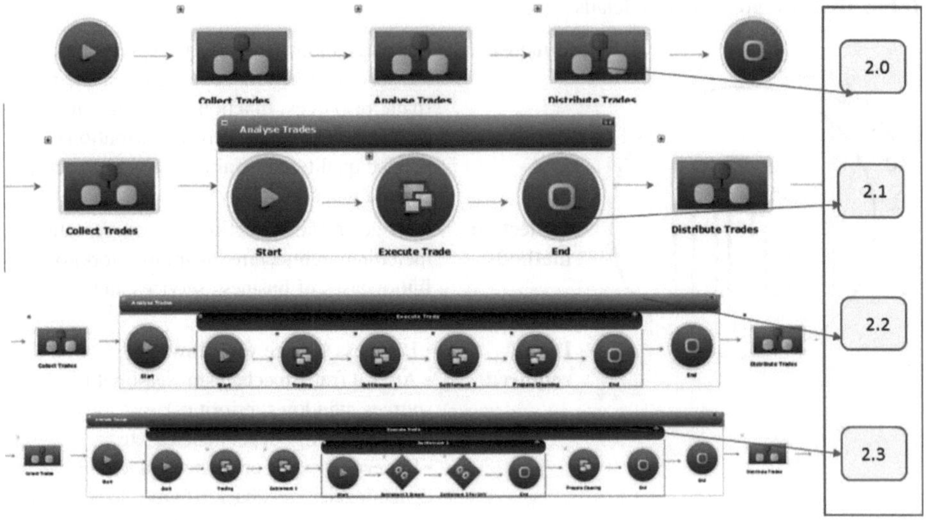

Fig. 16.4 X-Act® OBC Platform: service view, trading system

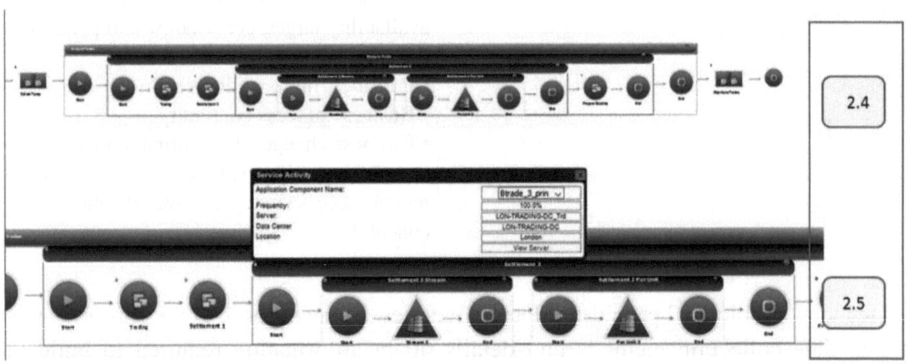

Fig. 16.5 X-Act® OBC Platform: service view, trading system, lowest logic that will be detailed in the Implementation View

Table 16.3 Service view interface definitions

Label	Definition
2.0	First level of service view divides process into sub-processes
2.1	Detailed structure for a sub-process
2.2	Translation of a sub-process structure into components
2.3	Division of components into tasks
2.4	Division of tasks into activities: the example here depicts a 4-level deconstruction logic, however the logic can expand to any number of levels as required
2.5	Activity is mapped to a physical demand of resources at a location

Service View Data Collection

The service view shows the organization of services top-down (i.e. service processes, sub processes, activities and logical executions) and therefore, the information required to build the model must be collected. Figure 16.6 provides an overview of the inputs necessary to

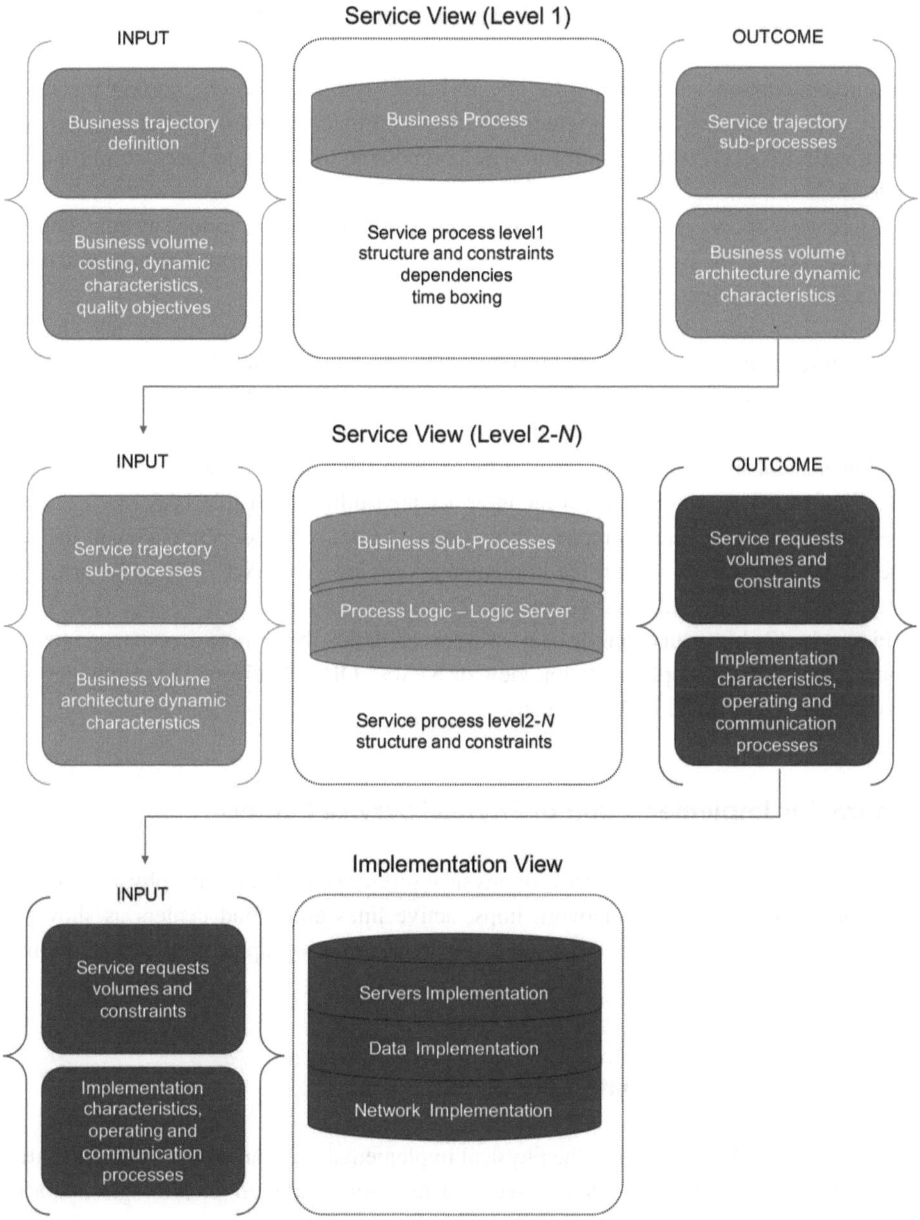

Fig. 16.6 Overview of service view model construction

build the service view model and the outcomes which then become the inputs necessary for construction of the lower level service views and subsequently implementation views. Table 16.4 provides a deeper overview of the purpose of the service view model, data collection methods and required depth of information.

Model Construction: Implementation View

The implementation view details the physical architecture of servers, sorting machines, supply and production chains. Figure 16.7 shows an example implementation view of a server within X-Act® OBC Platform. The components of the interface are outlined in Table 16.5.

Figure 16.8 shows an example of how users can populate the model by selecting the server type within the implementation view of X-Act® OBC Platform. The components of the interface are outlined in Table 16.6.

Figure 16.9 shows an example of how users can populate the model by selecting the manufacturer and technology options within the implementation view of X-Act® OBC Platform. The components of the interface are outlined in Table 16.7.

Figure 16.10 shows an example of how users can define the characteristics of activity components that share the same server instance within the implementation view of X-Act® OBC Platform. The components of the interface are outlined in Table 16.8.

Figure 16.11 shows an example of how users can define the dependencies of the data access layer per activity within the implementation view of X-Act® OBC Platform. The components of the interface are outlined in Table 16.9.

Figure 16.12 shows an example of how users can define the storage area management of candidates within the implementation view of X-Act® OBC Platform. The components of the interface are outlined in Table 16.10.

Geographic Implementation of Physical Service Centers

The geographic implementation view of physical service centers maps the physical location of service centers including network hops, active lines and cloud centers as shown in Fig. 16.13. The components of the X-Act® OBC Platform geographic interface are outlined in Table 16.11.

Implementation View Data Collection

The implementation view shows the physical implementation characteristics and operating environment including technology layers, data implementation technologies, storage

Table 16.4 Service model details

	**Purpose**:	Supports understanding and representation of the service structure, dependencies, sharing (data, resources, functionality, locations, arrival mechanisms, arrival distributions, service quality constraints, cost effectiveness constraints, seasonality)
	Collection methods:	Mainly through interviews, BPMN diagrams and/or the review of strategic business documents
	Data required:	• Business service organigram: units, departments, businesses, activities, sectors, etc. • Business processes, sub-processes, tasks, activities and sub activities • Arrival (rate, mechanism, seasonality, sources, windows, priorities) • Assets sharing/cooperative: data, resources, location, economies (do more for less), users, operators, etc. • "The branch" for each: organogram including parent/child, distribution, dependencies, business trajectory process name (the ultimate level in the view that leads to the service process view) • Performance constraints per branch (SLA, cost effectiveness, availability target, per window, etc.) • Critical success factors • Market, environment and business constraints: price pressure, globalization, regulation, deregulation, market consolidation, strategic orientations, sources of pumps and spikes • Priorities: high, medium and low • Business continuity • Risk maturity and criteria (in descending order): which business is highest, most critical, should have DR, constraints to scarify, etc. • Business changes, transformation, competition: triggers, functionality, arrival modes, access strategies, diversification, consolidation • Business goals: M&A, transformation, competitively dictated, sensitive to user demand, outsourcing, consolidation, etc.

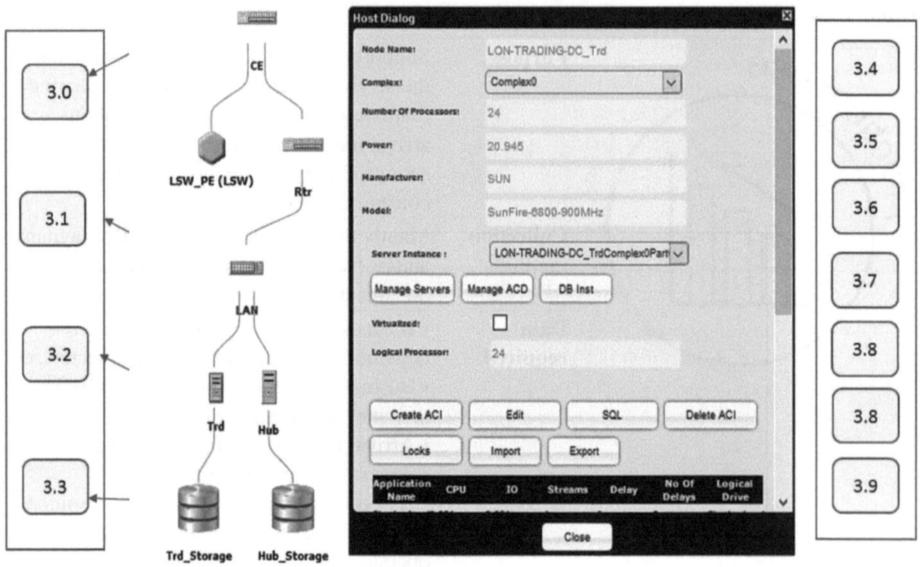

Fig. 16.7 Implementation view server selection

Table 16.5 Implementation view, server selection interface definitions

Label	Definition
3.0	Router
3.1	Switch
3.2	Server (can be IT server, sorting machine, robot, production engine, human, etc.)
3.3	Storage area (disk sub-system, data storage, storage hub, storage area, etc.)
3.4	Number of processing sources, power (reference to name in library)
3.5	Manufacturer (reference to name in library)
3.6	Name of the server in the service view
3.7	Role played by this server instance and its virtualization
3.8	Operations related to server deployment (ACI, database, locks, etc.)
3.9	All application(s) components running on the server (resources demand, parallelism, delays as imposed by the logic, etc.)

technologies, protocols, geographical coordinates, energy, space, time criticality, SLAs, SLGs (service level guaranteed). Figure 16.14 provides an overview of the inputs necessary to build the service view model and the outcomes which then become the inputs necessary for the analysis of risk and available prescriptive actions. Table 16.12 provides a deeper overview of the purpose of the service view model, data collection methods and required depth of information.

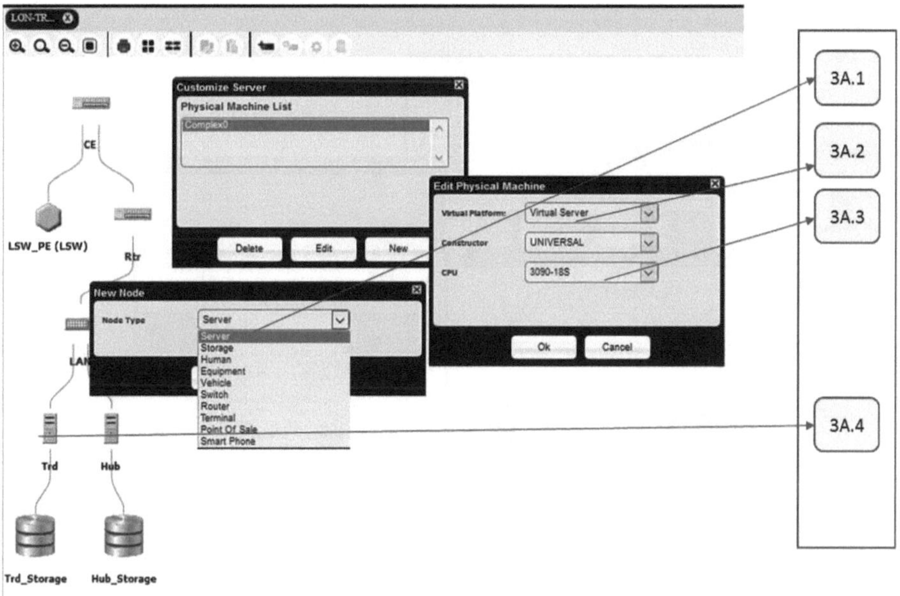

Fig. 16.8 Server type selection: human, storage, vehicle, router, etc.

Table 16.6 Server type selection interface definitions

Label	Definition
3A.1	Server Type
3A.2	Virtualization selection
3A.3	Server technology and operating environment
3A.4	Server selected in the Group Implementation View

Emulation Construction

After collecting the necessary data including processes, dynamics and NFRs, the user is ready to start the emulation process. The following two options of emulation construction are supported by X-Act® OBC Platform as detailed below and summarized in Fig. 16.15.

Option 1: Quick Start, Ideal Implementation

The quick start option provides a fast path to predictive insights. In this case, the emulator is constructed in real-time based upon the inputs of subject matter representatives and

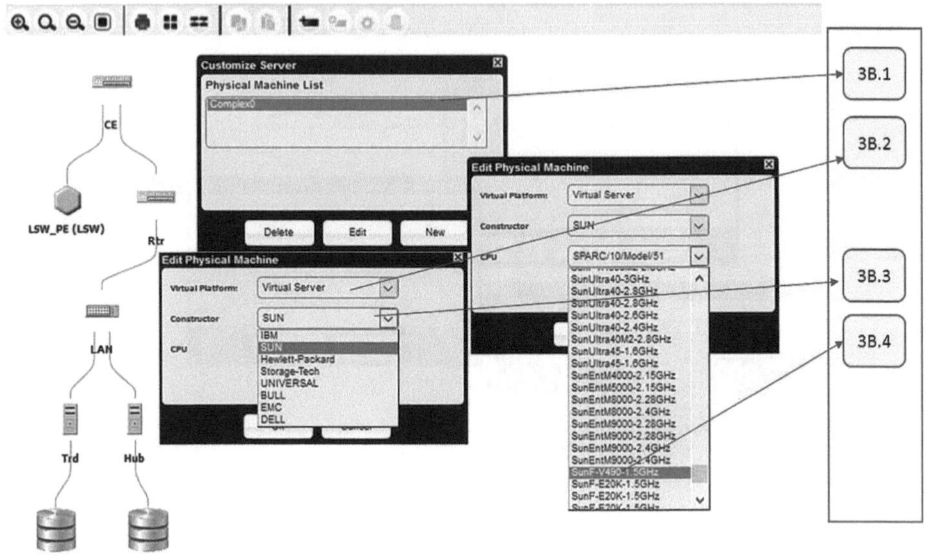

Fig. 16.9 Manufacturer and technology selections for IT server

Table 16.7 Manufacturer and technology selection interface definitions

Label	Definition
3B.1	Server complex name
3B.2	Virtualization status selection
3B.3	Server manufacturer taken from X-Act® Library of manufacturers
3B.4	Technology name within the X-Act® Library of benchmarks

dynamic patterns from the X-Act® libraries. The point and click features of the X-Act® OBC Platform make it very easy to update the model as knowledge is gained through interviews or the collection of data. Each level of the hierarchy relies on a list of objects that the user can change on demand and continuously update or augment as needed to match the business environment being modeled. Data associated to the objects represents best case practices and characteristics. Therefore, the emulator in this instance represents an ideal implementation.

Option 2: Detailed, Actual Implementation

In this case, the numbers that were used from the libraries in the quick start construct of the emulation are replaced by real measurements. The results of this construct fulfil two distinct purposes:

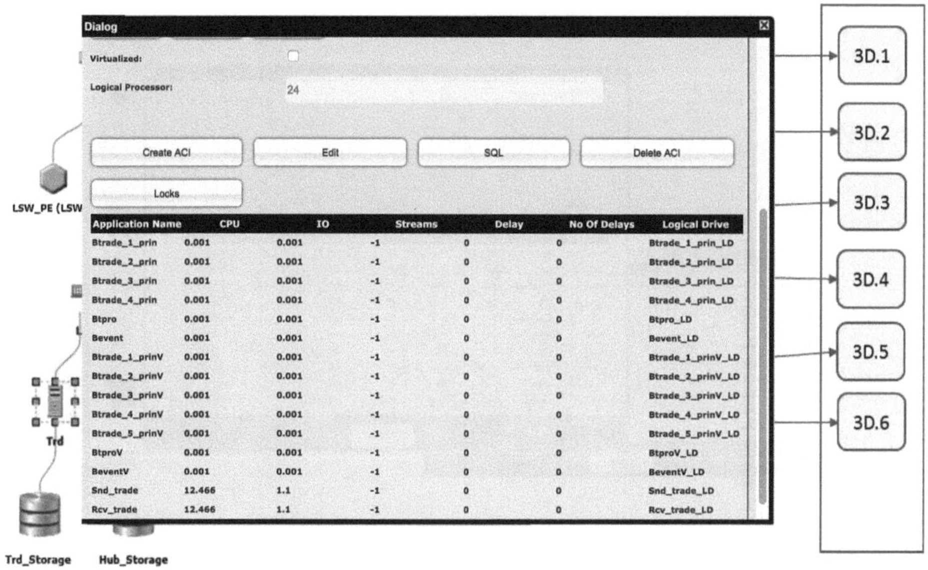

Fig. 16.10 Definition of activity component characteristics per server instance

Table 16.8 Selection of activity component characteristics interface definitions

Label	Definition
3D.1	Virtualization indication
3D.2	Data access will be explicated in the next view
3D.3	Sever demand in millisecond
3D.4	I/O's time in millisecond
3D.5	Group name
3D.6	Logical driver name

1. It allows the user to verify the representativeness of the emulator in comparison to a real instantiation and apply any calibration that is needed to represent the actual implementation.
2. Since the quick start construct represents an ideal implementation, the comparison of the quick start versus actual construct helps the user begin diagnosing any issues and identify which optimization actions are required. Any deviations in the model from the ideal representation will require interpretation including identifying the origin and causes of the deviation.

From experience gained through building hundreds of emulations for businesses, we have found that in most cases, the quick start construct is sufficient to compare,

Fig. 16.11 Definition of dependencies of data access layer per activity

Table 16.9 Dependency interface definitions

Label	Definition
3C.1	Name of store procedure
3C.2	Data access action
3C.3	Name of data access order
3C.4	Accessed table name
3C.5	Index for accessed table
3C.6	Frequency of access
3C.7	Cluster efficiency

benchmark, diagnose and predict the best-case scenario for system limits and find a potential singularity. Constructing a detailed emulation is necessary to support optimization and transformation programs. Using our model-based architecture (MBA) methodology, the real implementation construct helps plan and guide a successful project.

Goals Determine Best Approach

The best way to use the predictive ability of the emulator will be dependent on your risk analysis goals.

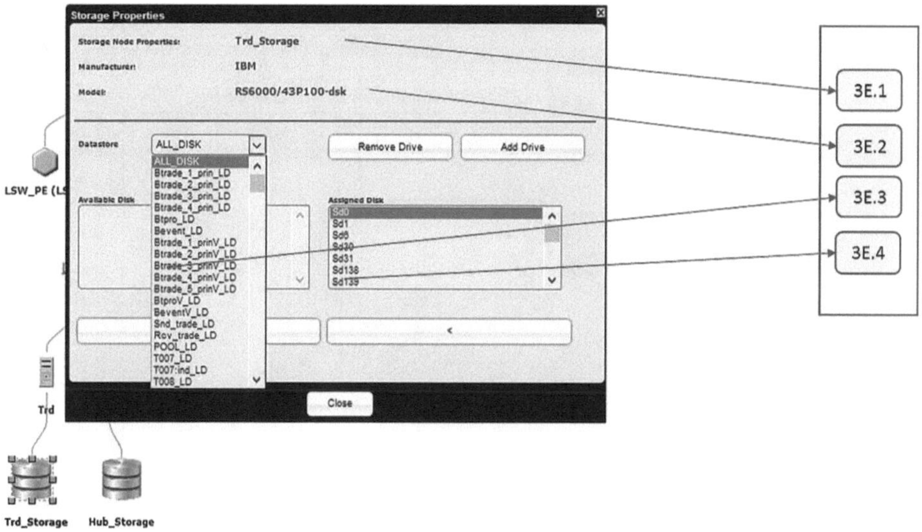

Fig. 16.12 Storage area management of candidates

Table 16.10 Storage area management interface definitions

Label	Definition
3E.1	Storage sub-system name
3E.2	Storage manufacturer
3E.3	Activities name for assigned storage
3E.4	Storage name

New system	When building a new business system, the emulator can be used to select the optimal infrastructure that will satisfy a business objective and service level guarantee as well as deliver the right support and predictable scalability to meet growing volume requirements. An emulator built using certified and pre-tested mathematical objects and data can support all types of *what-if* analysis—covering all possible models and patterns to support decisions. Experience shows that this approach supports a new era of systemic enterprise in which concepts are fully tested through emulation before any monetary or resource investments are made in the actual implementation.
Existing system	When optimization and transformation of an existing organization and its systems is the goal of the predictive analysis exercise, the user will need to build both the quick start construct and actual construct. Once both emulations have been built, the user will be able to identify the cause of an eventual deviation between ideal and actual as a first step. Obviously, this process will take more time than would be the case with a new system, since the objective is both a renewal as well as transformation. In this way, the emulator then becomes a field experimentation facility. Companies can typically expect to increase performance and reduce costs by a few orders of magnitude when following this process.

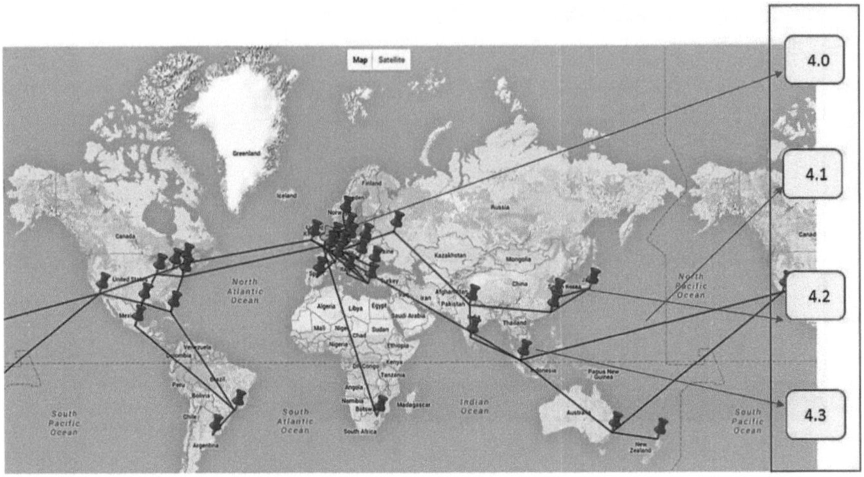

Fig. 16.13 Geographic implementation of physical services centers

Table 16.11 Geographic implementation of physical service centers interface definitions

Label	Definition
4.0	The physical service center within the geographic deployment
4.1	Network characteristics between physical centers
4.2	Virtualized service hubs
4.3	Cloud service within the geographic deployment

X-Act OBC Platform Operations Menu

Once the emulator has been constructed within X-Act® OBC Platform, the user can apply any number of operations to compute, show the results and other actions as necessary to formulate a risk management strategy or support a business decision. Figure 16.16 shows the operations menu and the corresponding definitions are provided in Table 16.13.

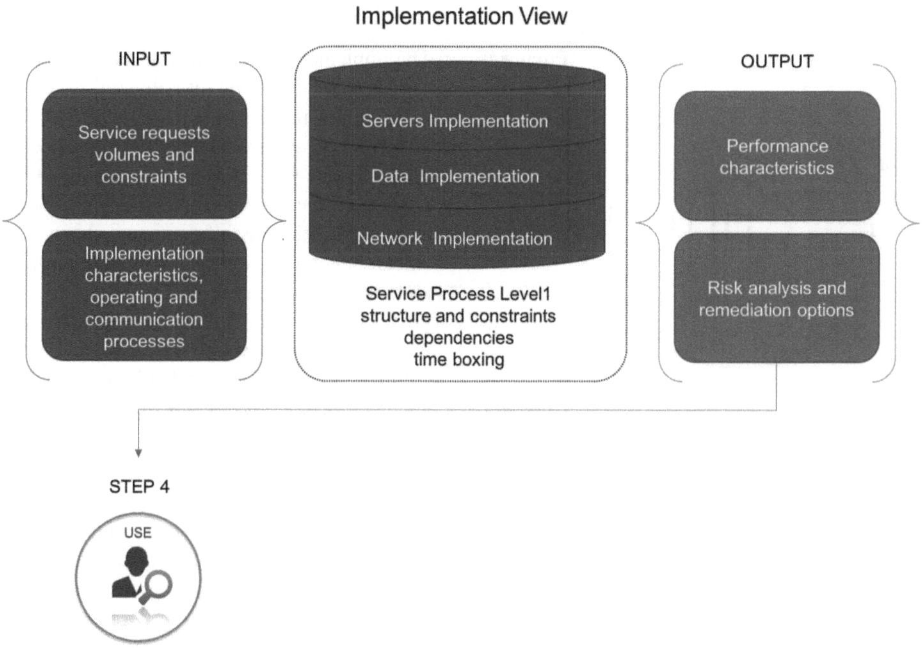

Fig. 16.14 Overview of implementation model construction

X-Act OBC Platform Computation Center

The X-Act® OBC Platform computation center relies on several parameters that allow users to identify problems and risks by exposing scenarios, which will produce a singularity. Figure 16.17 shows how the parameters of the emulation can be changed within the computation center to execute *what-if* scenarios, thus helping users identify a potential risk or diagnose the root cause of a problem. Table 16.14 provides further definitions of the computation center labels.

X-Act OBC Platform Results

Using the results provided by X-Act® OBC Platform, users can determine the maximum volume that will be delivered in optimal quality and cost as well as the point of chaos—allowing users to understand the conditions that will cause a system failure. These results allow users to predictively discover eventual risks and prescriptively support remedial

Table 16.12 Implementation model details

	**Purpose**:	The implementation model translates the service logic execution into physical performance metrics as reaction to arrival distributions, service quality constraints, cost effectiveness constraints and seasonality. This view represents interdependencies, demand sharing, partitioning, infrastructure choices and architecture as well as the internal services and external influencers which are the provoking forces of dynamic complexity that will be generated through contentions, conflicts, locks, failures and delays.
	Collection methods:	This information can be collected using extractors and system metrics. However, during the early stages of design or when creating a new business, it is unlikely that measurements will be available. In this case, X-Act® libraries of pre-built dynamic patterns can be used. The dynamic patterns made available through the X-Act® libraries are benchmarks that represent ideal metrics. Once the business system is physically available, a comparison between the benchmark metrics and actual implementation can be made to calibrate the emulator and keep it aligned with the actual implementation.
	Data required:	• System characteristics per activity • System requests per activity: arrival rate, mechanism, seasonality, sources, windows, priorities and system consumption metrics • Priorities, task distribution and virtualization properties • Data implementation characteristics (verbs: updates, select, insert and delete) and size of tables, indexes and store procedures composition • Performance constraints per branch: SLAs, cost effectiveness, availability target, per window, etc. • Business continuity • Cloud preferences • Risk maturity operating options (in descending order): which business is highest, most critical, business changes/ transformation/competition: triggers, functionality, arrival modes, accesses strategies, diversification, consolidation

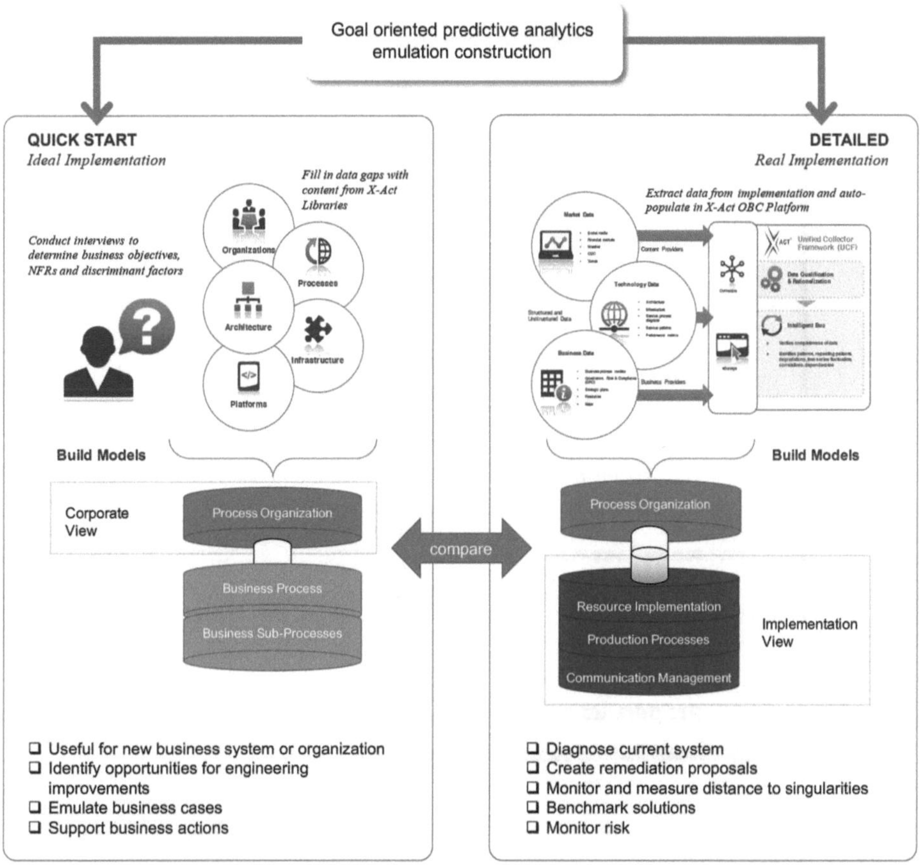

Fig. 16.15 Overview of emulation construction options when using X-Act® OBC Platform

decisions. Figure 16.18 shows the results sub-menu options which are further explained in Table 16.15.

Results: Business Orientation

X-Act® OBC Platform results can provide strategic business insights by detailing the maximum volume that can be delivered with optimal quality and cost as well as predicting the chaos point as detailed in Fig. 16.19 and further explained in Table 16.16.

X-Act® OBC Platform dashboards provide a universal view of risk with the Risk Index metric and quantify the risk posed by dynamic complexity through the Dycom Score per business service process as shown in Fig. 16.20 and further explained in Table 16.17.

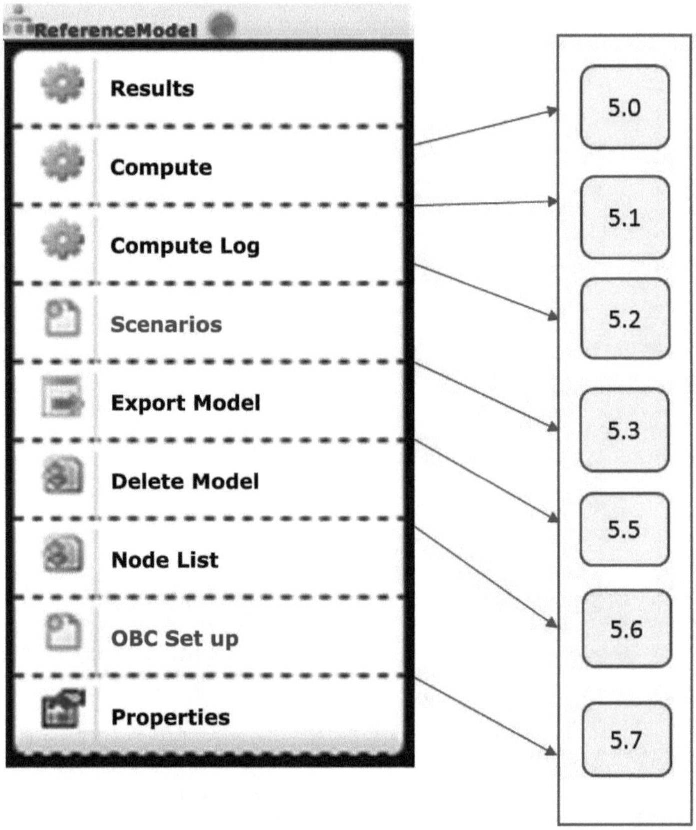

Fig. 16.16 X-Act® OBC Platform operations menu

Table 16.13 Operations menu definitions

Label	Definition
5.0	Results: provides multiple display options
5.1	Compute: computation center for single, multiple and predefined projection points
5.2	Compute Log: provides log of computations
5.3	Scenarios: lists multiple areas
5.4	Export Model: instantiation of emulator that corresponds to a specific set of initial conditions
5.5	Delete Model: removes model
5.6	Node List: overview of deployment nodes
5.7	Properties: overview of deployment properties

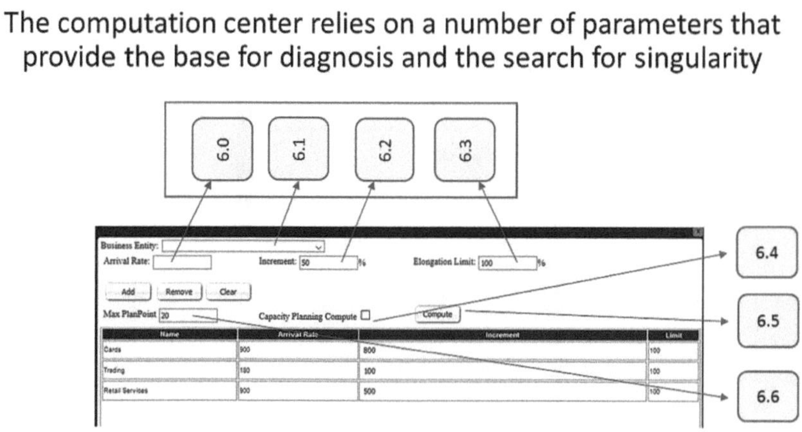

Fig. 16.17 Computation center parameters

Table 16.14 Computation center label definitions

Label	Definition
6.0	Initial arrival rate of a business process
6.1	Business process name (entity). Several business processes are allowed (as presented)
6.2	For multiple computation: step increments of arrival rate—could be many for many business processes
6.3	Limit for conflicts, contention of dynamic complexity origin
6.4	Specific step increments of arrival rate—could be many for many business processes
6.5	Single compute (if Max plan points = 0) or Multiple computation = Max plan points
6.6	Number of single computations that may allow system to hit eventual singularity point

From the X-Act® OBC Platform Overview Risk Index and Dycom Score Reporting Dashboard, users can diagnose problems by drilling down on a specific business service process to identify which component is causing the risk due to excessive dynamic complexity as shown in Fig. 16.21 and further explained in Table 16.18.

The X-Act® OBC Platform remediation dashboard helps users identify which action are necessary for improvement, determine the complexity of implementing the recommended actions and project the time necessary to complete the remedial actions as shown in Fig. 16.22 and further explained in Table 16.19.

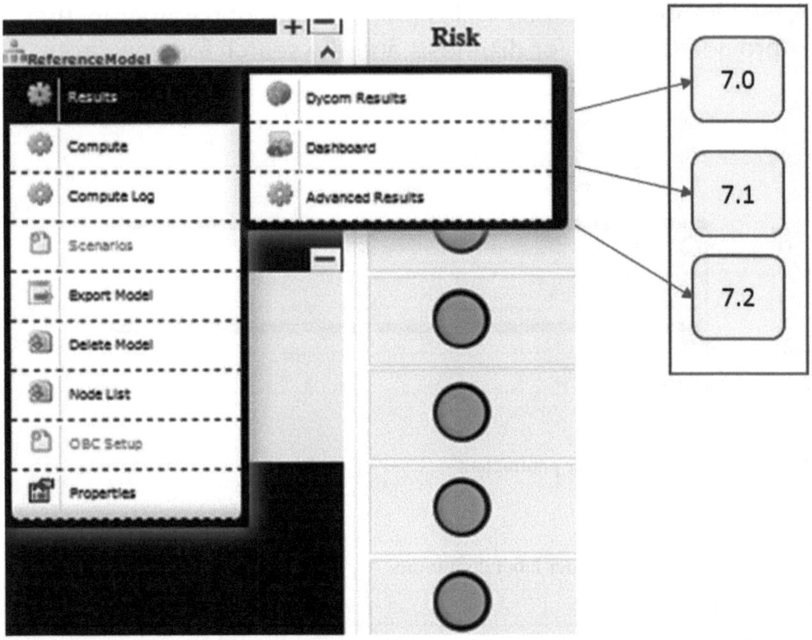

Fig. 16.18 X-Act® OBC Platform results sub-menu

Table 16.15 Results sub-menu definitions

Label	Definition
7.0	Dycom Results: determine the amount of inefficiencies that are due to internal dependencies or external deterministic factors. Dycom is a dimensionless metric. The results are given with risk evaluation metrics per business process. The discovery process points to the cause and allows for fixing and remediation.
7.1	Dashboard: These results, delivered as a dashboard, serve engineering teams and includes in depth details including service management, resources utilization and financial views
7.2	Advanced Results: provides access to advanced metrics such as Scalability Index, Service Quality Degradation Metrics, and Limits in terms of delivery capability, etc.

Results: Systemic Orientation

In the following section, we present the results that can be used by the re-engineering teams to translate the business diagnosis into a systemic action plan that covers optimization and transformation at both the logical (architecture) and physical (system infrastructure) levels.

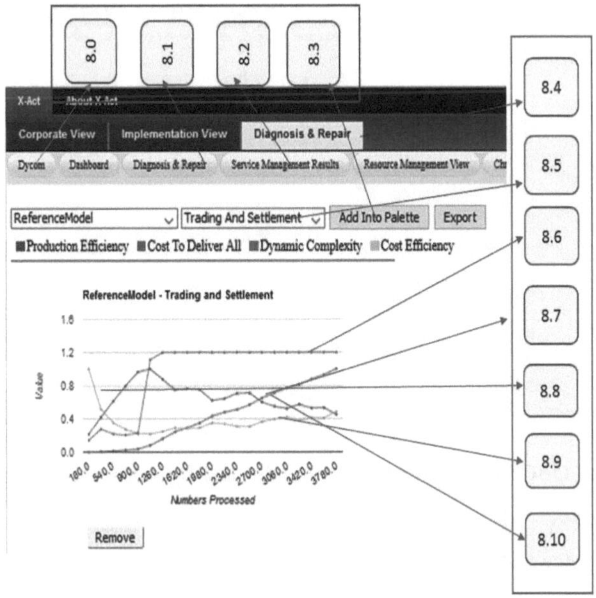

Fig. 16.19 X-Act® OBC Platform business orientation results visualization

Table 16.16 Business orientation results definitions

Label	Definition
8.0	Dycom: shows graphs presented in Fig. 16.20 and Table 16.17
8.1	Diagnosis and Repair: shows details presented in Figs. 16.21 and 16.22 and Tables 16.18 and 16.19
8.2	Service Management Results: shows results presented in Fig. 16.23 and Table 16.20
8.3	Add Into Palette: Adds the constituents of graphs per business process to the results space. In the example shown it would add 'Trading and Settlement' to the results space.
8.4	Diagnosis and Repair: shows the results which are presented in Figs. 16.23, 16.24 and 16.25
8.5	The graph results of one business process. In this example 'Trading and Settlement'
8.6	The results for the dynamic complexity at each computation plan point. The dynamic complexity results are capped at 100% for presentation clarity.
8.7	The graph shows the cost to deliver all business volume requests
8.8	Cost efficiency to deliver a unit business
8.9	The productivity efficiency: the revenue for business services
8.10	The intersection between 8.7 and 8.9 represents the singularity point, which must be avoided through prescriptive actions

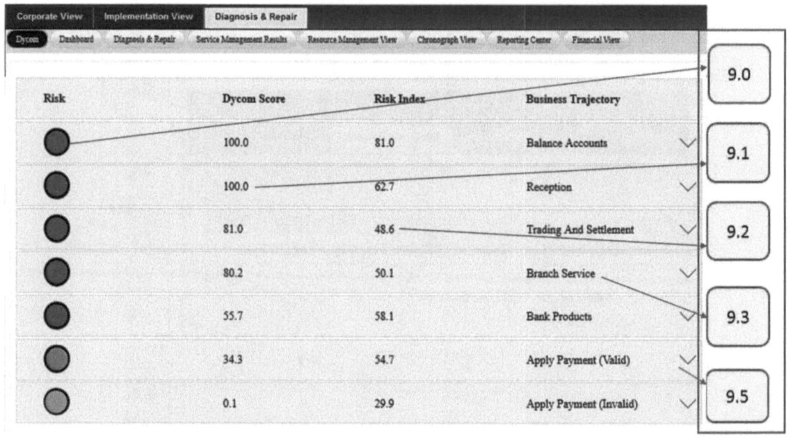

Fig. 16.20 X-Act® OBC Platform overview risk index and Dycom score reporting dashboard

Table 16.17 Overview risk index and Dycom score reporting interface definitions

Label	Definition
9.0	Risk Indicator: shows gravity of risk perception with green, yellow, orange or red indicators (boundaries of color indicators are adjustable on demand)
9.1	Dycom Score: indicates the impact of nonbusiness origins on the performance and cost—due to internal conflicts, contentions and locks and the impact of deterministic external factors.
9.2	Risk Index: represents the business risk due to Dycom (High/High) or lack of resources (Low/High)
9.3	The name of business process
9.4	The results are classified based on highest gravity process exposure downward
9.5	An indication that detailed results are following

Figure 16.23 shows the engineering dashboard that delivers the associated computed metrics so that re-engineering teams can understand in technical terms the business diagnosis. This dashboard facilitates plans to meet the optimization or transformation objectives. Dashboard definitions are provided in Table 16.20.

From the Engineering Dashboard, users can drill down into the Systemic Service Management view and presented in Fig. 16.24 to find the computed results of service tasks and activities per component and aggregated by business entity. Interface definitions are provided in Table 16.21.

Users can view the utilization by resource and process from the Resource Utilization view, presented in Fig. 16.25 with interface definition provided in Table 16.22.

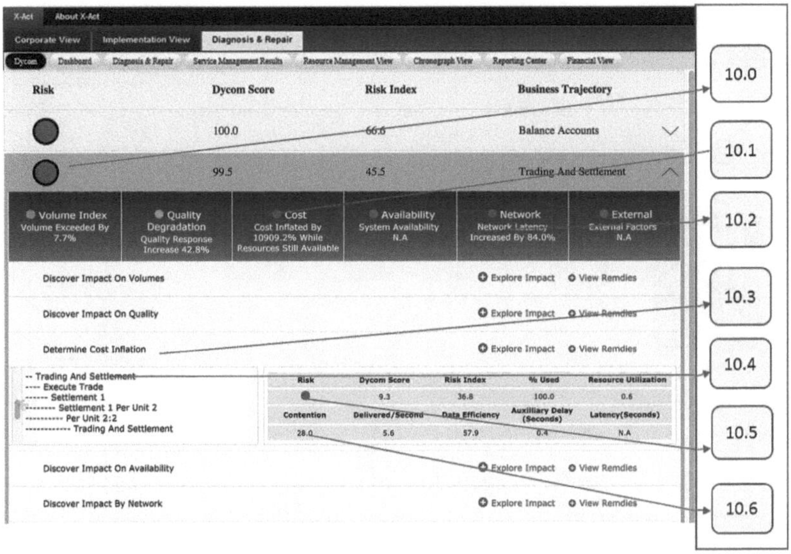

Fig. 16.21 X-Act® OBC Platform business process risk index and Dycom score reporting dashboard

Table 16.18 Business process risk index and Dycom score reporting interface definitions

Label	Definition
10.0	At the top of the list Dycom and Risk are organized in descending order from the highest to the lowest. When multiple scores are high, the tool privileges the Dycom Score since it is the most urgent problem that must be resolved to avoid a general degradation.
10.1	Provides the score and index values. Special attention must be given when both values are high. Typically, this would indicate that Dycom is most likely the cause of risk.
10.2	This field shows the area that is impacted. In this case, it exposes a cost inflation risk. By clicking on this, the user can determine which business component(s) are causing the risk.
10.3	By clicking on this link, the user can determine which business component(s) are causing the risk.
10.4	Details the component(s) and systemic details
10.5	By analyzing the details of business component computed attributes, the user can understand the origin of the problem.
10.6	And the user can identify the engineering action necessary to remediate its impact.

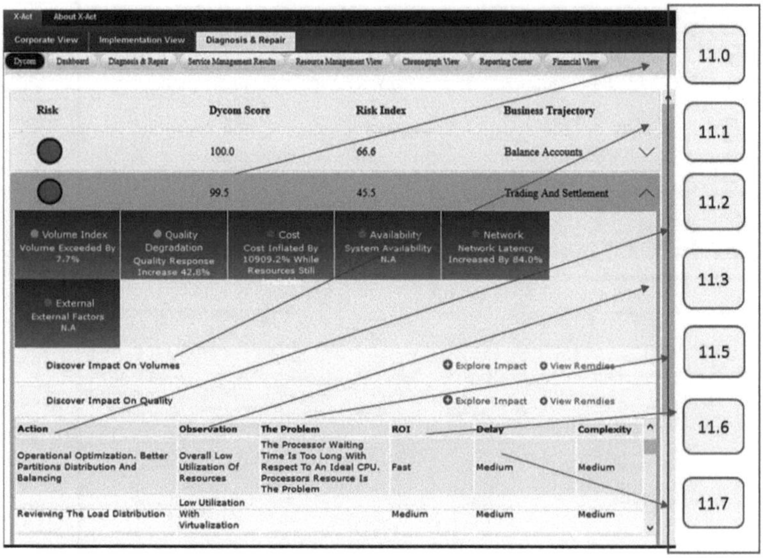

Fig. 16.22 X-Act® OBC Platform remediation dashboard

Table 16.19 Remediation dashboard definitions

Label	Definition
11.0	At the top of the list Dycom and Risk are organized in descending order from the highest to the lowest. When multiple scores are high, the tool privileges the Dycom Score since it is the most urgent problem to be resolved to avoid a general degradation.
11.1	Provides the score and index values. Special attention must be given when both values are high. Typically, this would indicate that Dycom is most likely the cause of risk.
11.2	Action: shows a series of proposed actions that could be used to remediate the computed diagnosis.
11.3	Observation: explains the nature of problem that needs to be solved through computation.
11.5	The Problem: computed diagnosis of the problem.
11.6	ROI: computed return on investment if we apply the action.
11.7	Delay: computed time to deliver and complexity to apply the action.

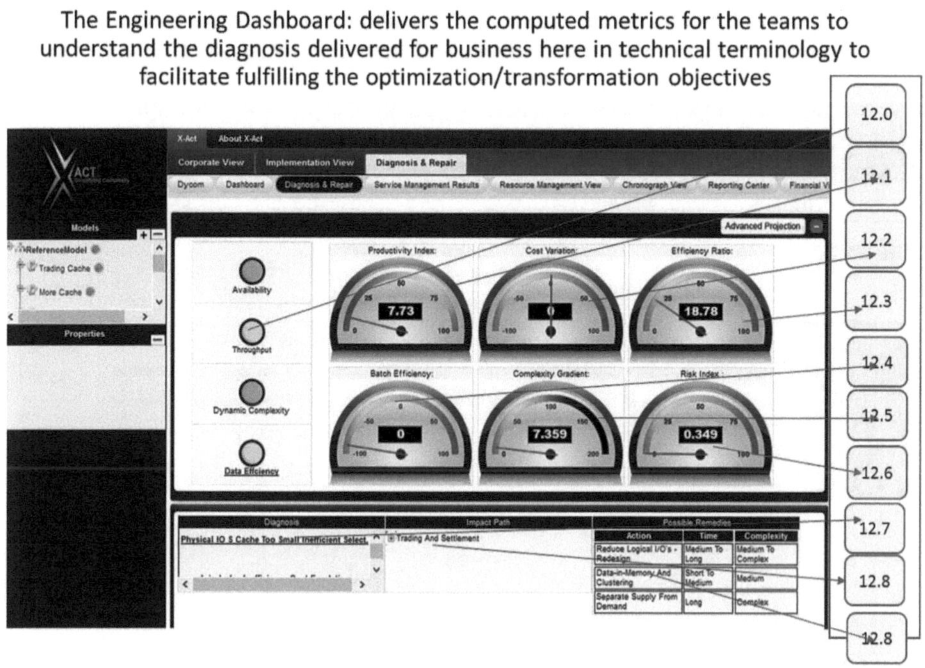

Fig. 16.23 X-Act® OBC Platform engineering dashboard

Table 16.20 Engineering dashboard definitions

Label	Definition
12.0	Key indicators communicate the status of availability, throughput, data access efficiency and dynamic complexity.
12.1	Productivity Index as proportion of a maximum, ideal and dynamic complexity free throughput is determined by the computation algorithm.
12.2	Cost Variation around the optimal cost in a stable, ideally loaded environment. Lower cost is possible if favorable mix can be achieved.
12.3	Efficiency Ratio shows the resources consumption by the productivity ratio.
12.4	Batch Efficiency determines the batch window to process, move or service the demand sequence.
12.5	Complexity Gradient expresses the non-business related activities that consume additional resources and impact quality and throughput.
12.6	Risk Index exposes risk due to the presence of dynamic complexity and/or lack of resources.
12.7	Diagnosis: reveals which system components are creating a problem.
12.8	Impact Path: shows the corresponding tree of causal impact.
12.9	Action: shows the computed action for remediation.

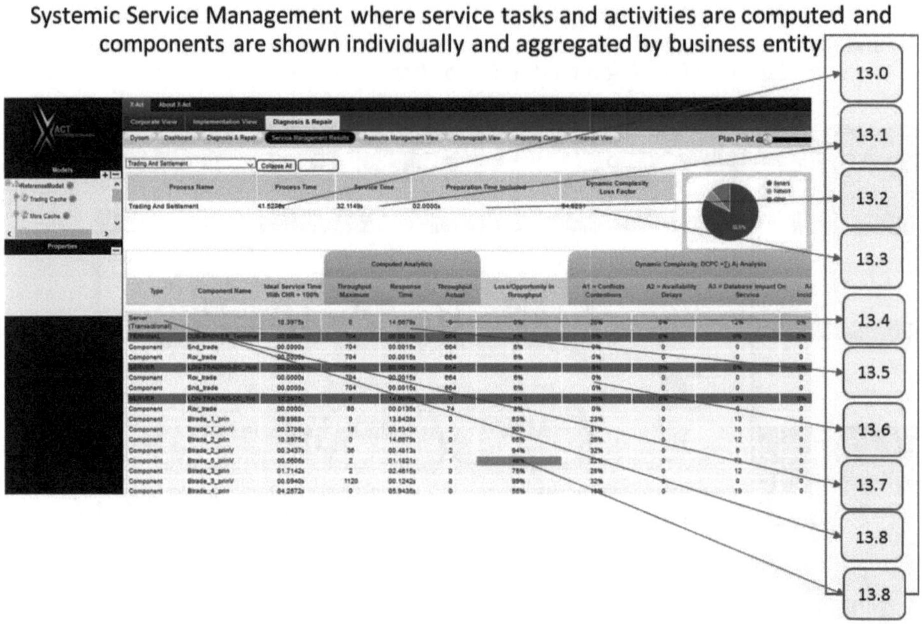

Fig. 16.24 X-Act® OBC Platform systemic service management view

Table 16.21 Systemic service management interface definitions

Label	Definition
13.0	Process Time: computed process time includes service time, waiting time, preparation time and the impact of all conflicts, contention, locks and other latencies.
13.1	Service Time: computed service time for the end-to-end process if it were dynamic complexity free
13.2	Preparation Time: accounts for human, traffic, other delays
13.3	Dynamic Complexity Loss Factor: Dynamic Complexity computed as a loss factor
13.4	Throughput Actual: computed throughput per component/server
13.5	Response Time: computed response time per component/server
13.6	Dynamic Complexity Analysis: computed dynamic complexity due to conflicts and contentions
13.7	Component name
13.8	Component server type (server, terminal, network, etc.)
13.9	Computed loss opportunity per component and resource

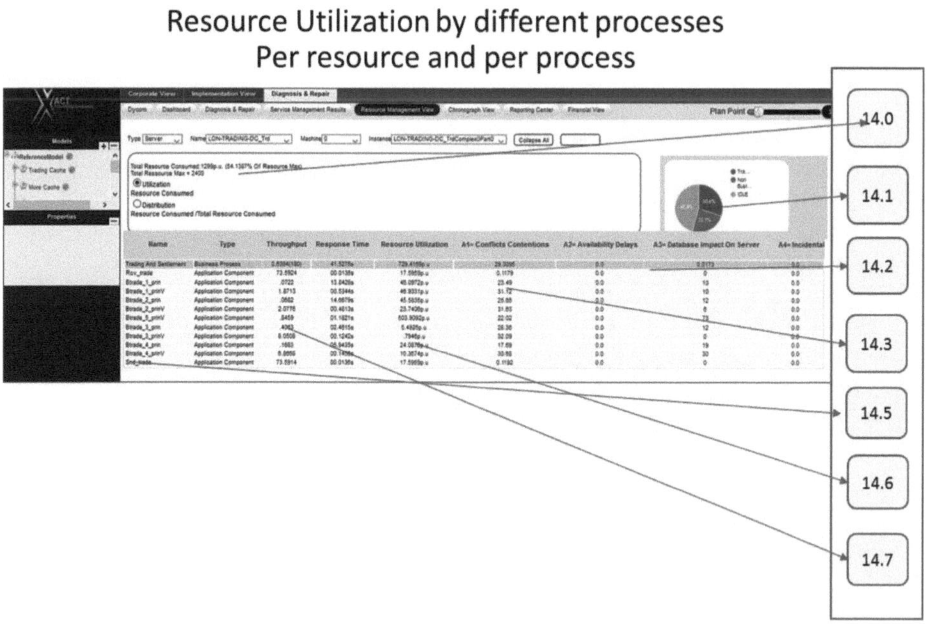

Fig. 16.25 X-Act® OBC Platform resource utilization view

Table 16.22 Resource utilization interface definitions

Label	Definition
14.0	Computed total utilization of a resource
14.1	Distribution of the utilization of a resource
14.2	Computed dynamic complexity due to data access
14.3	Computed dynamic complexity due to conflicts and contentions
14.5	Name of the component
14.6	Resource utilization per component
14.7	Throughput per component

17 Using X-Act OBC Platform Metrics for Predictive Diagnosis and Prescriptive Treatment of Risk

The further a mathematical theory is developed, the more harmoniously and uniformly does its construction proceed, and unsuspected relations are disclosed between hitherto separated branches of the science.
—David, Hilbert, German mathematician, known as one of the most influential and universal mathematicians of all time

In this chapter:

- Using Dycom score to determine if dynamic complexity is impacting system performance
- Monitoring Risk Index score to determine if systems have sufficient resources
- Determining whether a risk is imminent from the Dycom and Risk Index scores
- How X-Act® OBC Platform is used to maintain optimal productivity

Once an emulation has been computed and validated in X-Act® OBC Platform, the user is ready to predictively diagnose problems and prescriptively identify solutions. Dycom and Risk Index (RI) scores provided in the reporting dashboards help users understand if a current problem exists—or when a problem will arise using *what-if* scenarios—as well as anticipate the impact of any potential risk.

As detailed in the following sections, a high Dycom score lets users know that dynamic complexity is exerting a significant strain on the system being examined. A high RI score

N. Abu el Ata, A. Drucbert, *Leading from Under the Sword of Damocles*,
https://doi.org/10.1007/978-3-662-56300-7_17

indicates that there are not enough resources to meet system demands. When both Dycom and RI are high, a risk may be imminent.

By changing the emulated system parameters within X-Act® OBC Platform, users can predictively find which scenarios will cause a system disruption and evaluate the applicability of prescriptive solutions. This prepares the organization to proactively take any actions necessary to avoid future risk events.

High Dycom Score

A Dycom score over 30 will lead to a reduction in throughput, meaning that the cost to deliver the same volume will begin to escalate (see Fig. 17.1).

Users can identify which steps should be taken to keep the Dycom score below 30 by reviewing the suggested remedies within the diagnosis dashboard (see Fig. 17.2).

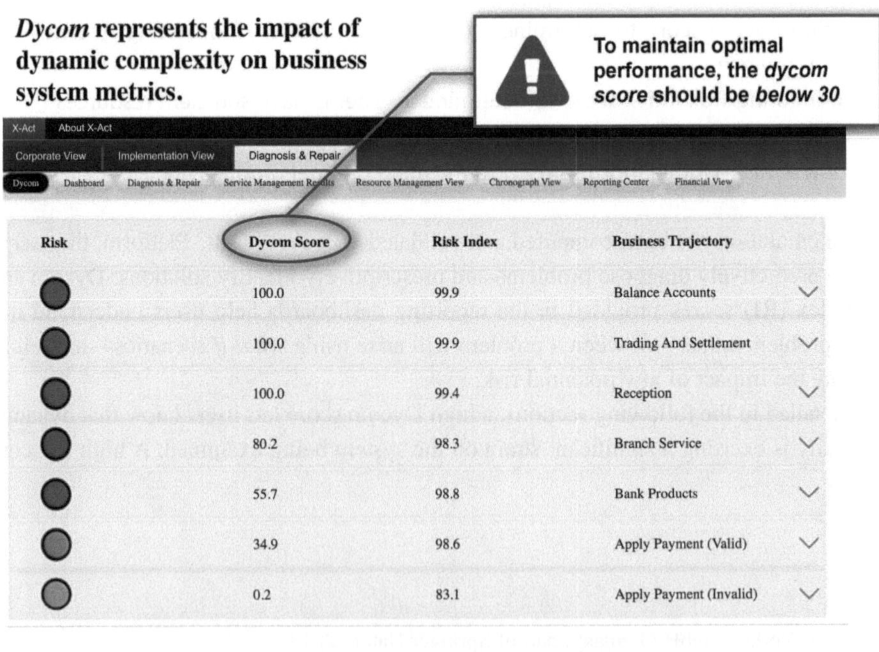

Fig. 17.1 Using Dycom score to measure impact of dynamic complexity

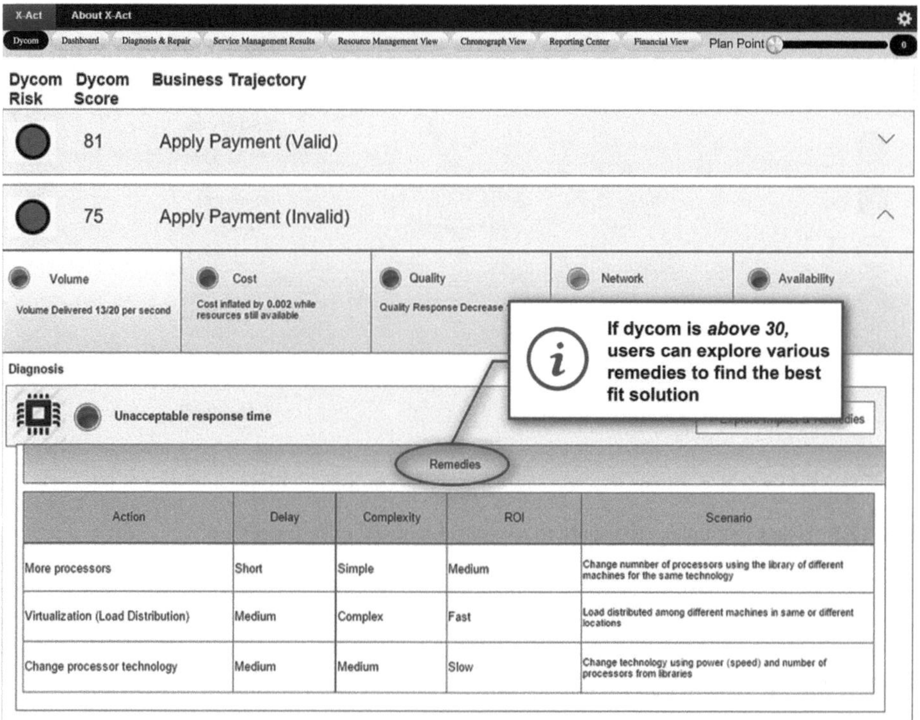

Fig. 17.2 Identifying the prescriptive remedies to reduce Dycom score

High RI and Low Dycom Scores

If RI is more than 40 but Dycom is less than 20, the risk is due to a lack of resources (see Fig. 17.3).

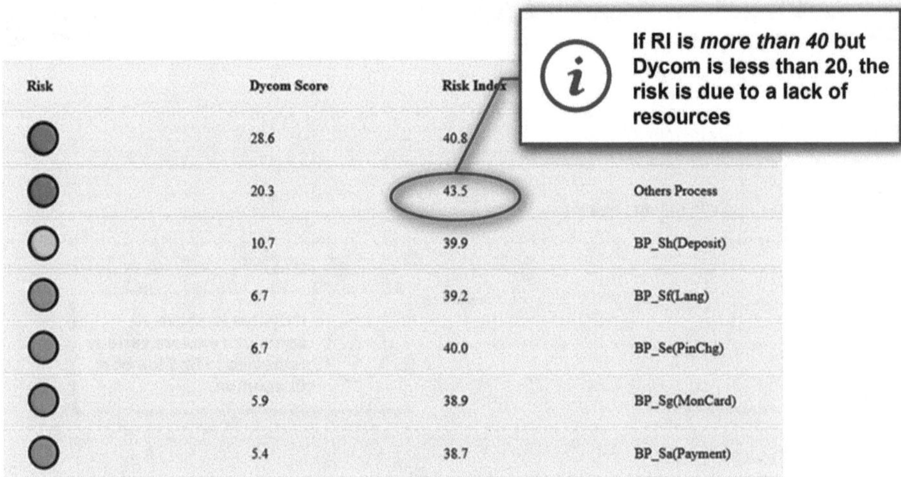

Fig. 17.3 Using risk index (RI) score to measure adequacy of resources

High RI and High Dycom Scores

If RI and Dycom are both greater than 60, a potential risk may be imminent (see Fig. 17.4).

If the problem persists, action should be taken immediately to avoid negative business outcomes.

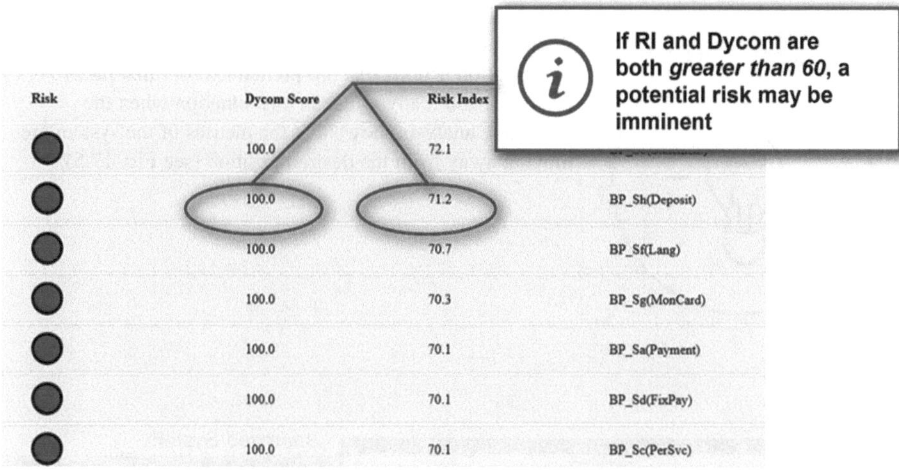

Fig. 17.4 High Dycom and Risk Index (RI) scores indicate a potential risk

Sudden Spike in RI and Dycom Scores

When RI and Dycom scores generally remain low, but spikes occur within short timeframes or under certain conditions, there is no need to worry about a potential risk forming.

For example, a system may be able to handle up to 100 transactions within a given timeframe. If the system receives over 100 transactions during this time, a degradation may occur. But if the system only receives a spike in transactions within a certain window of time—for instance during the lunch hour—and then normalizes, a risk will not form.

Optimizing Outcomes

Optimal productivity equates to the delivery of business goods or services at a minimum cost, while maintaining acceptable service quality. Through our research and use of X-Act® OBC Platform, we know that once we move beyond the point of optimal productivity, any additional increase in volume will cause a deterioration in productivity and an escalation in cost. Additionally, the enterprise is running sub-optimally before the optimal productivity point is reached.

key concept

To maintain a position of optimal productivity, X-Act® OBC Platform can be used to create a knowledgebase of optimization actions that are predefined (optimal patterns), evaluated and ready to use in any situation when the predictive analysis shows that the metrics of the system are moving away from the desired position (see Fig. 17.5).

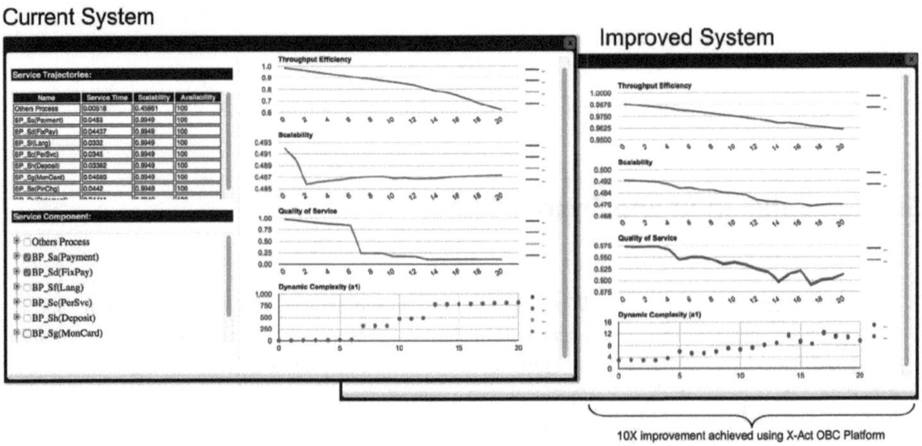

Fig. 17.5 Comparison of current system versus system with optimization actions applied

By using the predictive and prescriptive emulation capabilities offered by X-Act® OBC Platform, users can:

- Monitor the systemic enterprise characteristics and behavior in near real time
- Identify the root cause of any eventual limitation
- Use the predefined risk patterns to intervene at the right time with the right cure
- Continue to mature risk management programs by generating new patterns

Figure 17.6 summarizes how X-Act® OBC Platform's predictive and prescriptive emulation capabilities can be used to predict performance problems and maintain optimal business outcomes.

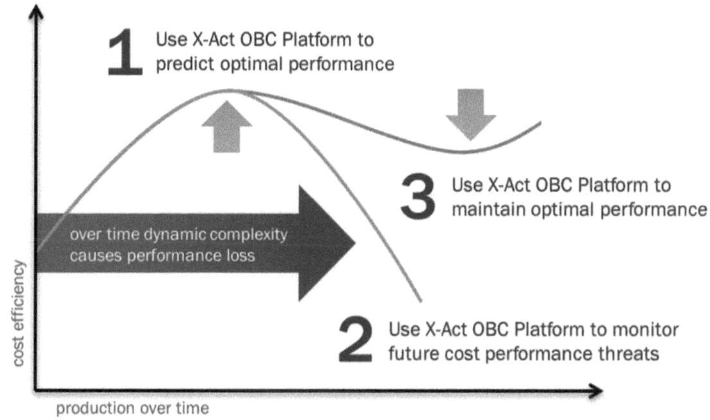

Fig. 17.6 Summary of how X-Act® OBC Platform is used to predict performance problems and maintain optimal business outcomes

Part II

Making Decisions Using X-Act OBC Platform Metrics: Example Cases

Case #1: Managing Corporate Risk

Global Payment Card Processing Company

18

Case Overview

Up until the late 1990s, third-party payment processing was a very lucrative business model. Then new market entrants created pricing pressures, which led to margin erosion for the established market leaders.

At the same time, modernization of processing platforms became necessary to support an expanding global economy and evolving market requirements, which included clearing transactions in a timely, accurate manner and reflecting in near real-time activities undertaken by the cardholder at anytime and anywhere in the world. Adding more functionality, such as reward programs and value-added services, became a key competitive differentiator.

As this market shift occurred, the leading payment processor was unprepared to meet changing market demands. Ongoing enhancements and modifications over multiple decades had led to decreased system efficiency, higher operational costs and made it difficult for the company to successfully undertake any large-scale re-engineering or system modernization projects.

The company needed better insights into the root cause of their current problems and perspective on future risks, as well as more efficient and reliable methods to identify and vet possible solutions. The predictive and prescriptive intelligence gathered using X-Act® OBC Platform supported a board-level re-engineering decision, tracked the program execution and verified the results—all while helping to manage and control the risks.

N. Abu el Ata, A. Drucbert, *Leading from Under the Sword of Damocles*,
https://doi.org/10.1007/978-3-662-56300-7_18

Case Highlights

Implementation characteristics	• 30-year-old payment card processing platform • Processing over 400 million credit and debit card accounts • Serving over 1400 banks offering credit and debit card services to businesses and consumers
Business goals	• Greatly reduce operational costs: The cost per transaction must be low enough to support competitive pricing • Regenerate competitive advantage: Identify opportunities to offer new and improved services • Support accurate cost based pricing: Determine true development and total cost of each transaction type and associated features
Challenges	• **Increasing complexity** caused by an over-stretched, aging implementation and external influencers • **Declining profit margins** caused by decreasing revenues while cost of doing business was escalating • **Managing reputation** during time of uncertainty due to market evolution and a growing number of competitive offerings • Overcoming slow time-to-market issues caused by a **lack of adaptability** of an aging payment processing platform
Business constraints	• **Cause no business disruption**: Nothing should prevent the organization from fulfilling its service commitments to existing issuers/clients • **Maximize flexibility** by using open structures: The engineering decisions should not in any way limit future development • **Move towards a component-based architecture**: When possible create a clear separation between information assets and replaceable components • **Allow for a phased approach**: The replacing of components and modernization efforts should be staged to support continuous improvement
Strategic options	• **Optimize**: Identify opportunities to optimize existing systems or sunset old components to do more, for less • **Transform**: Develop a re-engineering program to modernize the 30-year-old platform and execute a data profiling/cleansing project to improve platform performance • **Disrupt**: Replace the 30-year-old platform with new architecture and implementation to improve platform agility and performance with more efficient event processing capabilities

Getting Started, Stage 1: Build Emulator

The model of the business processes and underlying credit card processing platform were built using X-Act® OBC Platform following the steps outlined in Chap. 16 with case specific details provided in Step 1 and Step 2 below.

Step 1: Capture the Necessary Information

Often IT incorrectly assumes, in cases such as this one, that it is possible to consider the processing platform as a closed loop system that can be sufficiently modeled using big data automatically captured from system monitoring tools, which include only the related service processes and infrastructure of the system. However, dynamic complexity is created through a complex web of internal as well as external influences. To build a representative model and strategically guide a business level decision, a top down approach was essential to uncover dynamic complexity related risks.

Industry characteristics, business goals and strategic characteristics of the implementation needed to be understood.

This data was collected through: (1) interviews and workshops, (2) automatic collection of data and measurements, and (3) X-Act® libraries. Once the emulation was built, the model then was refined with data that was predictively created through analysis of emulation scenarios. Table 18.1 provides a further breakdown of the information we gathered and how it was obtained.

Gaining buy-in from business leaders was key to our success and made possible by clearly defining the goals of the project and how the expected outcomes would support a strategic business decision. Information collected related to industry characteristics and business goals included economics, competition and monitoring parameters covering 1-year period, next 3–5 years and any longer-term objectives.

Information collected related to strategic characteristics included:

- Organization of business, organization of service
- Business implementation structures, physical and logical resources, human resources

Table 18.1 Overview of information and data required for system modeling

Business characteristics and constraints	Technical analysis measurements	Patterns and peer evaluation	Fundamental analysis
Collected through interviews and formal questionnaires	Collected using automatic extractors	Populated from X-Act® pattern libraries	Predictively created through emulation scenarios
• Corporate strategy • Business • Competition • Activity pricing • Operational implementation • Activity costing • Service management • Obligations • Resources and management • Business cycles • Resource utilization • Peaks/valleys	• Resources/events • Resources utilization • Outstanding issues	• Best in class • Implementation strategies • Specificities	• Impact of external events • Impact of internal services • Impact of external service • Impact of internal event

- Business characteristics: volumes, quality constraints, geography, criticality, distribution windows
- Financial outlook, projections, constituents, priorities, resources, R&D
- Client relationships
- Competitive outlook: Now and future
- Possible disruption: innovation, business models
- Business discriminant factors: impacting settlement, external dependencies
- Supply chain
- Strategic goals

As with any organization which has established a good level of management maturity, the company already had most of the information necessary to build the model in strategic plans, competitive analysis, and business process analysis and architecture documents.

After collecting the corporate-level information through interviews and existing documentation, system, infrastructure and metrics were automatically collected and populated into the emulator using existing data or X-Act® OBC Platform connectors in cases where data automation practices were not already in place. Additionally, the assets contained in the X-Act® libraries were used whenever possible and as needed to fill in any data gaps and speed the data collection process.

Step 2: Build the Emulator

Multiple emulations were created to represent all operational scenarios and support multiple parameter scenarios. These emulations were built to support Stage 2 activities, which include predictively evaluating how changes in volumes, constraints and perception would impact the system in 3–5 years, as well as running speculative scenarios to identify points of failure in the system.

Corporate View

The corporate view was built from information gathered during Step 1 and included the following:

- Business and operational organizational definitions
- Volumes and constraints (subject to possible scenarios of change)
- Service processes

Service View

The service view was built using best-in-class components from X-Act® libraries and included the following:

- Division into sub-processes
- Interdependencies on common services

- Hierarchy to service logic
- Constraints

Implementation View

The implementation view was built using assets from X-Act® libraries and included the following:

- Geography
- Physical resources
- Physical components and structures
- Infrastructure
- Constraints

Figure 18.1 shows an example of how the model was populated using the X-Act® libraries and the point and click features of X-Act® OBC Platform.

Stage 2: Perform Diagnosis

Once the emulation was built, we used the predictive analytics capabilities of X-Act® OBC Platform to study current and predicted system behaviors as well as discover the root cause of current problems and understand future business risks. This was accomplished through

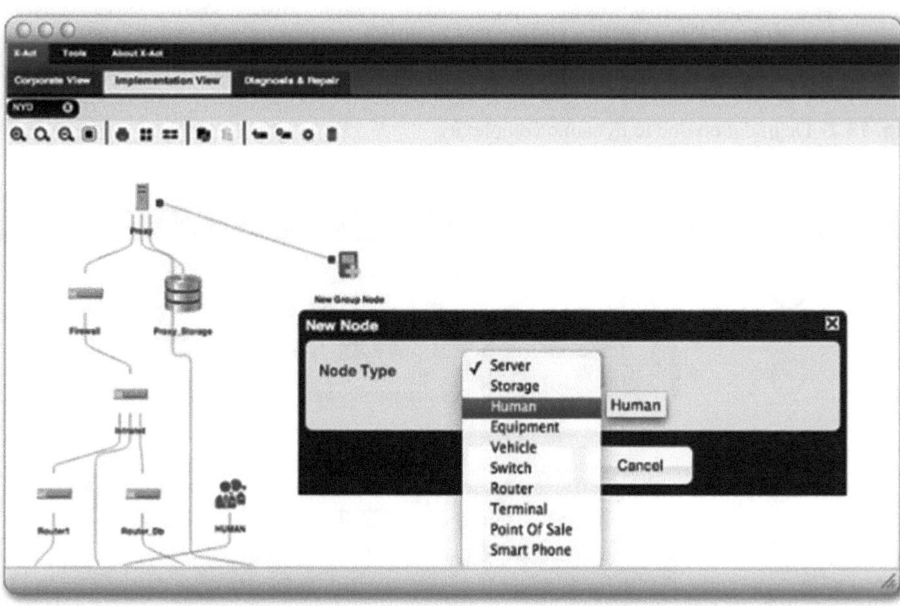

Fig. 18.1 Building model from library components in X-Act® OBC Platform

stress testing and sensitivity analysis, which allowed us to see how the system would behave at different volumes and how individual components would behave under stress.

As visually represented in Figs. 18.2 and 18.3, X-Act® OBC Platform metrics showed that:

- Dynamic complexity had increased by 300% over a 5-year period—mainly because system owners had been continuously and reactively making changes to the system as needed to meet business requirements without completely understanding the impact of those add-ons, which led to a deterioration of architecture.
- Revenue per unit had declined by 39%.
- Costs to deliver had escalated by 86%.
- Time to market cycles had lengthened from 1 week to 6 months.

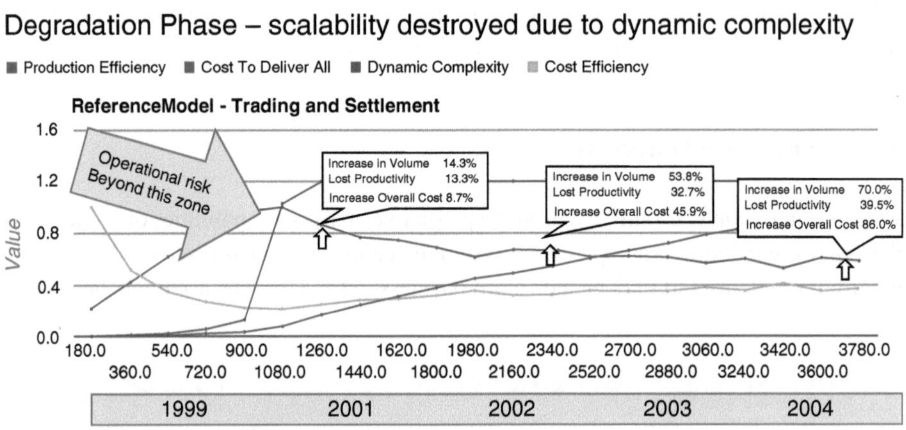

Fig. 18.2 Degradation due to dynamic complexity

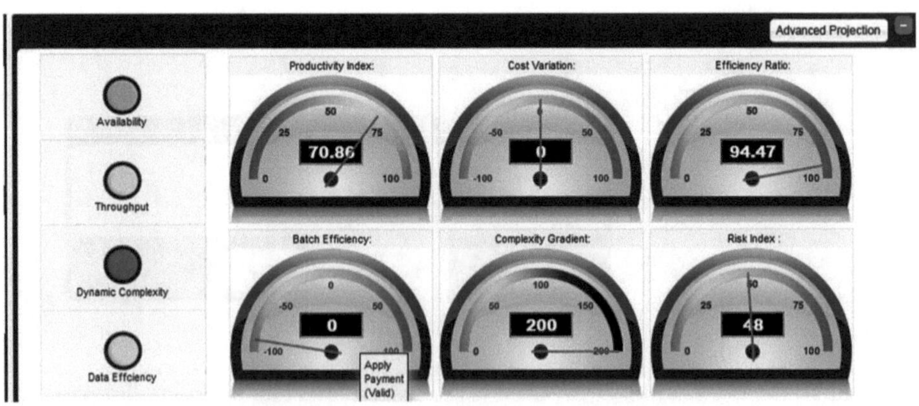

Fig. 18.3 X-Act® OBC Platform metrics

- The company began insourcing resources to offset pricing increases and bring costs back into alignment, however this threatened the advantages they had previously gained through a global outsourcing model.

Causal Analysis Results

System aging naturally led to severe efficiency problems, as aging was forced by reactive maintenance that never questioned the long-term impact of the fix on the overall implementation:

- Over several years, the business system aging had become so high that there was a real threat to margins (cost escalation doubled over 4 years)
- The annual aging ratio was higher than 20% and accelerating
- Processor utilization per unit of work had moved from 5 to 23 millisecond (ms) in 6 years
- The nominal throughput, measured in millions of cardholder accounts, went from 26 to just 12 for the same period and normalized infrastructure characteristics
- Time to market moved from 1 week to 6 months due to the increasing complexity, and therefore difficulty to enhance and test system updates before moving them into production

Stress Testing Analysis Results

Dynamic complexity poses a threat to corporate survival:

- The forward prediction showed an accelerating degradation that would create an unacceptable situation in terms of service quality and margin (revenue pressure and cost) within 3 years (see Fig. 18.4)

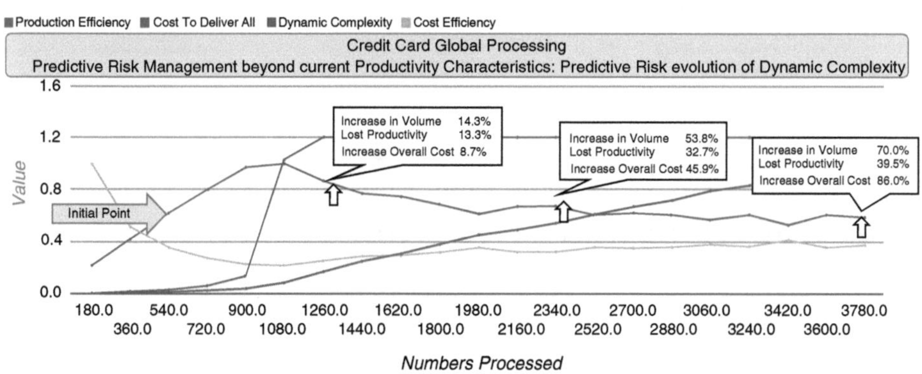

Fig. 18.4 X-Act® OBC Platform prediction revealed risk of accelerating system degradation

- Other competitive alternatives that were available in the market place offered less functionality, reduced flexibility and higher cost structures—meaning that business consolidation would not make sense
- Market growth would only be modestly attractive—since service pricing pressures would continue and even accelerate—unless the company could create new opportunities through new financial instruments or new ways to apply the card processing model for new applications and activities in banking, healthcare, taxes, transportation or other areas

Stage 3: Identify Prescriptive Actions

We then used the X-Act® OBC Platform to prescriptively emulate various remedial scenarios (see Fig. 18.5).

Optimization

The following optimization options were defined and the limitations of each scenario were exposed using X-Act® OBC Platform prescriptive emulation capabilities. Key findings were as follows:

- A rebuild of major implementation components would yield a 40% gain in volume
- Sun-setting old components would yield a 25% gain in resources utilization
- Re-implementing the posting and cycling data model would yield a 20% gain in productivity
- All options showed that operational risks would increase within 5 years due to continuous pressure on revenue and slow but still significant cost escalation

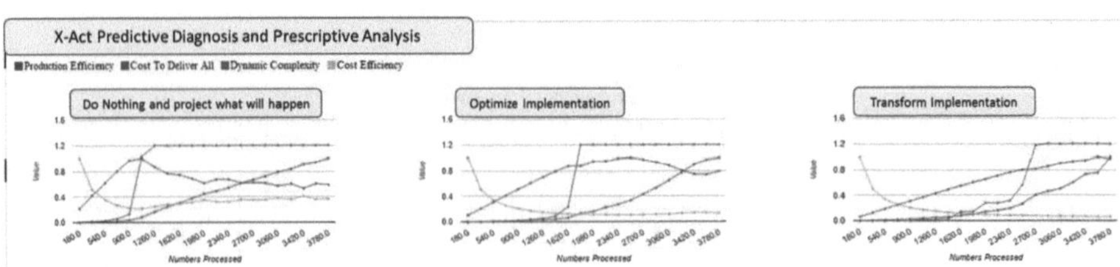

Fig. 18.5 X-Act® OBC Platform predictive diagnosis and prescriptive analysis

Transformation

All feasible transformation scenarios were explored. However, we identified the following obstacles based on the predictive emulation:

- The speed to deliver all transformation options were incompatible with corporate constraints
- The cost of transformation options was too high to be realistically considered—especially the cost for the data profiling/cleansing project
- Uncertainty about how the future evolution of the market would impact the current business model made any significant investment in the old implementation risky

Disruption

We used predictive emulation to explore disruption scenarios, such as new business models and innovative approaches that would allow the business to become more agile and better prepared to meet the evolving needs of the card processing industry. The following disruptive scenarios were proposed:

- Execute a corporate re-engineering project
- Deploy a new implementation that would allow for new types of event processing
- Reduce dependencies on intermediaries

Stage 4: Make Informed Risk Decision

The outputs of the X-Act® OBC Platform analysis were used to create an executive presentation of the immediate and future risks as well as proposed prescriptive solutions for consideration by the board. All risks and remedial options were evaluated based on their ability to meet stated business goals, which included greatly reducing operational costs and regenerating competitive advantage.

The board considered the presented options in terms of the following criteria:

- Limitations of scalability, volume, quality of service and cost
- Cost to make the change in terms of complexity, required resources/skills and dynamic ROI (the length of time until it becomes possible for the business to break even with its investment in a new dynamic environment)
- Time to deliver
- Adaptability
- Industry imposed risks such as obsolescence, market evolution and competitive outlook

Key Decision Considerations

The following factors were key to the board's decision:

- Scalability is predictable at increasing volumes until the system hits a new singularity point
- Beyond the singularity point, dynamic complexity takes over—leading to an escalation in costs, which is predicted to increase by 85% while yielding only a 70% increase in volume
- Dynamic complexity related risks are engendered from interdependencies that annihilate any improvement that could typically be gained by adding additional resources
- Time to deliver will continue to be a challenge and a source of rapid degradation
- Adaptability is modest as the system continuously leverages old assets to create new, adapted assets in response to new demands

Board Decision: Proceed with Optimization Project

Ultimately, the board decided that the optimization project was the only viable strategic option as it met business constraints and could deliver 48% more volume for 30% less cost (see Fig. 18.6).

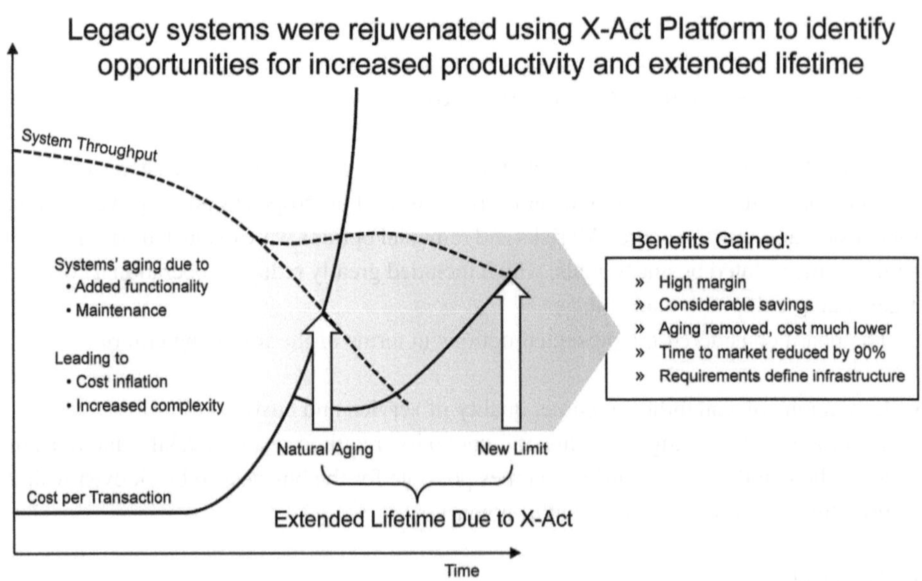

Fig. 18.6 Optimization project extended lifetime of system and met business constraints

However, the risk of obsolescence was a real threat to corporate survival. Through the analysis, it became clear that the current business model would only be sustainable for the short term and would become extinct as soon as alternative ecommerce and new business models began to proliferate. As such, it would be necessary to monitor market developments and further investigate longer term options if the business wished to defend its competitive advantage in the future.

Case #2: Managing Market Erosion Risk

19

Postal Services

Case Overview

Changing market factors often force entire industries to redefine their business strategy or face extinction. The postal industry today faces such a challenge, as postal organizations worldwide must evolve their strategies to survive the rising popularity of digital communications, the decline in traditional, physical mail volumes, and growing competition from private companies.

Market disruption quickly moved postal organizations from attractive economic and industrial models to an unbalanced financial corporate position with a major risk of obsolescence. To survive a market disruption of this magnitude, executive leaders of La Poste used X-Act® OBC Platform to identify and implement the right strategies to compensate for major shifts in customer demands—while managing costs without negatively impacting the quality of services.

Case Highlights

Implementation characteristics	• **Fourth largest** national postal services organization in the world • Handling over **15 billion pieces of mail and parcels** per year • Operating **17,000 postal services outlets**
Business goals	• Achieve **short-term cost reductions** without reducing quality of service (QoS) or mail volumes • Proactively **manage, plan and anticipate potential problems** across the end-to-end postal service supply chain • **Keep cost of operations in alignment** with predicted mail volumes and anticipated revenues

(continued)

N. Abu el Ata, A. Drucbert, *Leading from Under the Sword of Damocles*,
https://doi.org/10.1007/978-3-662-56300-7_19

	• **Offer new products or services** to maintain revenue as traditional mail volumes decline • Identify the most **effective pricing** based on competitive scenarios
Challenges	• **High cost of operations, infrastructure and provisioning** while facing a continuous decline in mail volume • **Deregulation and privatization** of postal services • Growing criticality of **accelerating delivery time** • **Finding the right skills** to enable greater automation and winning corporate commitment • **Political appropriation**
Business constraints	• **Maintain quality of service** (QoS) under any expected operational conditions • Preserve ability to **handle projected mail volumes** • **Reduce downtime** or impact of any service disruptions
Strategic options	• **Optimize**: Reduce number of sorting centers, build more exchange hubs and optimize treatment of daily unprocessed mail volumes • **Transform**: Train workforce and add new offers, such as hybrid mail and ecommerce, coupled to existing distribution channels • **Disrupt**: Move to a postal cloud and offer new goods and services to rural areas

Getting Started, Stage 1: Build Emulator

The model of the postal services processes and underlying mail distribution network were built in X-Act® OBC Platform following the steps outlined in Chap. 16 and further detailed below.

Step 1: Collect the Necessary Information

As this case included a supply chain management problem, it was necessary to capture all information that defined the end-to-end process—including steps, sorting centers, sorting machines, machine technologies and characteristics, human service centers, hubs, storage areas, trucks (capacities, speeds, traffic characteristics), distribution characteristics and constraints, incidents and problem solving options, business implementation classes, service geography, decision and workforce parameters.

Step 2: Build the Emulator

Using X-Act® OBC Platform, an emulator was built to represent the full postal environment: organization, processes, implementation, transportation, and physical and human dimensions.

Over a period of 15 weeks, more than eight million objects were modeled, covering the end-to-end service: time to deliver, quantities of different classes and costs.

Our emulation definitions and corresponding outcomes included the following three views to holistically represent the full environment:

Corporate View

The corporate view (Fig. 19.1) was built from information gathered during Step 1 and included the following:

- Business and operational definitions
- Volumes and constraints
- Service processes

Service View

The service view (Fig. 19.2) was built using best-in-class components from X-Act® libraries and included the following:

- Division into sub-processes (activities and tasks)
- Interdependencies on common services
- Hierarchy to service logic
- Constraints

Implementation View

The implementation view (Figs. 19.3 and 19.4) was built using newly constructed and existing assets from X-Act® libraries and included the following:

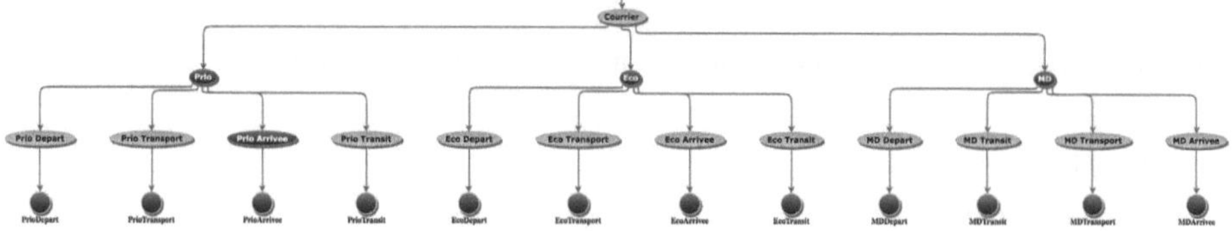

Fig. 19.1 X-Act® OBC Platform corporate view

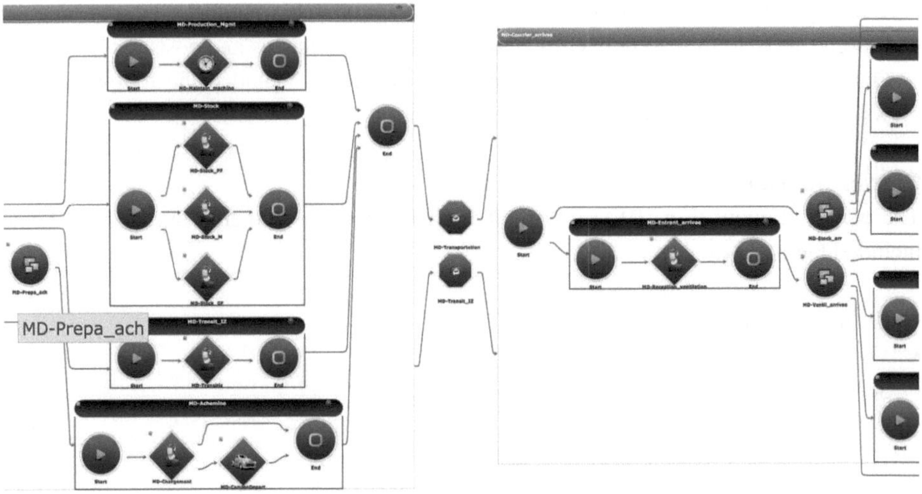

Fig. 19.2 X-Act® OBC Platform service view

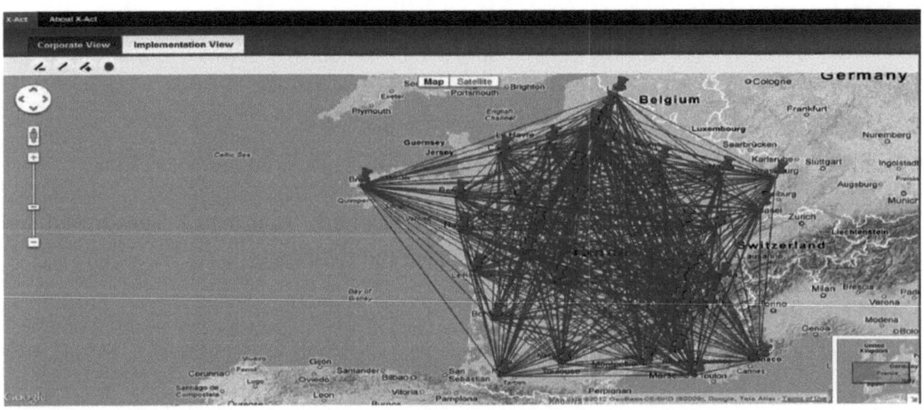

Fig. 19.3 X-Act® OBC Platform implementation view of mail sorting centers

- Geography
- Physical resources
- Physical components and structures
- Infrastructure
- Constraints

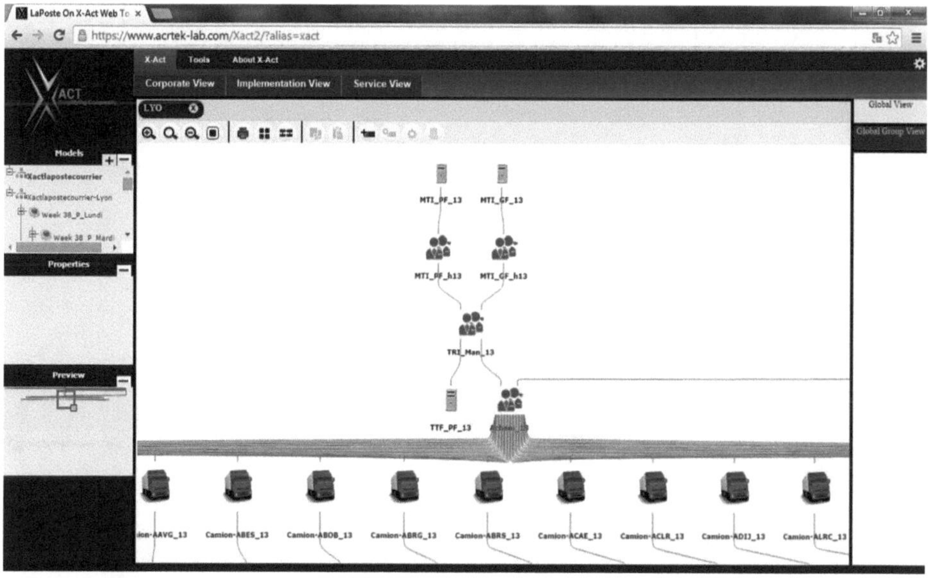

Fig. 19.4 X-Act® OBC Platform implementation view of mail transportation objects over the network of roads all are explicitly represented (size, capacity, dynamic conditions and environmental parameters

Stage 2: Perform Diagnosis

The mathematical emulation of the end-to-end postal services allowed us to proactively identify potential risks that could affect delivery time, temporal changes in volume and the cost of service for processes, technology, humans, logistics and organizations.

X-Act® OBC Platform metrics at the global level showed that the risk was high for marketing and economy classes of mail (see Fig. 19.5).

At the detailed level, service management per process metrics, resources management and financial management were evaluated to determine the root causes of risks (see Fig. 19.6).

Through our analysis (see Fig. 19.7), it became clear that priority mail carried the least risk, while marketing and economy classes of mail had a Dycom above 30 (meaning that the cost to deliver the same volume will begin to escalate) and Risk Index score near or above 30 (meaning that the risk on business is medium but may escalate and should be carefully monitored).

Risk	Dycom Score	Risk Index	Business Trajectory
	100.0	43.4	Md
	99.6	40.7	Eco
	6.3	27.9	Prio

Fig. 19.5 X-Act® OBC Platform global view of risk metrics

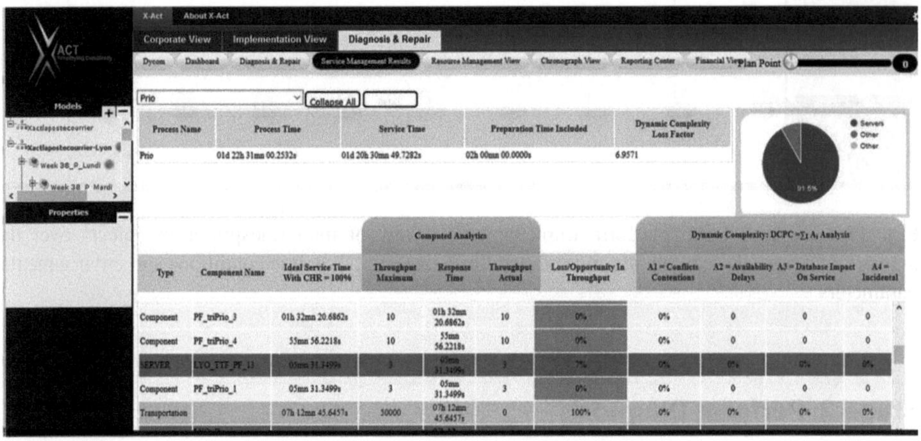

Fig. 19.6 X-Act® OBC Platform service management view of risk causes

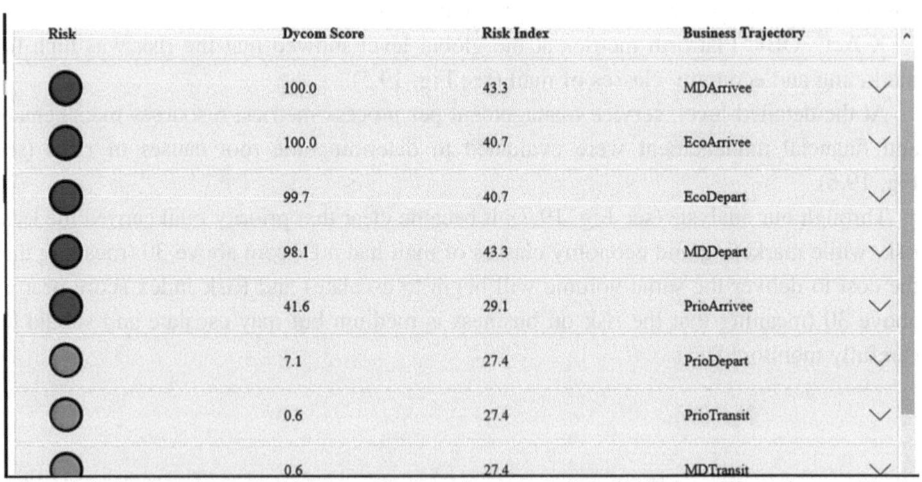

Risk	Dycom Score	Risk Index	Business Trajectory
	100.0	43.3	MDArrivee
	100.0	40.7	EcoArrivee
	99.7	40.7	EcoDepart
	98.1	43.3	MDDepart
	41.6	29.1	PrioArrivee
	7.1	27.4	PrioDepart
	0.6	27.4	PrioTransit
	0.6	27.4	MDTransit

MD = Marketing class mail | Eco = Economic stamped mail | Prio = First class mail

Fig. 19.7 X-Act® OBC Platform Dycom and risk index dashboard. *MD* marketing class mail, *Eco* economic stamped mail, *Prio* first class mail

Stage 3: Identify Prescriptive Actions

Using the *what-if* capabilities of X-Act® OBC Platform, we identified the optimal balance between projected mail traffic volumes versus the cost of operations and quality of service.

Decisions to reduce the number of sorting centers or increase dependency on automation technologies were proven before changes or investments were made.

Optimization

The following optimization options were defined and the limitations of each scenario were exposed using X-Act® OBC Platform prescriptive emulation capabilities. Key findings were as follows:

- Reducing the number of sorting centers to reduce overall cost and increasing transportation costs didn't affect service quality
- Building more exchange hubs would improve performance
- Optimized treatment of daily volumes of unprocessed mail and parcels left over from the previous day is critical
- Synchronization of sorting output and transportation is important to monitor
- Handling of incidents should be defined through X-Act® OBC Platform real-time monitoring

Transformation

All feasible transformation scenarios were explored and the following key findings were revealed through our predictive and prescriptive emulation of scenarios:

- Training the workforce to deliver service faster would change dynamics
- Adding new offers, such as hybrid mail and ecommerce coupled to existing distribution channels, could compensate for the decline in mail volumes
- Real time monitoring could be used to expose risks and inform actions in time to avoid negative outcomes

Disruption

We used predictive emulation to explore disruption scenarios, such as new business models and innovative approaches that would allow the business to become more agile and better prepared to meet the evolving needs of the citizens it served. The following disruptive scenarios were proposed:

- Move to a postal cloud
- Offer IT services for rural areas
- Deliver goods and services to rural areas

Stage 4: Make Informed Risk Decision

The outputs of the X-Act® OBC Platform analysis were used to create an executive presentation of the immediate and future risks as well as proposed prescriptive solutions for consideration by management. All risks and remedial options were evaluated based on their ability to meet stated business goals, which included reducing operational costs while meeting QoS and volume demands.

Management considered the presented options in terms of the following criteria:

- Risk on the delivery of mail constraint
- Right time maintenance to avoid multiple-phase management of assets
- Cover the different dynamics that correspond to a day in the week, a week in a month, seasons and geographic activities
- Cost of operations (end-to-end)
- Rerouting in case of incidents

Key Decisions

The following were key decisions:

- Reduce number of sorting centers
- Reduce the transportation options to one
- Launch advanced training programs
- Support business diversification
- Implement the new business process using predictive risk monitoring supported by X-Act® OBC Platform

Case #3: Managing Operational Risk 20

Global Supply Chain

Case Overview

In this case, a global fast food franchise with more than 36,000 outlets served worldwide was undertaking a massive $250 million USD project to create a global customer relationship management (CRM) and supply chain management (SCM) system. Each restaurant required the timely delivery of perishable and non-perishable ingredients prior to opening each day. The project was initiated to reduce operational risks and streamline processes. The system in development was based on a proven third-party IT application that used an Oracle platform, Oracle financials and application servers.

Partway into the project, management became uncertain about the new system's ability to meet the stated business objectives. The situation was politically charged as considerable capital and resources had already been dedicated to the project. However, before continuing, management wanted to be assured that the new system would scale with adequate quality of service (QoS) and could be maintained. Additionally, they wanted a clear understanding of the cost implications.

X-Act® OBC Platform was used to evaluate the operational risks of the proposed project and identify prescriptive solutions that would allow for the optimization of the fast food giant's just-in-time supply chain.

Case Highlights

Implementation characteristics	• Global fast food franchise with CRM and SCM system serving more than **36,000 outlets served worldwide**
Business goals	• **Improve agility, resiliency and transparency** of supply chain management platform

(continued)

N. Abu el Ata, A. Drucbert, *Leading from Under the Sword of Damocles*,
https://doi.org/10.1007/978-3-662-56300-7_20

	• **Reduce costs** • **Scale** to deliver more goods in less time
Challenges	• **Speed** of global deployment requirements place pressure on supply • **Maintaining improvements in margin** as cost escalation threatens revenues • **Uncertainty** about future evolution and direction of market • **Slow adaptability** impacts time to market capabilities • **Managing reputation**
Business constraints	• **Timely delivery** of perishable and non-perishable ingredients before restaurant opening each day
Strategic options	• **Optimize:** Identify opportunities to do more, for less with the business processes implementation, consider whether proposed updates can achieve an acceptable ROI, look for opportunities for infrastructure optimization and better operational management as well as ways to reduce storage, transportation and leftover • **Transform:** Develop a re-engineering program to modernize the global process, improve operational management, regional specifics and service processes that involve perishable and non-perishable SKU's • **Disrupt:** Replace the supply chain with new architecture and implementation to improve platform agility, resiliency and transparency

Getting Started, Stage 1: Build Emulator

The model of the global supply chain was built in X-Act® OBC Platform following the steps outlined in Chap. 16 and further detailed below.

Step 1: Collect the Necessary Information

To build a representative model and strategically guide a business level decision, it was necessary to model the entire supply chain and business process to uncover dynamic complexity related risks. This data was collected through a series of workshops and interviews with business stakeholders.

Industry Characteristics and Business Goals

- Economics, competition and monitoring parameters covering 1-year period, next 3–5 years and any longer-term objectives

Strategic Characteristics

- Organization of business, organization of service
- Business implementation structures, physical and logical resources, human resources

- Business characteristics: volumes, quality constraints, geography, criticality, distribution windows
- Financial outlook, projections, constituents, priorities, resources, R&D
- Client relationships
- Competition outlook: now and future
- Possible disruption: innovation, business models
- Business discriminant factors: impacting settlement, external dependencies
- Supply chain
- Strategic goals

Step 2: Build the Emulator

Multiple emulations were created to represent all operational scenarios and support multiple parameter scenarios. These emulations were built to support Stage 2 activities which include predictively evaluating how changes in volumes, constraints and perception would impact the system in 3–5 years, as well as running speculative scenarios to identify points of failure in the system.

Our emulation definitions and corresponding outcomes included the following three views to holistically represent the full systemic enterprise:

Corporate View

The corporate view was built from information gathered during Step 1 and included the following:

- Business and operational definitions
- Volumes and constraints
- Service processes

Service View

The service view was built using best-in-class components from X-Act® libraries and included the following:

- Division into sub-processes
- Interdependencies on common services
- Hierarchy to service logic
- Constraints

Implementation View

The implementation view was built using assets from X-Act® libraries and included the following:

- Geography
- Physical resources
- Physical components and structures
- Infrastructure
- Constraints

Stage 2: Perform Diagnosis

Once the emulation was built, we used the capabilities of X-Act® OBC Platform to analyze historical and predicted system behaviors to identify risks.

X-Act® OBC Platform metrics showed that:

- Dynamic complexity increased by more than 180% over a period of 3 years due to continuous system add-ons and reactive management of risk, which deteriorated the architecture
- Revenue per unit declined by 22% over the same period and the cost escalated by 60%
- Time to market moved from a 1 week to 6-month cycle

Stage 3: Identify Prescriptive Actions

We then used the X-Act® OBC Platform to prescriptively emulate various remedial scenarios.

Optimization

The following optimization options were defined and the limitations of each scenario were exposed using X-Act® OBC Platform prescriptive emulation capabilities. Key findings were as follows:

- Recommendation to cancel the global CRM project due to lack of control over the SCM system and its ability to meet on-time constraints
- Sun-setting old components in the current deployment would deliver a 20% gain
- Re-implementing the data model for posting and cycling and selecting the right level for database management system (DBMS) would achieve a 30% gain
- All options showed that risk would be significant in the 3rd year due to continuous pressure on revenue combined with moderate cost escalation

Transformation

The current transformation project was evaluated. However, the emulation showed that the CRM/SCM project would not be able to meet business requirements within the approved budget. Previous business process analysis and mapping had lacked the dynamic behaviors, therefore underestimated the risks due to dynamic complexity. Our analysis showed that:

- The selected infrastructure was highly restrictive
- Locks, contentions and bandwidth issues at the various endpoints would prevent the supply chain system from reliably achieving its purpose

Disruption

We used predictive emulation to explore disruption scenarios, such as new business models and innovative approaches that would allow the business to become more agile and better prepared to avoid a major supply chain disruption. The following disruptive scenarios were proposed:

- Corporate reengineering
- A new implementation that allow for new types of event processing

Stage 4: Make Informed Risk Decision

The insight gained through X-Act® OBC Platform allowed corporate management to make a very difficult decision with confidence. The X-Act® OBC Platform emulation showed that the proposed system would not meet business objectives in terms of capacity, cost and QoS. Our findings were unexpected. Multiple risks were identified under sensitivity analysis of future operational scenarios. There were simply too many locks, contentions and bandwidth issues at the various endpoints for the supply chain system to reliably achieve its purpose.

Subsequent design analysis and examination of re-architecture alternatives based on our MBA methodology confirmed this result. A viable architecture was eventually identified, but it would cost considerably more than what was originally planned. Based on the money already spent and the additional funds required to realistically achieve the desired business goals, the project was deemed to have insufficient return on investment (ROI) to justify the continuation of the project. Through the cancellation of the project, the corporation realized an economic benefit of over $170 million in risk avoidance. Had they continued, they would have either gone over budget or ended up with a non-viable system. In this case, it was much more prudent to adopt an evolutionary strategy rather than a disruptive one.

Management Decision: Cancel Disruption Project, Proceed with Optimization

Through the predictive insights provided by X-Act® OBC Platform, management could evaluate and understand the limitations of the proposed system and justify a re-definition of the project to focus on the following goals:

- Improve the current implementation in terms of performance and cost
- Continually assess new versions of the business implementation using the MBA methodology to verify that proposed changes will meet business expectations
- Reduce costs through infrastructure downsizing
- Optimize the application to run daily without adding dynamic complexity to other applications using the same infrastructure and data resources per country

Looking Forward

Management now uses X-Act® OBC Platform to evaluate new business implementation models, such as blockchain, and assess whether the proposed changes will adequately address business requirements by:

- Increasing volume
- Speeding delivery
- Reducing costs
- Ensuring predictability

Case #4: Managing Risk of Cost Escalation and Service Quality Degradation

21

National Healthcare Services

Case Overview

Currently many governments are struggling to contain the cost of reliable and equitable healthcare systems. The efficiency of the system is necessary to support the wellness of citizens as well as the economic and social progress of the country. By applying our proposed universal risk management methods, healthcare system stakeholders can gain the insights needed to create continuous cost management programs by identifying opportunities to improve cost efficiency without reducing the quality of care or excluding individuals who need access to universal healthcare services.

In this case, X-Act® OBC Platform was used to evaluate how the efficiency of a healthcare system could be improved by using blockchain technology and a shared ledger to increase preventive and proactive intervention and reduce any unnecessarily overhead due to repetitive analysis and diagnosis for the same case by consolidating patient history.

Case Highlights

Implementation characteristics	• Seventeen major metropolitan hospitals • Covering all healthcare specialties • Offering universal services to citizens
Business goals	• Offer the best global healthcare with reduced cost • Allow much more preventive healthcare • Provide telemedicine and monitoring at the right time
Challenges	• High cost of care which averages about $5000 per citizen per year in most European countries or $8500 in US • Redundancy of medical tests and services due to inability to coordinate efforts and synch medical records

(continued)

N. Abu el Ata, A. Drucbert, *Leading from Under the Sword of Damocles*,
https://doi.org/10.1007/978-3-662-56300-7_21

	• Chronic insurance deficits • Difficult to collect data necessary to research cause and effect of illnesses and diseases • Entropic support creates a heavy burden due to legal costs • Complexity of offering preventive medicine and proactive treatment at the right time to avoid higher long-term costs
Business constraints	• Control cost • Deliver procedures faster • Better coordination • More efficient monitoring
Strategic options	• Optimize: Use predictive prescription to identify optimal treatment of patients, reduce costs and speed-up processes • Disrupt: Use a shared distributed ledger to achieve better coordination and immediate administration of patient records

Getting Started, Stage 1: Build Emulator

The model of the healthcare system was built in X-Act® OBC Platform following the steps outlined in Chap. 16 and further detailed below.

Step 1: Capture the Necessary Information

For such an ambitious project, it was necessary to collect information and data that reflected the experience pertaining to the healthcare system within and among the hospitals that would be part the emulation exercise. This included information about related departments, typical treatment cycles, time of treatment per function, dependencies, sources of delay, cost structures, geographic coordinates, service constraints, human resources and any other impacts.

Information collected related to industry characteristics and business goals included economics, competition and monitoring parameters covering 1-year period, next 3–5 years and any longer-term objectives.

Information collected related to strategic characteristics included:

- Organization of business, organization of service
- Business implementation structures, physical and logical resources, human resources
- Business characteristics: volumes, quality constraints, geography, criticality, distribution windows
- Financial outlook, projections, constituents, priorities, resources, R&D
- Healthcare treatment and service classes
- Current and future service constraints
- Possible disruption through innovation or new business models
- Business discriminant factors that impact settlement or external dependencies

- Supply chain
- Strategic goals
- Best in class characteristics

Step 2: Build the Emulator

Using X-Act® OBC Platform, an emulator was built to represent the healthcare environment: organization, processes, implementation, transportation, and physical and human dimensions.

Over a period of 12 weeks, we built the model covering 280,000 objects and 3000 dependencies (direct and indirectly induced delays).

Our emulation definitions and corresponding outcomes included the following three views to holistically represent the full environment:

Corporate View

The corporate view was built from information gathered during Step 1 and included the following:

- Business and operational definitions
- Volumes and constraints
- Service processes

The corporate view shows the six business processes that represent the individual parts of the healthcare system (see Fig. 21.1). Under the proposed project, each business process uses permissioned, shared ledgers to securely exchange and maintain patient care information.

Service View

The service view was built using best-in-class components from X-Act® libraries and included the following:

- Division into sub-processes
- Interdependencies on common services
- Hierarchy to service logic
- Characteristics of services
- Constraints

Implementation View

The implementation view was built using assets from X-Act® libraries and included the following:

- Geography
- Physical resources

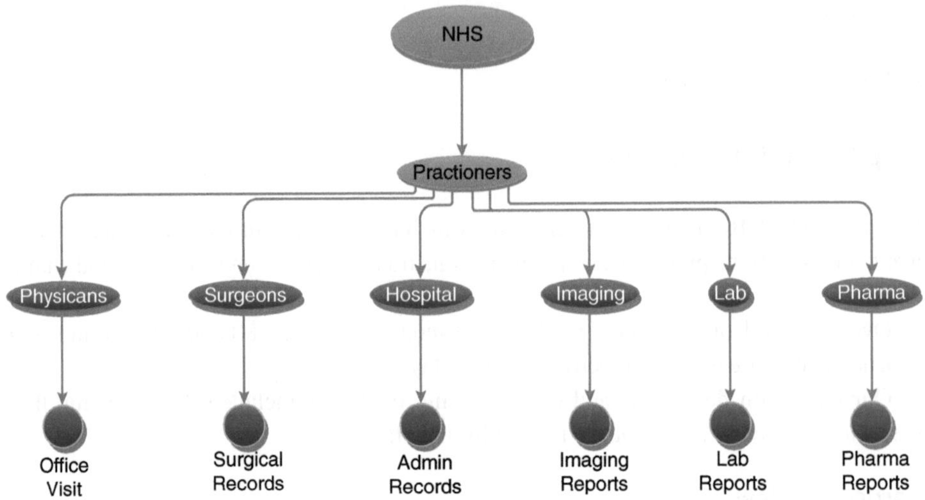

Fig. 21.1 X-Act® OBC Platform corporate view

- Physical components and structures
- Infrastructure
- Constraints

Figure 21.2 shows the implementation view of the UNMC hospital in Omaha with staff and patients, as well as internal services and hospital ledger servers. Similar models of medical offices and facilities are defined for Kearney and Lincoln, Nebraska.

Stage 2: Perform Diagnosis

Once the emulation was built, we used the *what-if* capabilities of X-Act® OBC Platform to analyze predicted system behaviors to identify whether the system could deliver per business expectations.

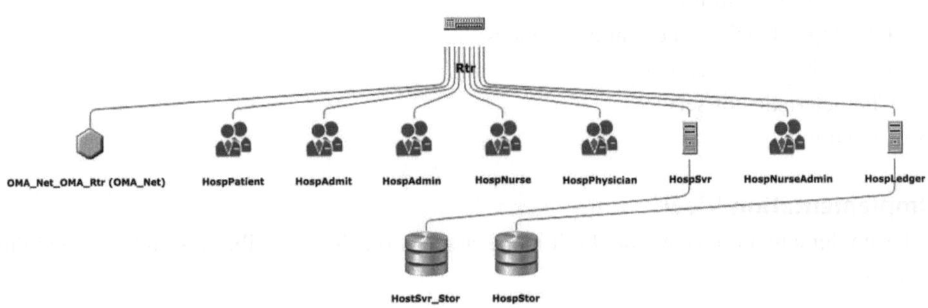

Fig. 21.2 X-Act® OBC Platform implementation view of UNMC Hospital

As visually represented in Fig. 21.3, X-Act® OBC Platform metrics showed that:

- The human activities in the process created delays
- Upgrading human effort could off-set loss of cycles that leads to escalating costs and may generate outdated analysis and imaging

At planned volumes of healthcare activities in the current system, both Dycom and RI are predicted to be high (see Fig. 21.4)—indicating that a risk is eminent and prescriptive actions should be taken to avoid negative outcomes.

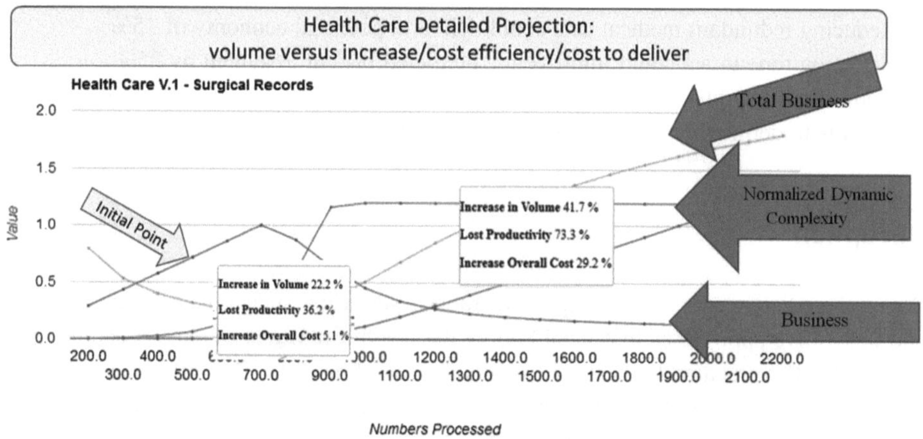

Fig. 21.3 X-Act® OBC Platform prediction revealed declines in productivity and increasing costs

Risk	Dycom Score	Risk Index	Business Trajectory
	91.8	52.0	Admin Records
	15.5	60.4	Office Visit
	13.7	61.2	Surgical Records
	9.7	60.3	Pharma Reports
	7.7	60.3	Imaging Reports
	2.3	59.7	Lab Reports

Fig. 21.4 X-Act® OBC Platform predicted Dycom and RI scores

Stage 3: Identify Prescriptive Actions

We then used the X-Act® OBC Platform to prescriptively emulate various remedial scenarios.

Optimization and Transformation

Using X-Act® OBC Platform prescriptive emulation capabilities, it was clear that significant benefits could be gained through better coordination among different services and processes. Key findings were as follows:

- Reducing redundant medical acts could deliver a potential economy of 15%
- Reducing time to act could improve the predicted patient treatment by 25%
- Additional benefits could be gained by evaluating required effort versus potential benefits to define the right and optimal course of action

Disruption

We used predictive emulation to explore disruption scenarios, such as new business models and innovative approaches that would allow the healthcare organization to become more agile and better prepared to meet the evolving needs of patients. The following disruptive scenario was proposed: A move to shared distributed ledger using blockchain technology would support organizational goals including better coordination and immediate administration of patient records.

Stage 4: Make Informed Risk Decision

The outputs of the X-Act® OBC Platform analysis were used to create an executive presentation of the immediate and future opportunities for consideration by management. All project risks and remedial options were evaluated based on their ability to meet stated organizational goals.

Looking Forward

Management will use X-Act® OBC Platform to evaluate new business implementation models, such as blockchain, and assess whether the proposed changes will adequately address business requirements by:

- Increasing volume
- Speeding delivery
- Reducing costs
- Ensuring predictability

Case #5: Managing Risk of Corporate Integration

22

Global Financial Institution

Case Overview

Often in global organizations, data becomes segmented by business lines and geographical boundaries as the business grows. This creates barriers in optimizing the performance of systems, managing risks across borders and cross selling services. With many separate lines of business independently offering services such as insurance, credit cards, retail banking, and corporate and investment banking, this global financial institution had client data spread across as many as ten disparate systems. The executive team realized that data integration was necessary to better serve clients, cross sell services and accurately measure and mitigate risk based upon a holistic risk profile for each activity.

However, managing an integration project of this scope always introduces new, unexpected risks, which can ultimately hijack the intend gains and anticipated advantages of the proposed system. In this case, X-Act® OBC Platform was used to evaluate the operational risks and identify prescriptive solutions that would allow for the successful integration of data across all the financial institution's client services.

Case Highlights

Implementation characteristics	• Global financial institution • Issues over 15% of all US credit cards • Originates over $130 billion in US loans • Provides retail, investment, wealth and private banking products and services

(continued)

N. Abu el Ata, A. Drucbert, *Leading from Under the Sword of Damocles*,
https://doi.org/10.1007/978-3-662-56300-7_22

Business goals	• Identify client cross selling opportunities across lines of business • Keep pace with competitive financial service offerings and technological prowess • Accurately measure and mitigate risk based upon a holistic risk profile for each activity
Challenges	• Continuous margin erosion • Duplication of resources across multiple divisions and activities • Sales and marketing insights limited by divisional activities with little strategic overlap or integration between business lines • Uncompetitive time to market • Managing reputation in times of uncertainty
Business constraints	• A staged approach is preferable over a big bang approach • Corporate collaboration will replace consensus • Justification is necessary before implementing chosen solution
Strategic options	• Optimize: of business processes, implementation architecture and service processes, as well as implementation of predicted operational risk management, automation and common infrastructure • Transform: Use common services for business processes, implement a coordinated architecture and monitor and treat operational risk globally • Disrupt: Implement a common universal view of client data

Stage 1: Build Emulator

The model of the global banking processes and underlying infrastructure were built in X-Act® OBC Platform following the steps outlined in Chap. 16 and further detailed below.

Step 1: Collect the Necessary Information

To build a representative model and strategically guide the integration project, it was necessary to model the entire client services process as it existed as well as the proposed system to uncover dynamic complexity related risks and identify the most appropriate prescriptive solutions. The necessary information and data pertaining to all divisions, processes, applications and infrastructure, as well as, the corporate, business and technical objectives were collected through automated data collection processes as well as workshops and interviews with business stakeholders as necessary to fill in any information gaps.

Step 2: Build the Emulator

Using X-Act® OBC Platform, an emulator was built to represent the global bank: organizations, services, and implementation. Over a period of 18 weeks, more than four million objects were modeled to cover the full scope of the global banking business.

Our emulation definitions and corresponding outcomes included the following three views to holistically represent the full environment:

Corporate View

The corporate view was built from information gathered during Step 1 and included the following (see Fig. 22.1):

- Business and operational definitions
- Volumes and constraints
- Service processes

Service View

The service view (see Fig. 22.2) was built using best-in-class components from X-Act® libraries as well as newly created assets and included the following:

- Division into sub-processes
- Interdependencies on common services
- Hierarchy to service logic
- Constraints

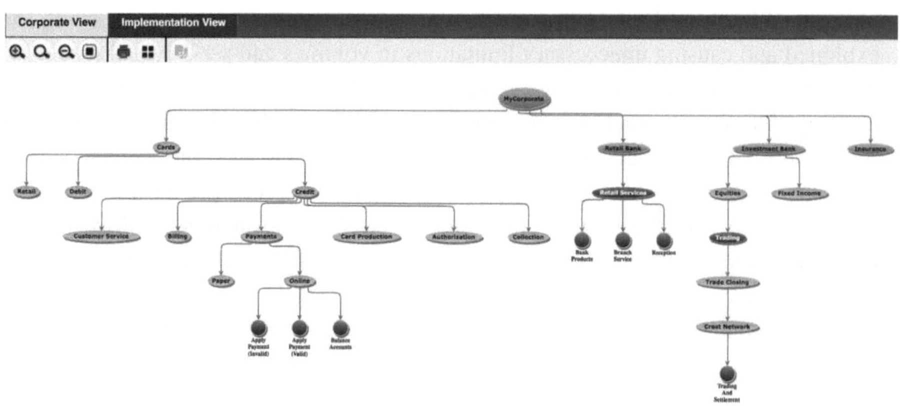

Fig. 22.1 X-Act® OBC Platform corporate view of global bank

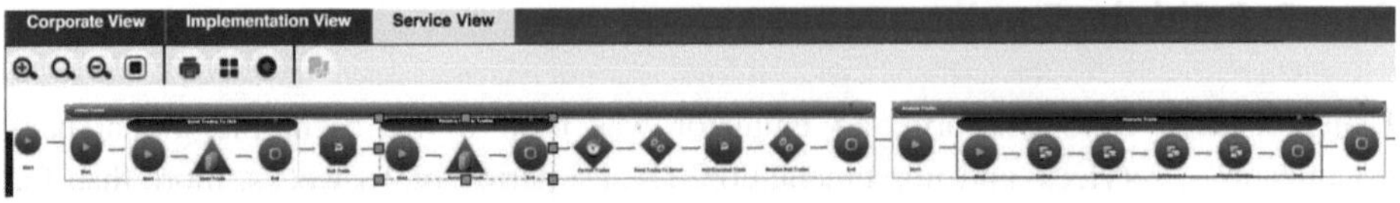

Fig. 22.2 X-Act® OBC Platform: service view of trading and settlement services

Implementation Views

The implementation views (see Figs. 22.3 and 22.4 as examples) were built using pre-modeled components from X-Act® libraries as well as newly created assets and included the following:

- Geography
- Physical resources
- Physical components and structures
- Infrastructure
- Constraints

Stage 2: Perform Diagnosis

Once the emulation was built, we used the capabilities of X-Act® OBC Platform to analyze historical and predicted system behaviors to identify the root cause of current problems and understand future business risks.

- Our risk analysis predicted that the business integration project as planned may cause unintended harm to the financial institution by preventing the assets from being fully exploited and causing unnecessary limitations in volumes and service quality
- The forward prediction showed an accelerating degradation that would result in an unacceptable situation (in terms of service quality, revenue pressure and cost) within the foreseeable future and left untreated may threaten corporate survival
- Creating a common infrastructure provided an attractive incentive for the business by supporting the consolidation of client attributes, allowing intelligent CRM, enabling cross marketing of services, as well as reducing redundant tasks, however proceeding with the project as planned would introduce service quality issues
- Predictive emulation defined a path to optimal operations while keeping the evolution of risk under close surveillance
- All patterns discovered during the predictive diagnosis stage, as well as any others collected over time were used to create a knowledge base to support our proposed universal risk management approach through the implementation of smart automation and advanced problem detection

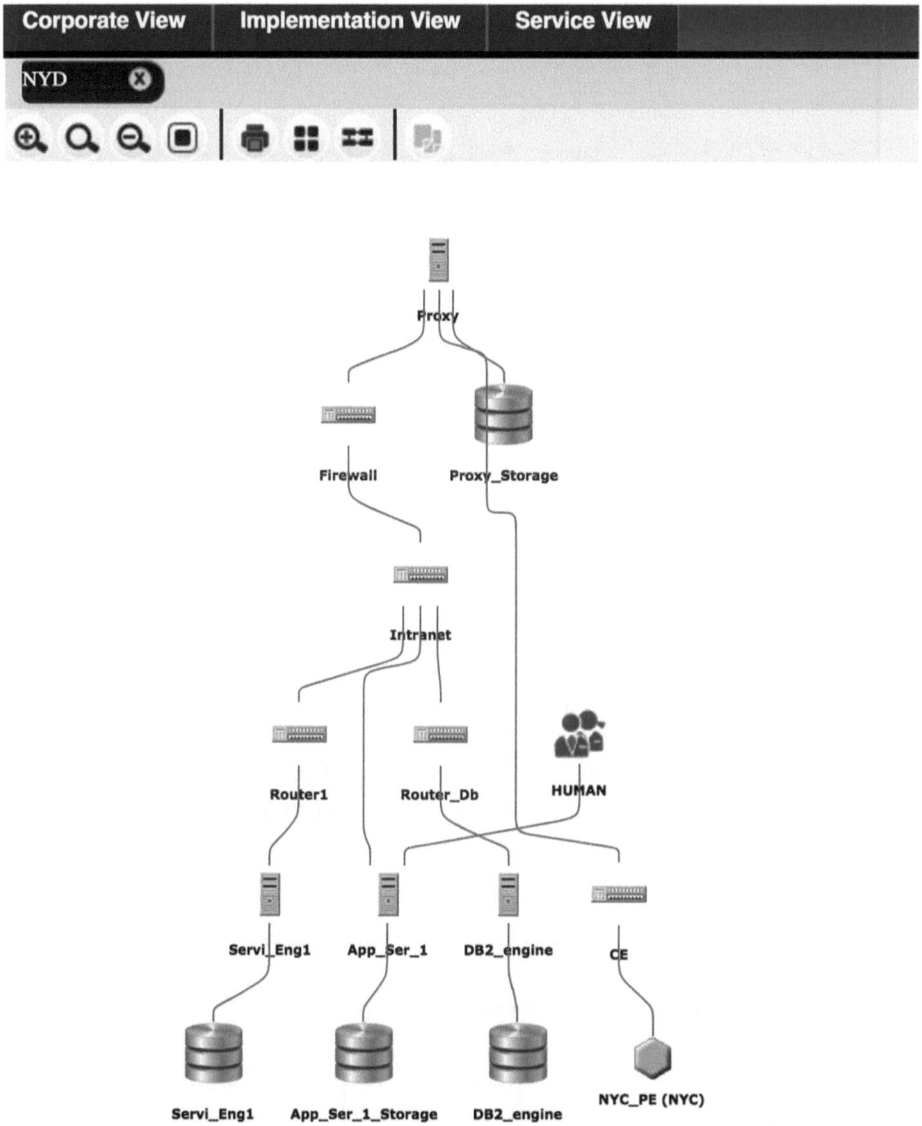

Fig. 22.3 X-Act® OBC Platform: implementation view of a datacenter

X-Act® OBC Platform metrics showed that:

- Due to continuous add-ons, dynamic complexity grew by 200% over a period of 5 years because changes were reactive and deteriorated architecture
- Revenue per unit improved due to consolidation to +10%, but then declined by 30% over 5 years, while the cost escalated by from −10% to +110% over the same period

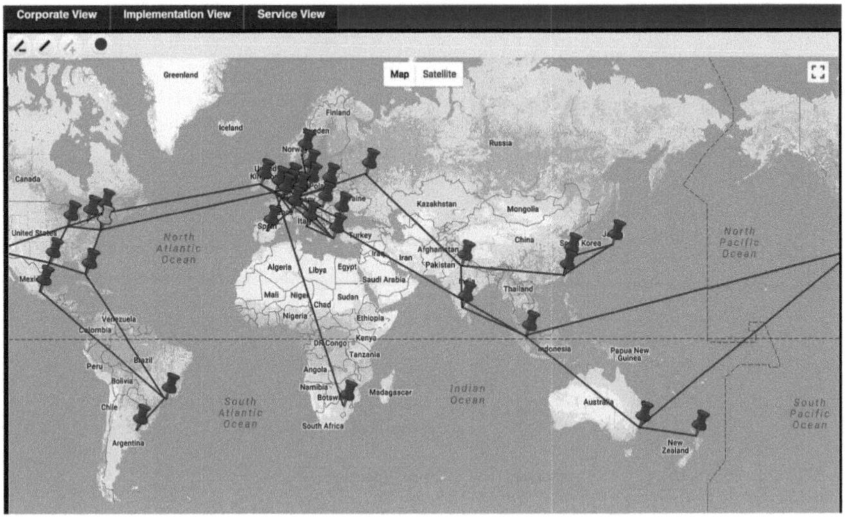

Fig. 22.4 X-Act® OBC Platform: implementation view mapping of datacenters

- Time to market moved from 6 months to 3 week cycles, then started to build up on the 3rd year to 6 month cycles again
- System behaviors could be reliably predicted for the next 4 years

In our analysis (Fig. 22.5), we found that one of the banking systems could go from 540 transactions per second to 900, but then the system performance started to degrade again.

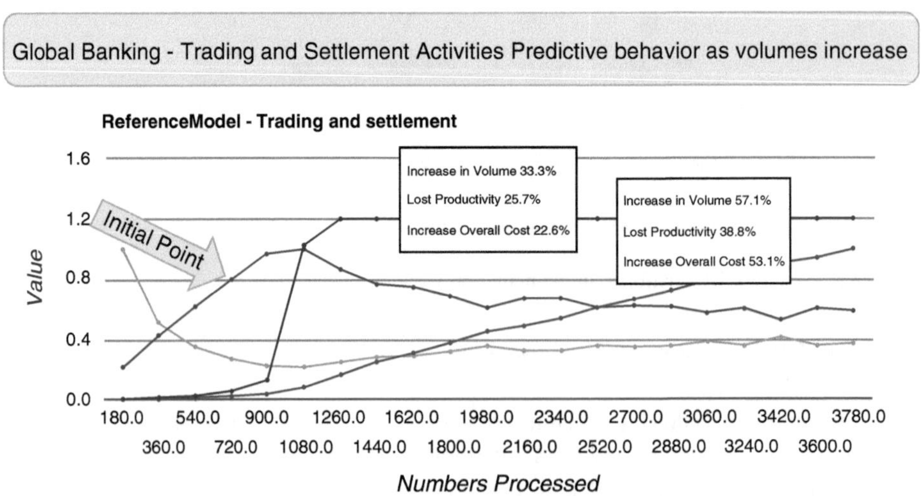

Fig. 22.5 X-Act® OBC Platform analysis of global banking activity

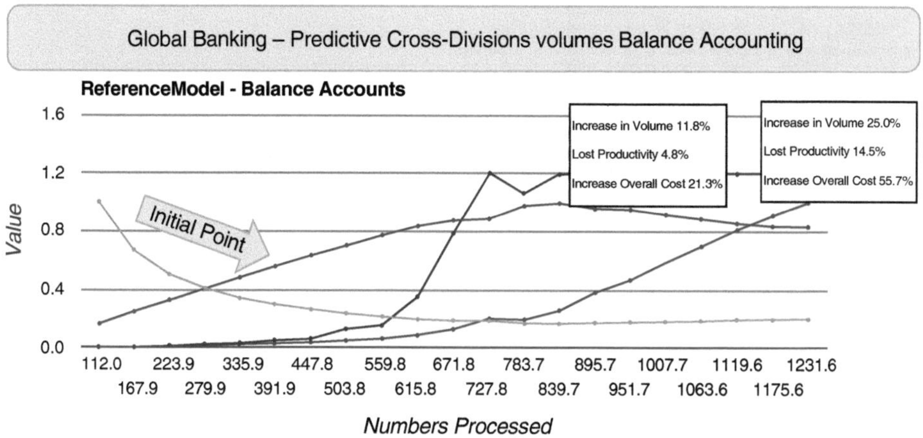

Fig. 22.6 X-Act® OBC Platform analysis of cross-division volumes

Figure 22.6 shows that once the cross-division balance account more than doubled, the cost built up again.

Stage 3: Identify Prescriptive Actions

We then used the X-Act® OBC Platform to prescriptively emulate various remedial scenarios.

Optimization

The following optimization options were defined and the limitations of each scenario were exposed using X-Act® OBC Platform prescriptive emulation capabilities. Key findings were as follows:

- Implementing a common infrastructure would yield a 45% gain in resources availability for more volume
- Sun-setting old components would yield a 15% gain in the system's ability to process more volume
- Re-implementing the data model would yield a 20% gain in service quality and throughput
- All options showed that operational risks would increase within 5 years due to continuous pressure on revenue and gradual cost escalation

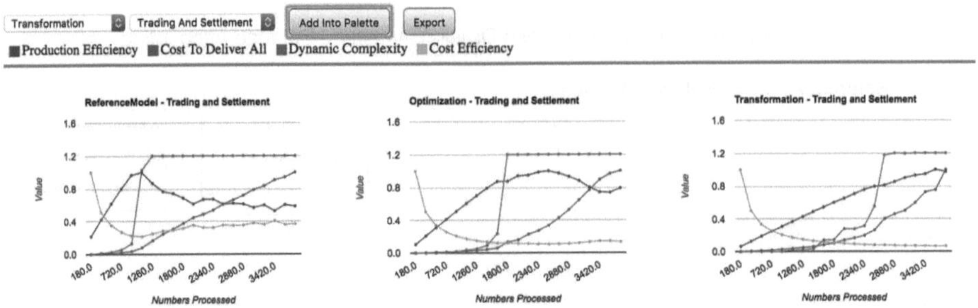

Fig. 22.7 Prescriptive risk mitigation and performance gains exposed through X-Act® OBC Platform

Transformation

Options to transform assets into a modern platform were explored. Key findings included the following (see Fig. 22.7):

- The speed to deliver the renewal project would be compatible with corporate constraints
- A data profiling/cleansing exercise should be executed and continuously revisited to weigh the advantages
- It would be beneficial to integrate any uncertainty about the future business model in a variable geometry architecture

Disruption

We used predictive emulation to explore disruption scenarios, such as new business models and innovative approaches that would allow the business to become more agile and better prepared to meet the evolving needs of the banking industry. The following disruptive scenarios were proposed:

- Execute corporate reengineering
- Use new implementation that would allow for new types of events processing
- Reduce dynamic complexity through smart interdependencies management

Stage 4: Make Informed Risk Decision

The outputs of the X-Act® OBC Platform analysis were used to create an executive presentation of the immediate and future risks as well as proposed prescriptive solutions for consideration by management. All risks and remedial options were evaluated based on their ability to meet stated business goals.

Management Decisions:

- Start by consolidating an advanced level of modern infrastructure to deliver the service to business application assets through a common bus
- Separate the business application assets into two levels: (1) heavy duty engines that would be responsible for delivering the services to all business components forming the second level, and (2) the access to the engines would be achieved through another bus that would deliver the parameterization, constraints and access to a data layer
- The data layer would be responsible for delivering, receiving, organizing and cleansing the data for the business
- Prioritizations, streaming, scheduling and dispatching would be performed in the buses
- X-Act® OBC Platform would be used to predict, prescribe and remediate operational risk through its OBC real-time surveillance monitoring capabilities
- The high level of adaptability ensured by such optimization process would ensure full alignment between the business and its implementation

Conclusion 23

Making a Commitment to Maturing Risk Management

In life, we often want to believe that we will somehow be able to escape any harm caused by future events or circumstances. In general, this attitude of blind optimism persists because we do not know how to deal with something that may appear as a surprise. While science—particularly from the seventeenth century forward—has established causality as a base for phenomenology, people continue to believe in *luck*. This is especially true in the case of complex events, which are difficult for us to otherwise explain. No doubt, the foretelling of many *RISK* events is beyond human comprehension.

But ultimately, hope is not a useful business strategy. Through our research and promotion of new methods and technologies, our objective is turn the management of risk into science, and in doing so deliver the right approach to discover the scope of circumstances that lead to an eventual risk, predict when a risk may impact an organization, identify the root cause that makes the risk event plausible and determine how to mitigate any unwanted risks before it is too late.

Our quest to establish a scientific approach to risk management became feasible only after we discovered that dynamic complexity systematically leads to risk. A major reason that risk appears as a surprise is that businesses lack the tools necessary to observe the evolution of dynamic complexity overtime within an operational structure—whether it be an enterprise, government activity, financial institution, economic implementation strategy or even medical conditions.

Our contribution to the science of risk is based on the determination of dynamic complexity—including its frequency of change and amplitude of impact. Using these discoveries, businesses can now determine the moment in time when the evolution of dynamic complexity will become predominant, causing the system to become inefficient and consequently prepare for the coming risk.

N. Abu el Ata, A. Drucbert, *Leading from Under the Sword of Damocles*,
https://doi.org/10.1007/978-3-662-56300-7_23

Replacing Hope with Knowledge

Users of X-Act® OBC Platform can mathematically predict risk events through system emulation to discover under which conditions dynamic complexity will absorb resources and takeover the planned yield, thereby deteriorating the expected quality and quantity while inflating costs. These foresights are necessary to improve the maturity of risk management practices because when *risk* is out-of-control any manifestations of unwanted system behaviors will otherwise appear as a surprise—leaving an organization no choice but to reactively manage the risk.

Often our methods and technologies are put into place after a major risk event has unexpectedly appeared. While there are certainly benefits to be gained at this point, best in class companies use X-Act® OBC Platform to continuously monitor risk as it evolves and validate any planned changes (see Fig. 23.1). Obviously, some systems—including enterprises, economic, financial or automotive systems—are more prone to dynamic complexity and consequently to the associated risk than others. This imparts a responsibility to build the right systems and solutions from the start to minimize dynamic complexity and control its evolution.

Within the current competitive and ever-changing business climate, companies with the most mature risk management practices will establish a defendable market advantage.

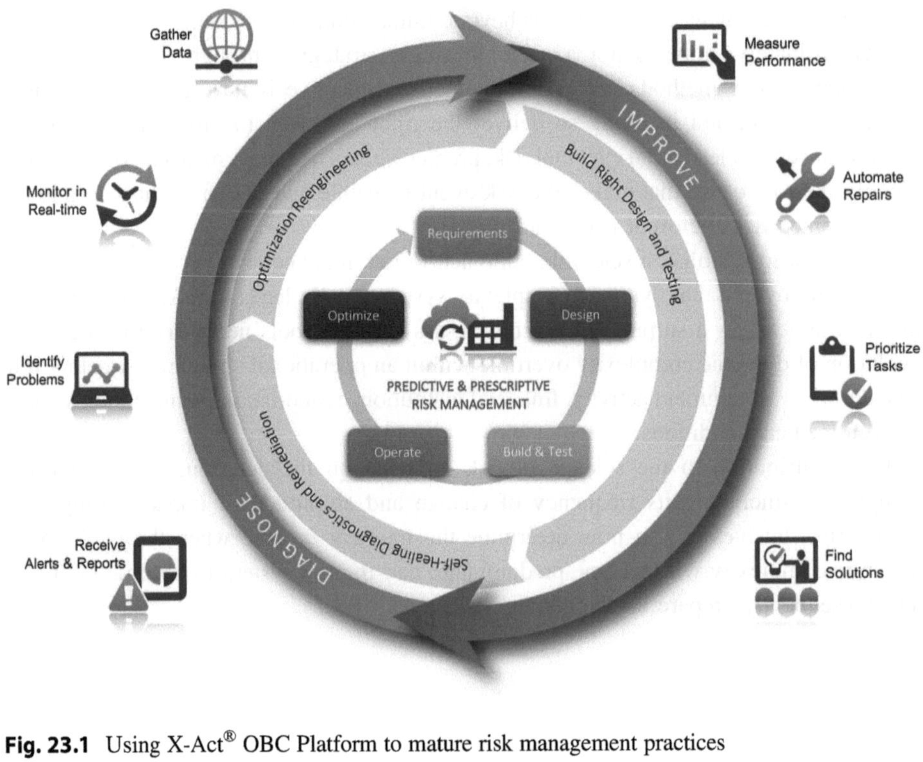

Fig. 23.1 Using X-Act® OBC Platform to mature risk management practices

When it becomes possible to quickly, cost-effectively and predictably execute against business strategy and plans, innovation can flourish and organizations can respond more agilely to changing market requirements.

Getting Started with a Phased Approach

For many companies, the move towards universal risk management will begin with a single project, but ultimately it takes more than technology for companies to successfully operationalize a prescriptive approach to risk management. An enterprise-wide strategy is necessary to promote an analytics-driven culture. A phased approach can help companies demonstrate the value of prescriptive risk management, while building organizational buy-in for a centralized universal risk management service (see Fig. 23.2).

Phase One

While there are many opportunities to define, and achieve strategic universal risk management goals, it is most advisable to start by identifying a single, high-priority project. The goal is to quickly demonstrate success and prove gains can be realized through the applied use of prescriptive emulation. Using X-Act® libraries of pre-built models and assets, the start-up phase can be as short as 10 weeks to enable a rapid return on investment.

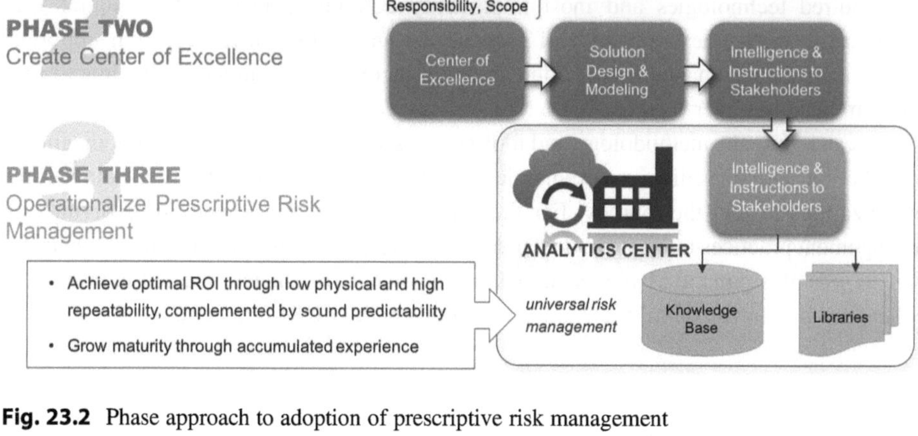

Fig. 23.2 Phase approach to adoption of prescriptive risk management

Phase Two

Move towards the shared services approach by first assembling a Center of Excellence within a line of business (LOB). Create a small cross-functional team of business, production design and delivery stakeholders that can work together effectively as a team. Previous analytics experience is not required—X-Act® OBC Platform is simple enough for business users while powerful enough for operational teams. During this phase, define the governance, process, responsibility and scope of the enterprise-wide Center of Excellence.

Phase Three

Consolidate decentralized Centers of Excellence to create a centrally managed services organization capable of providing enterprise-wide universal risk management services.

Thriving in the Fourth Industrial Revolution

Improving the maturity of entrenched risk management practices is undoubtedly hard work, fraught with many challenges. And while those that lack transparency into the root causes of dynamic complexity related risks may well still achieve growth, it may be unprofitable growth. Businesses that approach dynamic complexity as a strategic concern will—with the right decision support tools—create space within which to grow and secure a real competitive advantage.

This book offers the scientific foundation to build new systems and determine the right moment to mitigate risk in an existing structure. The presented cases show how others have achieved considerable results through better control and more efficient processes to predict a future risk while it is still possible to react and correct the outcome. Ultimately, each organization will need to customize their application of this scientific methodology, adopt the required technologies and most importantly commit to making the cultural shift necessary to reject the acceptance of surprises as an excuse not to deal with important phenomena that will happen more often and with increasing amplitude as the time to fix a problem becomes ever scarcer.

We can define the methodology and toolset necessary to cover the prediction, diagnosis, remediation and surveillance of dynamic complexity related risks, but we cannot force organizations to join the journey. For those that recognize the urgency of evolving risk management practices to meet the demands of our modern business environment, we invite you to join the pursuit of universal risk management excellence and learn from your colleagues that have committed themselves to this path at URMgrp.com.

X-Act OBC Platform

Glossary of Terms

Term	Definition
Actions	A change proposed to deliver better results.
Advanced projections	Provides predictions in the form of four metrics at various points of workload/arrival increase. These points may correspond to either fixed or variable changes.
Aging acceleration (A^2)	Represented by the A^2 metric, measures the speed of inflation in resource consumption for the same business and quality of service between two dates. The inflation is generally due to an increase in static and/or dynamic complexity.
Architecture	Defined in three layers: (1) business and its functions and processes, (2) implementation of the functions and their data, and (3) the exchanges between the functions. For IT implementations, it includes infrastructure as the choice of servers, hardware components and software tools such as RDBMS. For other environments, it includes the physical implementation components such as sorting machines, robots, vehicles and humans.
Availability	The time during which resources are available to deliver the business within the window of measurements.
Average degree of multiprogramming	Average number of transactions or customers that are concurrently executing in a system.
Batch extension index	Represents the time extension of batch window due to either higher business requirements or system efficiency impact.
Bottleneck	Resource that saturates first as workload intensity increases. It is the resource with the highest service demand.
Business value chain	Defines the relation between different layers of process management in the enterprise.
Business workload	The workload that represents the flow of generated transactions due to business processes.

(continued)

N. Abu el Ata, A. Drucbert, *Leading from Under the Sword of Damocles*,
https://doi.org/10.1007/978-3-662-56300-7

Term	Definition
Busy time	The time during which a service is utilized (not idle).
Cache hit ratio	This ratio describes the activity of the cache memory. The ratio is equal to the number of logical I/O staying in the cache memory relative to the total number of logical I/O. The other part transforms into physical disk I/Os.
Cache memory	Memory holding data designed to speed up subsequent accesses to the same data. Although caching techniques have been most often applied to processor memory access, they also have been used for data accessibility.
Calibration	Technique used to alter the parameters of a reference model of an actual system (system or application in operation or in test), so that the output parameters of the resulting calibrated model matches the performance of the actual system being modeled.
Chronograph view	Represent the time-series of the business service timing for each component crossed end-to-end and the comparison between ideal and actual sub-process time slots.
Clustering concept	Process by which many components are grouped into clusters of similar components.
Complex	A server could be decomposed into several complexes (or machines). The complexes could be of different models, types or manufacturing, or under different operating systems. The complexes can share the same disk configuration.
Complex flow	The goal of the complex flow is to offer the possibility of describing a flow from its origin to its destination by segments; each segment could have unique characteristics. So, a flow can have two or more parallel paths.
Complexity disruptors (Vector of causes)	An X-Act® OBC Platform metric that represents the causes that provoke the propagation of risk due to dynamic complexity. These causes may be direct or indirect, internal or external, dormant and appear under certain conditions, or deficient by design.
Complexity index (Lost opportunity)	An X-Act® OBC Platform metric that is computed by mathematical emulation. It represents the loss of opportunity due to contentions, conflicts, management overhead, and combinatorial factors provoked by the presence of dynamic complexity.
Conflicts	If two transaction candidates look for the same resource(s), a conflict occurs causing one of the transactions to wait.
Contingency analysis	Forecast the different events, which could arrive, and then determine their impacts on the behavior of the Information System. These events could be classified by their contingency rate.
Cost inflation	The additional cost to a baseline cost that is necessary to deliver a service.
Cost inflation rate	Cost inflation for the same business and quality of service between two dates.
Cost variation index	Represents the variations in resource consumptions due to resources management and the dynamic situation of such resources at a point in time.

(continued)

Term	Definition
Dashboard	Systemic presentation of performance, dynamic complexity and risk and their evolution corresponding to different business/system volumes for an insanitation of initial conditions: architecture, infrastructure and resources.
Degree of complexity (Dependencies)	An X-Act® OBC Platform qualitative and quantitative metric that varies from tight and strong coupling to loose and weak coupling that can be used to discover the evolution of dynamic complexity and define the policy to reduce it or mitigate its inflation.
Delay (Implementation)	Time to market in business terminology.
Delay queue	Queue time spent before activity is processed.
Determine cost inflation	By comparing the cost before and after a change in initial conditions, a scenario of change in internal structure or due to external influencers.
Diagnosis	The formal process of X-Act® interpretation of n-metric computation to discover impacts on business service.
Diagnosis and repair	The systemic engineering view of the diagnosis at task and activity level, how and what to remediate and the position of the diagnosed component in the hierarchy.
Discover impacts on availability	Studying impact of change in process or architecture to allow recovery, and business continuity.
Discovery activity	Diagnosis to discover secondary bottlenecks and other degradations that are only partially dependent on the load growth (aging, complexification of databases)
Distributed system	The distributed system computing model is predicated based on the notion of splitting the work to be performed by an application between different types of processes—the workstation of the user, the servers of SQL, Data or Applications. The servers accept the requests for data from the user and return results to the user.
Dycom	Represents degree of: Dependencies among components forming a business system. High degree of dependencies shows high risk of generating dynamic complexity that threats efficiency, increases unproductive cost portion and reduces the quality of service. Dependencies that produces a feedback: example, a feedback could be equivalent to n dependencies. That happens if the production line produces leftover that needs to be further treated Coverage of impact analysis (elements like priorities, locks, volumes, discriminant factors such as pay-in at the right moment, default payment etc.) All elements of the Dycom vector are computed by the Perturbation theory, so the indicator will be given in the form of Dycom = $(x_1, x_2, x_3 \ldots, x_n)$
Dycom score	A measure of the impact of dynamic complexity. It is a dimensionless metric that can be adapted to represent the true perception of decision maker about the relative importance among four metrics: service quality, service quantity, service cost and service availability.

(continued)

Term	Definition
Dynamic complexity, Type I *Due to conflicts, contentions and latencies*	A measure of the relative magnitude of computed response time compared to the basic service time with no delays. Hundred percent indicates that the computed response time is 100% longer than the basic service time that would be required to accomplish the business service with no delays or locks. When the value is small, the only way to improve response time is to reduce the basic service time. A large value indicates that resource contention is causing undue delays or locks.
Dynamic complexity, Type II *Throughput*	Indicates the loss in throughput due to an increase in service time caused by the transformation of logical demand in memory into a physical execution that may or may not result into additional contention on physical resources. Increases in service time may be accompanied by a decrease in contentions as the distribution of resources is disjointed from the previous case.
Dynamic complexity, Type III *Availability*	If a resource availability problem occurs, dynamic complexity increases, which then causes loss in productivity and elongation of response time.
Dynamic complexity, Type IV *Incidentals*	Incidental issues such as changes in business environment, priorities, sequencing, induced effects that impact system performance.
Dynamic complexity, Type V *Transport Atypical Latency*	Delays due to unforeseeable network, transport and or triage disorders.
Dynamic ROI	The length of time until it becomes possible for a new business enterprise to break even within its dynamic environment.
Elapsed time	Total time spent by a job from its submission until its completion. This corresponds to the response time concept, except that it is generally used for batch workloads.
Elongation ratio	The ratio between the actual average response time of a task and what the response time would be if the task ran alone in the system without any resource contentions. In other words, the elongation ratio is the normalized response time with respect to the execution time without wait. It corresponds to Dynamic Complexity, Type I.
Engineering efficiency (E^2)	Compares the cost of equipment utilization compared to the total cost of equipment installed. Higher numbers are generally indicative of well utilized equipment, but there may be little room for further growth if the efficiency is too high.
Explore impacts	Generally used in *what-if* scenario management, it shows the impact on quality, quantity and cost metrics, and the risk index due to a new dynamic complexity calculation.
Financial singularity	The moment the revenue (productivity efficiency) becomes lower that the cost to deliver the business. Generally, dynamic complexity is the main cause as it consumes resources in ways that were never planned and therefore reduces the availability of resources to serve the intended business goals.

(continued)

Term	Definition
Margin index	A measure of margin efficiency. It compares actual margin to total possible margin. The total possible margin is computed using the results of the system limit, while the actual margin is based upon the iteration selected. Negative margins are displayed as 0. They can occur when there is not enough business throughput to cover the cost of resource utilization.
Operational compute	Multiple computations in X-Act® OBC Platform covering a window in time. After aggregation, a service trajectory, a process, sub-process or component will be seen as an end-to-end service.
Optimized model	Definition of best-case emulation within X-Act® OBC Platform, where the remediation actions are evaluated and grouped in one scenario.
Plan point	It is the number of single computations that each correspond to a specific business service volume. In the absence of predefined business volume sequence, the tool proposes fixed interval increases or decreases. Plan point is used for sizing, research of singularity or SLA verification.
Process time	The end-to-end time to deliver a business process. It may include steps, involve sub-processes, go through different branches, involve a feedback, locks, left-over, etc.
Productivity degradation ratio	Productivity degradation due to faster limit attainability.
Productivity index	Compares the business revenue delivered by the reference architecture within cost and service constraints compared to total possible revenue. The total possible revenue is determined from the system limit computation while the business revenue delivered is based upon the iteration currently selected. Examples of productivity include throughput, number of cars, pieces of mail, number of subscriptions, etc.
Project name, description	The name given to an emulator. Under an emulator many models may exist. Each will correspond to an instantiation of the emulator with a proper set of initial conditions.
Quality degradation	The ratio between response time and service time. It represents how much additional time is needed to deliver a business.
Reporting center	Provides a menu of import/export, results formatting, predefined report-formats and pattern libraries.
Residence time	Total time spent by a request, transaction or program at a resource.
Resolution engine	Mathematical set of equations that represent the internal dynamics of multi-device and multi-discipline service centers.
Resources management view	Systemic view of computed resource utilization per server, service object and business service object.
Response time	The elapsed time between task initiation and task completion.
Response time/elapsed time	The time required to deliver a task that will call upon other resources and consequently cause delays due to conflicts, contentions, rerouting or interruptions.

(continued)

Term	Definition
Risk index (RI)	Function of the impact of dynamic complexity or rarefication of resources or both on business.
Scalability index	A relative value between 0 and 1. Numbers closer to one indicate that adding more hardware will be aligned to equivalent increase in business throughput that is near the investment in resources. Numbers closer to zero indicate that the service process may not benefit as well from a simple increase in resources.
Scenario Manager (editor)	It partially automates the process of altering the information system model to reflect the re-engineering action(s).
Sensitivity analysis	Incremental increase of the workload on a few components in the value chain (functions, application components, servers, network components) again up to an elongation of the response time of such component >100%.
Service component, task, activities	The systemic view of service. It is a hierarchy of horizontal or vertical sequences, representing the logic demand for physical resources.
Service management view	Systemic view of system task/activity components that compose a business service process, including each task and activity computed performance metrics with special emphasis for the computed dynamic complexity at each resource and service center including communication and data accesses.
Service quality	A relative number showing the extent of degradation in response time as the iterations increase the business workload. A sharp down slope in this graph reveals the point at which the system may no longer support service time requirements.
Service time	The computed time of service free of any conflict, contention, lock or delay for whatever reason. This metric is one of the useful goal-oriented-analytics in X-Act® OBC Platform that allows users to benchmark an impact-free baseline.
Simple compute	Computes a single point at a time to identify bottlenecks, shortage in resources and eventual degradation in quantity, quality or cost.
Singularity, chaotic point	Represents the point beyond which a degradation becomes unacceptable with subsequent points having unpredictable behavior.
System domain	The results of a model executed in the system domain mode will include only the system management domain and the network traffic. They exclude the business and application domains.
Throughput	Rate at which users, terminals or messages complete a process. Measured in number of complete transactions per unit of time.
Throughput efficiency	A relative value comparing the computed business throughput to the requested business arrival rate. Numbers closer to one indicate that the system can meet the demand presented. An efficiency closer to zero indicates that the system is not able to keep up with demand and many arrivals are not being processed within the service constraints.

(continued)

Term	Definition
Transaction	This is an online processing class that groups components that arrive at a computer system with a given arrival rate.
Transmission control protocol	The most common transport layer protocol used on the Internet as well as on Ethernet LANs.
Utilization rate	The ratio that indicates the amount of resources consumed by a particular task or group.
View remedies	Shows the list of actions automatically proposed by X-Act® OBC Platform to remediate a situation. All actions are evaluated and organized by impact, complexity, speed to deliver and expected return.
Volume index	The rapport between the business volume and the volume of delivered service to provide a ratio of quantity requested to quantity delivered.
X-Act® diagnosis report	For each process and component, the diagnosis report itemizes the bottlenecks, saturation and locking that affects service quality, quantity and/or cost.
X-Act® remediation action	Provides possible remedial actions automatically suggested by X-Act® OBC Platform, organized by order of benefit, complexity and time to deliver.

Universal Risk Management

Glossary of Terms

Term	Definition
Accuracy	How close you are to a true or accepted value.
Business requirements	The static and dynamic objects that are necessary to perform business.
Causal deconstruction	A seven-stage scientific methodology that is used to understand the constituent components of a system and any dependencies among them by establishing the base dynamics, deconstructing complexity, constructing an emulator, predicting singularities, comparing to actual system, defining improvements and monitoring the execution.
Chaos theory	A field of study in mathematics that studies the behavior of dynamical systems that are highly sensitive to initial conditions and describes the behavior of dynamical systems that states evolve with time and under certain servicing conditions.
Chaotic point (see also Singularity)	Represents the point beyond which a degradation becomes unacceptable with subsequent points having unpredictable behavior.
Database management system (DBMS)	Collection of programs that enable the users to create and maintain databases.
Differential equations	A mathematical equation that relates some function with its derivatives. In applications, the functions usually represent physical quantities, the derivatives represent their rates of change, and the equation defines a relationship between the two. Because such relations are extremely common, differential equations play a prominent role in many disciplines including engineering, physics, economics, and biology.

(continued)

N. Abu el Ata, A. Drucbert, *Leading from Under the Sword of Damocles*,
https://doi.org/10.1007/978-3-662-56300-7

Term	Definition
Discriminant factors	Those factors that impact the performance, cost and service quality delivered by a system. They are of Business origin, generated by elements composing the architecture, infrastructure and methods of operations. They are at the origin of service behavior and outcome fluctuations.
Dynamic complexity	The contentions, conflicts, locks, and delays that result from binding a system and generated through dependencies, feedback, operating organization, optimizers and enforcement mechanisms in a system.
Dynamic pattern	A pattern that has a dynamic signature requesting resources, characterized by specific behavior and business demands.
Dynamic signature	Used to certify dynamic patterns. The dynamic signature is determined by computing the amount of resources used to bind the compound pattern.
Emulation	Mathematical transformation of a system that encapsulates all characteristics, dynamic behaviors and dependencies among system components to reproduce the same exact behavior, and adheres to all the rules of the system being emulated so that predictive analysis can be performed.
Emulative deconstruction theory	A set of methods, rules, and tooling that allows conceptual, virtual, and/or physical dismantlement of structures into components, building blocks, interdependencies, interactions, and other dynamics to understand, predict, reconstruct, and operate improved, transformed, or innovated structures.
Measure	A numerical value to help metrication, replace variables in a mathematical structure or together with causal analysis in comparison between situations.
Metric	A qualitative and quantitative measure used to evaluate an outcome or indicate a status.
Model-based architecture (MBA)	A patented architecture approach that extends and relaxes some missing layers in service-oriented architecture (SOA). It defines six-layer definitions of a target architecture for a scalable, cost efficient and optimally controlled system dynamics that represents a business, its non-functional requirements and its discriminant factors.
Non-functional requirement (NFR)	A requirement that specifies criteria that can be used to judge the operation of a system, rather than specific behaviors. This should be contrasted with functional requirements that define specific behavior or functions.
Operational constraints	Internal and external elements that may impact non-functional requirements (NFRs)
Operational risk	Risks that arise due to choices about design and use of processes to create and deliver goods and services. They can include production errors, substandard raw materials, and technology malfunctions.
Optimal business control (OBC)	A set of management, data collection, analytics, machine learning and automation processes through which management predicts, evaluates, and, when necessary, responds to mitigate complexity risks that hinder the realization of business goals.

(continued)

Term	Definition
Pattern	A recurring object or event.
Perturbation theory	Mathematical methods for finding an approximate solution to a problem, by starting from the exact solution of a related problem. A critical feature of the technique is a middle step that breaks the problem into "solvable" and "perturbation" parts. Perturbation theory is applicable if the problem at hand cannot be solved exactly, but can be formulated by adding a "small" term to the mathematical description of the exactly solvable problem.
Predictive model	Dynamic model that represents a developed system prior to moving to operations.
Reference model	A model that represents a modeled system with acceptable accuracy.
Response time	The time required to deliver a task that will call amount others on resources and consequently subject to delays due to conflicts, contentions, rerouting or interruptions.
Service constraints	Characteristics that reveal how a non-functional requirement (NFR) is implemented.
Simulation	A system that behaves *similar to* something else, but is implemented in an entirely different way. It provides the basic behavior of a system, but may not necessarily adhere to all of the rules of the system being simulated. It is there to give you an idea about how something works.
Singularity	A point at which a given mathematical object is not defined or not well-behaved, for example infinite or not differentiable.
Systemic enterprise	Systemic enterprise is a dynamic view of organizational structure, which supports an integrated 'systems based' enterprise and business management approach using advanced forms of predictive mathematical emulation to understand how complex dynamics may cause a breakdown of critical business implementation and maintain a forward-looking view of what system changes are needed to meet the long-term goals of the business.
Target architecture	Business and system architecture definition based on Model-Based-Architecture's guidelines, principles and characteristics.
Universal risk management methodology	A five-stage process that supports a scientific methodology of risk management through risk perception, modeling, discovery, mitigation and monitoring.

Index

N. Abu el Ata, A. Drucbert, *Leading from Under the Sword of Damocles*,
https://doi.org/10.1007/978-3-662-56300-7

MIX
Papier aus verantwortungsvollen Quellen
Paper from responsible sources
FSC® C105338

If you have any concerns about our products,
you can contact us on
ProductSafety@springernature.com

In case Publisher is established outside the EU,
the EU authorized representative is:
Springer Nature Customer Service Center GmbH
Europaplatz 3, 69115 Heidelberg, Germany

Printed by Libri Plureos GmbH
in Hamburg, Germany